Super Easy Diabetic Cookbook for Beginners

1800+ Days Delicious, Low-Sugar & Low-Carbs Recipes Book for Pre Diabetic, Type 2 Diabetes | A 30-Day Meal Plan for Better Eating Habits

Inez R. Judge

Copyright© 2023 By Inez R. Judge
All rights reserved worldwide.

No part of this book may be reproduced or transmitted in any form or by any means, electronic or mechanical, including photo- copying, recording or by any information storage and retrieval system, without written permission from the publisher, except for the inclusion of brief quotations in a review.

Warning-Disclaimer

The purpose of this book is to educate and entertain. The author or publisher does not guarantee that anyone following the techniques, suggestions, tips, ideas, or strategies will become successful. The author and publisher shall have neither liability or responsibility to anyone with respect to any loss or damage caused, or alleged to be caused, directly or indirectly by the information contained in this book.

Table of Contents

Chapter 1   Breakfasts……/8
Chapter 2   Beans and Grains……/20
Chapter 3   Poultry……/27
Chapter 4   Beef, Pork, and Lamb……/38
Chapter 5   Fish and Seafood……/49
Chapter 6   Snacks and Appetizers……/59
Chapter 7   Vegetables and Sides……/66
Chapter 8   Vegetarian Mains……/74
Chapter 9   Stews and Soups……/83
Chapter 10   Desserts……/91
Chapter 11   Salads……/98
Chapter 12   Pizzas, Wraps, and Sandwiches……/107
Appendix 2: The Dirty Dozen and Clean Fifteen……/109
Appendix 2: The Dirty Dozen and Clean Fifteen……/110
Appendix 3: Recipe Index……/111

INTRODUCTION

Are you tired of feeling like a superhero with a kryptonite weakness when it comes to sugar? Well, fear not my fellow diabetics, because I have the perfect solution for you! Welcome to the Diabetic Diet Cookbook, where we believe that managing diabetes doesn't have to mean sacrificing flavor or fun! This cookbook is your guide to delicious and nutritious meals that will help you stay on track with your diabetic diet while satisfying your taste buds. Introducing the ultimate diabetic diet cookbook, filled with delicious recipes that will have you feeling like a true champ. Say goodbye to boring, tasteless meals and hello to a world of flavor and excitement.

What is Diabetes?

Well, diabetes is like that one annoying friend who never leaves your side. You know the one who always wants to tag along, even when you're trying to have a good time? Yeah, that's diabetes. But unlike that friend, diabetes brings a lot of baggage with it. Think of it like a group of rowdy teenagers throwing a party in your bloodstream, wrecking the place and causing chaos. But fear not, with a little effort and some good habits, you can kick diabetes to the curb and enjoy life without any unwanted guests.

Now, let me tell you more about diabetes. It is a chronic condition that affects millions of people worldwide. It is a disease that is characterized by high blood sugar levels, which can lead to a range of health problems, including heart disease, kidney damage, blindness, and nerve damage.

If you or someone you know has diabetes, it is important to understand the importance of managing the condition through a healthy lifestyle.

Types of Diabetes

There are three main types of diabetes: Type 1, Type 2, and Gestational Diabetes. Each type has different causes, symptoms, and treatment options.

※ **Type 1 Diabetes:**

Type 1 diabetes is an autoimmune disorder in which the immune system attacks the cells in the pancreas that produce insulin. This results in a complete lack of insulin production, and individuals with Type 1 diabetes require daily insulin injections to manage their blood sugar levels. Here are something you have to know about Type 1 diabetes.

➢ Typically diagnosed in childhood or adolescence

➢ Symptoms include increased thirst, frequent urination, weight loss, and fatigue

➢ Treatment includes insulin injections, blood sugar monitoring, and following a healthy diet and exercise regimen

➢ There is no known cure for Type 1 diabetes, and management is lifelong

※ **Type 2 Diabetes:**

Type 2 diabetes is the most common form of diabetes, accounting for approximately 90% of cases. It occurs when the body becomes resistant to insulin or doesn't produce enough insulin to meet the body's needs. Here are something you need to know about Type 2 diabetes.

➢ Typically diagnosed in adulthood, but can occur at any age

➢ Symptoms include increased thirst, frequent urination, blurred vision, slow healing of cuts or wounds, and fatigue

➢ Treatment includes lifestyle changes such as following a diabetic diet, regular exercise, and weight loss, as well as medication and insulin therapy in some cases

Type 2 diabetes can often be prevented or delayed through lifestyle changes

※ **Gestational Diabetes:**

Gestational diabetes occurs during pregnancy and affects approximately 10% of pregnant women. It is caused by hormonal changes that affect insulin production and sensitivity. Here are something you need to know about gestational diabetes.

➢ Typically diagnosed during the second or third trimester of pregnancy

➢ Symptoms may be mild or non-existent, but can include increased thirst, frequent urination, and blurred vision

➢ Treatment includes following a healthy diet, regular exercise, and monitoring blood sugar levels. In some cases, insulin therapy may be required

Gestational diabetes typically goes away after pregnancy, but increases the risk of developing Type 2 diabetes later in life

Why We are Diagnosed with Diabetes?

Diabetes is a common disease, affecting millions of people worldwide. According to the International Diabetes Federation, over 463 million adults between the ages of 20 and 79 were living with diabetes in 2019, and this number is expected to increase to 700 million by 2045. In the United States alone, more than 34 million people have diabetes, and 88 million adults have prediabetes, a condition that increases the risk of developing type 2 diabetes. Diabetes affects people of all ages and ethnicities, and it can lead to serious health complications if left untreated.

People can be diagnosed with diabetes for a variety of reasons, including:

➢ **Genetics:** Family history can play a role in the development of diabetes.

➢ **Lifestyle factors:** Poor diet, lack of exercise, and obesity can increase the risk of developing diabetes.

➢ **Age:** Diabetes is more common in older adults.

➢ **Gestational diabetes:** Pregnant women can develop diabetes, which usually goes away after giving birth.

➢ **Medical conditions:** Certain medical conditions, such as pancreatic disease, can increase the risk of developing diabetes.

Regardless of the cause, managing diabetes is crucial for overall health and well-being.

Why Diabetic Diet?

One of the most effective ways to manage diabetes is

through a diabetic diet. A diabetic diet is a healthy eating plan that is designed specifically to help people with diabetes in various ways. The history of the diabetic diet dates back to the early 20th century when it was believed that carbohydrates were the primary cause of high blood sugar levels. In the 1950s, low-carbohydrate diets were popularized, but they were later found to be ineffective in managing diabetes. In the 1970s, the concept of glycemic index (GI) was introduced, which measures the impact of carbohydrates on blood sugar levels. Today, the best diabetic diet is one that is low in fat, sodium and added sugars, and high in fiber, whole grains, fruits, and vegetables.

Helps control blood sugar levels: A diabetic diet can help regulate blood sugar levels, which is important for managing diabetes. When you eat foods that are high in carbohydrates, your body breaks them down into glucose, which is a type of sugar. If you have diabetes, your body may not be able to produce enough insulin to keep your blood sugar levels in check. By following a diabetic diet, you can help regulate your blood sugar levels and reduce your risk of complications.

➢ **Promotes weight loss:** A diabetic diet often emphasizes lean proteins, whole grains, and vegetables, which can help with weight loss and maintenance. Obesity is a major risk factor for diabetes, and losing weight can help reduce your risk of developing the condition. By following a diabetic diet, you can eat foods that are low in calories and high in nutrition, which can help you lose weight and improve your overall health.

➢ **Reduces risk of heart disease:** A diabetic diet can be heart-healthy, as it typically includes foods that are low in saturated and trans fats. People with diabetes are more likely to develop heart disease than people without diabetes. This is because high blood sugar levels can damage the blood vessels in your heart and increase your risk of developing plaque buildup. By following a diabetic diet, you can reduce your risk of heart disease by eating foods that are low in saturated fat and cholesterol.

➢ **Provides balanced nutrition:** A diabetic diet can provide all the necessary nutrients, while also limiting foods that can be harmful for people with diabetes. In addition to managing your blood sugar levels, losing weight, and reducing your risk of heart disease, a diabetic diet can also provide you with balanced nutrition. By eating a variety of foods from all the food groups, you can ensure that your body is getting the nutrients it needs to stay healthy.

About Diabetes and Diabetic Diet

About diabetes and diabetic diet, there are some terms for you to know.

1. Glycemic Index (GI): It is a measure of how quickly a particular food raises blood sugar levels. Foods with a high GI cause a rapid increase in blood sugar, while low GI foods cause a slower, more gradual increase.

2. Carbohydrate Counting: This method involves tracking the number of carbohydrates in each meal or snack and balancing them with insulin or medication doses. This helps to maintain consistent blood sugar levels throughout the day.

3. Plate Method: It is a simple way to plan meals by dividing the plate into sections for different types of foods. For example, half the plate should be filled with non-starchy vegetables, a quarter with lean protein, and a quarter with whole grains or starchy vegetables.

4. Exchange Lists: These are lists of foods grouped together based on their macronutrient content, such as carbohydrates, protein, and fat. This method offers more flexibility in meal planning and allows for substitutions within each food group.

5. Insulin-to-Carb Ratio (ICR): This is a personalized ratio that determines how much insulin is needed to cover a specific amount of carbohydrates. It helps to maintain consistent blood sugar levels and prevents spikes or drops.

6. Sugar Alcohols: These are sweeteners commonly used in diabetic-friendly foods and beverages. They have fewer calories and less impact on blood sugar than regular sugar, but may cause digestive issues in some people if consumed in excess.

Should and Shouldn't

So, what should you eat on a diabetic diet? A diabetic diet typically includes foods that are low in carbohydrates, sugar, and fat. This includes fruits, vegetables, whole grains, lean meats, and low-fat dairy products. It is also important to avoid foods that are high in sugar, such as candy, soda, and baked goods. Feeling a bit confused? Just read on!

➢ **Focus on whole foods:** Whole foods such as fruits, vegetables, whole grains, lean proteins, and healthy fats are nutrient-dense and provide a range of vitamins, minerals, and fiber. They also have a low glycemic index, which means they don't cause a sudden spike in blood sugar levels.

➢ **Limit processed foods:** Processed foods such as white bread, sugary drinks, and packaged snacks are high in refined carbohydrates and can cause blood sugar levels to rise rapidly. These foods should be avoided or limited as much as possible.

➢ **Choose low glycemic index foods:** Foods with a low glycemic index are slow to digest and are less likely to cause a sudden spike in blood sugar levels. Examples include sweet potatoes, legumes, oats, and non-starchy vegetables.

➢ **Watch portion sizes:** Eating too much of any food can cause blood sugar levels to rise. Portion control is key when it comes to managing diabetes. Measuring out servings and using smaller plates can help keep portion sizes in check.

➢ **Consider carb counting:** Carbohydrate counting is a common method used by diabetics to manage blood sugar levels. It involves tracking the number of carbohydrates in foods and adjusting insulin doses accordingly.

➢ **Stay hydrated:** Drinking plenty of water can help keep blood sugar levels stable and prevent dehydration, which can cause blood sugar levels to rise.

➢ Avoid sugary drinks: Sugary drinks such as soda and juice are high in refined sugar and can cause blood sugar levels to spike. Water, unsweetened tea, and coffee are better options.

➢ **Choose healthy fats:** Healthy fats such as those found in nuts, seeds, and avocados can help improve insulin sensitivity and reduce inflammation in the body.

➢ **Be mindful of alcohol consumption:** Alcohol can cause blood sugar levels to drop, so it's important to drink in moderation and always with food. It's also important to monitor blood sugar levels after drinking to ensure they don't drop too low.

In summary, a diabetic diet involves making healthy food choices, focusing on whole foods, limiting processed foods, choosing low glycemic index foods, watching portion sizes, considering carb counting, staying hydrated, avoiding sugary drinks, choosing healthy fats, and being mindful of alcohol consumption. By following these guidelines, diabetics can manage their blood sugar levels and reduce the risk of complications associated with the disease.

Then, what about the "shouldn't do"? Here are several foods that people with diabetes should avoid or limit in their diet.

➢ **Sugary drinks:** Sugary drinks like soda, fruit juice, and sports drinks can cause a rapid increase in blood sugar levels. These drinks also contain a lot of calories and can lead to weight gain, which can exacerbate diabetes symptoms.

➢ **Processed foods:** Processed foods like chips, crackers, and baked goods are often high in refined carbohydrates, which can lead to spikes in blood sugar levels. These foods also tend to be high in calories and low in nutrients, which can contribute to weight gain and other health problems.

➢ **Fried foods:** Fried foods like french fries and fried chicken can be high in saturated and trans fats, which can raise cholesterol levels and increase the risk of heart disease. These foods can also contribute to weight gain and worsen diabetes symptoms.

➢ **Alcohol:** Drinking alcohol can cause a rapid increase in blood sugar levels, particularly if consumed on an empty stomach. Alcohol can also interfere with diabetes medications and increase the risk of hypoglycemia (low blood sugar).

➢ White bread, rice, and pasta: Foods made from white flour can cause a rapid increase in blood sugar levels, as they are quickly broken down into glucose. Whole grain options like brown rice, whole wheat bread, and quinoa are better choices, as they are higher in fiber and nutrients and can help regulate blood sugar levels.

➢ **Sweets and desserts:** Sweets and desserts like candy, cake, and ice cream are high in sugar and calories and can cause a rapid increase in blood sugar levels. These foods should be limited or avoided in a diabetes-friendly diet.

➤ **High-fat dairy products:** High-fat dairy products like whole milk, cheese, and cream can be high in saturated and trans fats, which can raise cholesterol levels and increase the risk of heart disease. Low-fat or fat-free options are better choices.

By avoiding or limiting these foods, people with diabetes can better manage their blood sugar levels and reduce the risk of complications associated with the disease. It's also important to focus on eating whole foods like fruits, vegetables, lean protein, and whole grains, which can provide essential nutrients and help regulate blood sugar levels.

Others Tips for You

➤ **To make a diabetic diet more diverse.** It is important to choose a variety of nutrient-rich foods that are low in fat, sodium, and sugar. According to the American Diabetes Association (ADA) guidelines, individuals with diabetes should focus on getting carbohydrates from vegetables, whole grains, fruits, and legumes. Incorporating a range of colorful vegetables such as spinach, kale, broccoli, and carrots can add diversity to a diabetic diet. Additionally, lean meats, fish, and poultry can provide protein, while low-fat dairy products can supply calcium and vitamin D. It is important to consult with a registered dietician who is knowledgeable about diabetes nutrition to develop a personalized meal plan that caters to individual food preferences and lifestyle.

➤ **To calculate overall calories for each meal.** It is an important part of managing a diabetic diet. To calculate calories, you need to know the calorie content of each food item you consume and the serving size. Most packaged foods have nutrition labels that provide this information. You can also use online calorie calculators to get an estimate of the calories in whole, unprocessed foods. To make things easier, you can use a food diary or a calorie tracking app to keep track of your calorie intake throughout the day. It is essential to consult with a healthcare professional or registered dietician to determine the appropriate calorie intake for your specific needs.

➤ **To exercise regularly and monitor your blood sugar levels.** By staying active and monitoring your blood sugar levels, you can help manage your diabetes and reduce your risk of complications.

For instance, you can aim for moderate-intensity aerobic activity per week, incorporate strength training exercises at least 2-3 times per week, choose exercises that you enjoy and can do consistently. And remember, monitor your blood sugar levels before, during, and after exercise. Don't forget to stay hydrated and wear proper footwear! When you are doing exercises, consider working with a certified diabetes educator or personal trainer to create a safe and effective exercise plan. Remember to consult with your healthcare provider before starting any new exercise routine. They can help you determine what exercises are safe for you based on your individual health needs and medical history.

In conclusion, if you have diabetes, it is important to understand the benefits of following a diabetic diet. By managing your blood sugar levels, losing weight, reducing your risk of heart disease, and providing balanced nutrition, a diabetic diet can help you lead a healthier and happier life. So, talk to your doctor, registered dietitian or a healthcare provider to learn more about how a diabetic diet and exercises can benefit you.

Start to Cooking

I hope you have discovered some new and exciting recipes to add to your meal plan. Remember, managing diabetes doesn't have to be all doom and gloom. Managing diabetes is about making small, sustainable changes to your lifestyle, and with the help of a dietician, you can create a personalized meal plan that works for you.

With this cookbook by your side, you'll be able to fight off the evil villain known as type 2 diabetes and feel like the superhero you truly are. So, what are you waiting for? It's time to put on your apron and join the fight against diabetes, one meal at a time! Keep on cooking and keep on smiling!

30 Days Diabetic Diet Meal Plan

DAYS	BREAKFAST	LUNCH	DINNER	SNACK/DESSERT
1	Blueberry Oat Mini Muffins	Italian Zucchini Boats	Herbed Spring Peas	Cucumber Roll-Ups
2	Corn, Egg and Potato Bake	Chickpea-Spinach Curry	Celery and Apple Salad with Cider Vinaigrette	Zucchini Hummus Dip with Red Bell Peppers
3	Sausage Egg Cup	Stuffed Peppers	Chicken, Cantaloupe, Kale, and Almond Salad	Southern Boiled Peanuts
4	Spaghetti Squash Fritters	Italian Tofu with Mushrooms and Peppers	Chinese Chicken Salad	Hummus with Chickpeas and Tahini Sauce
5	Overnight Berry Oats	Italian Bean Burgers	Black-Eyed Pea Sauté with Garlic and Olives	Spicy Cajun Onion Dip
6	Brussels Sprout Hash and Eggs	Tex-Mex Rice 'N' Beans	Greek Stuffed Eggplant	Instant Popcorn
7	Breakfast Panini	Farmers' Market Barley Risotto	Baked Chicken Dijon	Low-Sugar Blueberry Muffins
8	Sunrise Smoothie Bowl	Edamame and Walnut Salad	Seitan Curry	Orange Praline with Yogurt
9	Mini Breakfast Quiches	Sweet Beet Grain Bowl	Palak Tofu	Banana Pineapple Freeze
10	BLT Breakfast Wrap	Rainbow Quinoa Salad	Roasted Veggie Bowl	Baked Berry Cups with Crispy Cinnamon Wedges
11	Ginger Blackberry Bliss Smoothie Bowl	Mandarin Orange Chicken Salad	No-Tuna Lettuce Wraps	Oatmeal Cookies
12	Tropical Steel Cut Oats	Texas Caviar	Stuffed Portobello Mushrooms	Creamy Orange Cheesecake
13	Mandarin Orange–Millet Breakfast Bowl	Chicken and Vegetables with Quinoa	Vegetable Burgers	Oatmeal Chippers
14	Pizza Eggs	Dirty Forbidden Rice	Steak Gyro Platter	Cherry Delight
15	Cinnamon-Almond Green Smoothie	BBQ Lentils	Caprese Eggplant Stacks	Candied Pecans
16	Orange Muffins	Colorful Rice Casserole	Instant Pot Hoppin' John with Skillet Cauli "Rice"	Baked Parmesan Crisps
17	Cinnamon Wisp Pancakes	Southwestern Quinoa Salad	Stuffed Portobellos	Sweet Potato Oven Fries with Spicy Sour Cream

DAYS	BREAKFAST	LUNCH	DINNER	SNACK/DESSERT
18	Avocado and Goat Cheese Toast	BBQ Bean Burgers	Edamame Falafel with Roasted Vegetables	Hummus
19	Bran Apple Muffins	Green Chickpea Falafel	Pra Ram Vegetables and Peanut Sauce with Seared Tofu	Crab-Filled Mushrooms
20	Oat and Walnut Granola	Sage and Garlic Vegetable Bake	Orange Tofu	No-Added-Sugar Berries and Cream Yogurt Bowl
21	Smoked Salmon and Asparagus Quiche Cups	Spicy Couscous and Chickpea Salad	Tuna Steak	Garlic Kale Chips
22	Fresh Blueberry Pancakes	Broccoli "Tabouli"	Coconut-Ginger Rice	Creamy Pineapple-Pecan Dessert Squares
23	Sweet Potato Toasts	Mediterranean Chicken Salad	Veggies and Kasha with Balsamic Vinaigrette	Spiced Rice Pudding
24	Harvest Blackberry Quinoa Bowl	Three Bean and Basil Salad	Thai Red Lentils	Apple Crunch
25	Goji Berry Muesli	Blueberry and Chicken Salad on a Bed of Greens	Italian Roasted Vegetables	Berry Bubble
26	Crustless Potato, Spinach, and Mushroom Quiche	Herbed Tomato Salad	Brown Rice–Stuffed Butternut Squash	Apple Cinnamon Bread Pudding
27	Asparagus and Bell Pepper Strata	Moroccan Carrot Salad	Thai Broccoli Slaw	Goat Cheese–Stuffed Pears
28	Italian Frittata	Salmon Niçoise Salad	Steak with Bell Pepper	Grilled Watermelon with Avocado Mousse
29	Breakfast Farro with Berries and Walnuts	Make-Ahead Apple, Carrot, and Cabbage Slaw	Sunflower-Tuna-Cauliflower Salad	Frozen Mocha Milkshake
30	Southwestern Egg Casserole	Warm Sweet Potato and Black Bean Salad	Scallops in Lemon-Butter Sauce	Banana Bread Nice Cream

Chapter 1   Breakfasts

Blueberry Oat Mini Muffins

Prep time: 12 minutes | Cook time: 10 minutes | Serves 7

½ cup rolled oats	½ cup plain Greek yogurt
¼ cup whole wheat pastry flour or white whole wheat flour	2 tablespoons pure maple syrup
½ tablespoon baking powder	2 teaspoons extra-virgin olive oil
½ teaspoon ground cardamom or ground cinnamon	½ teaspoon vanilla extract
⅛ teaspoon kosher salt	½ cup frozen blueberries (preferably small wild blueberries)
2 large eggs	

1. In a large bowl, stir together the oats, flour, baking powder, cardamom, and salt. 2. In a medium bowl, whisk together the eggs, yogurt, maple syrup, oil, and vanilla. 3. Add the egg mixture to oat mixture and stir just until combined. Gently fold in the blueberries. 4. Scoop the batter into each cup of the egg bite mold. 5. Pour 1 cup of water into the electric pressure cooker. Place the egg bite mold on the wire rack and carefully lower it into the pot. 6. Close and lock the lid of the pressure cooker. Set the valve to sealing. 7. Cook on high pressure for 10 minutes. 8. When the cooking is complete, allow the pressure to release naturally for 10 minutes, then quick release any remaining pressure. Hit Cancel. 9. Lift the wire rack out of the pot and place on a cooling rack for 5 minutes. Invert the mold onto the cooling rack to release the muffins. 10. Serve the muffins warm or refrigerate or freeze.

Per Serving:
calories: 117 | fat: 4g | protein: 5g | carbs: 15g | sugars: 4g | fiber: 2g | sodium: 89mg

Veggie-Stuffed Omelet

Prep time: 15 minutes | Cook time: 10 minutes | Serves 1

1 teaspoon olive or canola oil	½ cup fat-free egg product or 2 eggs, beaten
2 tablespoons chopped red bell pepper	1 tablespoon water
1 tablespoon chopped onion	Pinch salt
¼ cup sliced fresh mushrooms	Pinch pepper
1 cup loosely packed fresh baby spinach leaves, rinsed	1 tablespoon shredded reduced-fat Cheddar cheese

1 In 8-inch nonstick skillet, heat oil over medium-high heat. Add bell pepper, onion and mushrooms to oil. Cook 2 minutes, stirring frequently, until onion is tender. Stir in spinach; continue cooking and stirring just until spinach wilts. Transfer vegetables from pan to small bowl. 2 In medium bowl, beat egg product, water, salt and pepper with fork or whisk until well mixed. Reheat same skillet over medium-high heat. Quickly pour egg mixture into pan. While sliding pan back and forth rapidly over heat, quickly stir with spatula to spread eggs continuously over bottom of pan as they thicken. Let stand over heat a few seconds to lightly brown bottom of omelet. Do not overcook; omelet will continue to cook after folding. 3 Place cooked vegetable mixture over half of omelet; top with cheese. With spatula, fold other half of omelet over vegetables. Gently slide out of pan onto plate. Serve immediately.

Per Serving:
calorie: 140 | fat: 5g | protein: 16g | carbs: 6g | sugars: 3g | fiber: 2g | sodium: 470mg

Sausage Egg Cup

Prep time: 10 minutes | Cook time: 15 minutes | Serves 6

12 ounces (340 g) ground pork breakfast sausage	¼ teaspoon ground black pepper
6 large eggs	½ teaspoon crushed red pepper flakes
½ teaspoon salt	

1. Place sausage in six 4-inch ramekins (about 2 ounces / 57 g per ramekin) greased with cooking oil. Press sausage down to cover bottom and about ½-inch up the sides of ramekins. Crack one egg into each ramekin and sprinkle evenly with salt, black pepper, and red pepper flakes. 2. Place ramekins into air fryer basket. Adjust the temperature to 350°F (177°C) and set the timer for 15 minutes. Egg cups will be done when sausage is fully cooked to at least 145°F (63°C) and the egg is firm. Serve warm.

Per Serving:
calories: 268 | fat: 23g | protein: 14g | carbs: 1g | net carbs: 1g | fiber: 0g

Spaghetti Squash Fritters

Prep time: 15 minutes | Cook time: 8 minutes | Serves 4

2 cups cooked spaghetti squash	almond flour
2 tablespoons unsalted butter, softened	2 stalks green onion, sliced
1 large egg	½ teaspoon garlic powder
¼ cup blanched finely ground	1 teaspoon dried parsley

1. Remove excess moisture from the squash using a cheesecloth or kitchen towel. 2. Mix all ingredients in a large bowl. Form into four patties. 3. Cut a piece of parchment to fit your air fryer basket. Place each patty on the parchment and place into the air fryer basket. 4. Adjust the temperature to 400°F (204°C) and set the timer for 8 minutes. 5. Flip the patties halfway through the cooking time. Serve warm.

Per Serving:
calories: 146 | fat: 12g | protein: 4g | carbs: 7g | sugars: 3g | fiber: 2g | sodium: 36mg

Avocado and Goat Cheese Toast

Prep time: 5 minutes | Cook time: 0 minutes | Serves 2

2 slices whole-wheat thin-sliced bread (I love Ezekiel sprouted bread and Dave's Killer Bread)	½ avocado
	2 tablespoons crumbled goat cheese
	Salt

1. In a toaster or broiler, toast the bread until browned. 2. Remove the flesh from the avocado. In a medium bowl, use a fork to mash the avocado flesh. Spread it onto the toast. 3. Sprinkle with the goat cheese and season lightly with salt. 4. Add any toppings and serve.

Per Serving:
calories: 137 | fat: 6g | protein: 5g | carbs: 18g | sugars: 0g | fiber: 5g | sodium: 195mg

Overnight Berry Oats

Prep time: 5 minutes | Cook time: 0 minutes | Serves 2

1 cup rolled oats	fat nondairy milk (plus more
1 cup raspberries or mixed	for serving, if desired)
berries (such as blueberries,	½ tablespoon chia seeds
strawberries, and blackberries),	2 tablespoons coconut nectar
fresh or frozen	or pure maple syrup
1 cup + 1–2 tablespoons low-	Pinch of sea salt

1. In a bowl or large jar, combine the oats, berries, milk, chia seeds, nectar or syrup, and salt. Cover and refrigerate overnight (or for at least several hours). Serve with more milk to thin, if desired, and also try some additional add-ins.

Per Serving:
calorie: 326 | fat: 5g | protein: 9g | carbs: 64g | sugars: 21g | fiber: 14g | sodium: 205mg

Brussels Sprout Hash and Eggs

Prep time: 15 minutes | Cook time: 15 minutes | Serves 4

3 teaspoons extra-virgin olive oil, divided	2 garlic cloves, thinly sliced
1 pound Brussels sprouts, sliced	¼ teaspoon salt
	Juice of 1 lemon
	4 eggs

1. In a large skillet, heat 1½ teaspoons of oil over medium heat. Add the Brussels sprouts and toss. Cook, stirring regularly, for 6 to 8 minutes until browned and softened. Add the garlic and continue to cook until fragrant, about 1 minute. Season with the salt and lemon juice. Transfer to a serving dish. 2. In the same pan, heat the remaining 1½ teaspoons of oil over medium-high heat. Crack the eggs into the pan. Fry for 2 to 4 minutes, flip, and continue cooking to desired doneness. Serve over the bed of hash.

Per Serving:
calories: 158 | fat: 9g | protein: 10g | carbs: 12g | sugars: 4g | fiber: 4g | sodium: 234mg

Corn, Egg and Potato Bake

Prep time: 20 minutes | Cook time: 1 hour | Serves 8

4 cups frozen diced hash brown potatoes (from 2-lb bag), thawed	10 eggs or 2½ cups fat-free egg product
½ cup frozen whole-kernel corn (from 1-lb bag), thawed	½ cup fat-free small-curd cottage cheese
¼ cup chopped roasted red bell peppers (from 7-oz jar)	½ teaspoon dried oregano leaves
1½ cups shredded reduced-fat Colby–Monterey Jack cheese (6 oz)	¼ teaspoon garlic powder
	4 medium green onions, chopped (¼ cup)

1 Heat oven to 350°F. Spray 11x7-inch (2-quart) glass baking dish with cooking spray. In baking dish, layer potatoes, corn, bell peppers and 1 cup of the shredded cheese. 2 In medium bowl, beat eggs, cottage cheese, oregano and garlic powder with whisk until well blended. Slowly pour over potato mixture. Sprinkle with onions and remaining ½ cup shredded cheese. 3 Cover and bake 30 minutes. Uncover and bake about 30 minutes longer or until knife inserted in center comes out clean. Let stand 5 to 10 minutes before cutting.

Per Serving:
calories: 240 | fat: 11g | protein: 16g | carbs: 18g | sugars: 2g | fiber: 2g | sodium: 440mg

Breakfast Panini

Prep time: 10 minutes | Cook time: 10 minutes | Serves 2

2 eggs, beaten	2 slices tomato
½ teaspoon salt-free seasoning blend	2 thin slices onion
2 tablespoons chopped fresh chives	4 ultra-thin slices reduced-sodium deli ham
2 whole wheat thin bagels	2 thin slices reduced-fat Cheddar cheese

1 Spray 8-inch skillet with cooking spray; heat skillet over medium heat. In medium bowl, beat eggs, seasoning and chives with fork or whisk until well mixed. Pour into skillet. As eggs begin to set at bottom and side, gently lift cooked portions with spatula so that thin, uncooked portion can flow to bottom. Avoid constant stirring. Cook 3 to 4 minutes or until eggs are thickened throughout but still moist and creamy; remove from heat. 2 Meanwhile, heat closed contact grill or panini maker 5 minutes. 3 For each panini, divide cooked eggs evenly between bottom halves of bagels. Top each with 1 slice each tomato and onion, 2 ham slices, 1 cheese slice and top half of bagel. Transfer filled panini to heated grill. Close cover, pressing down lightly. Cook 2 to 3 minutes or until browned and cheese is melted. Serve immediately.

Per Serving:
1 Panini: calories: 260 | fat: 7g | protein: 15g | carbs: 32g | sugars: 5g | fiber: 2g | sodium: 410mg

Tropical Steel Cut Oats

Prep time: 5 minutes | Cook time: 5 minutes | Serves 4

1 cup steel cut oats	1 (2-inch) vanilla bean, scraped (seeds and pod)
1 cup unsweetened almond milk	Ground cinnamon
2 cups coconut water or water	¼ cup chopped unsalted macadamia nuts
¾ cup frozen chopped peaches	
¾ cup frozen mango chunks	

1. In the electric pressure cooker, combine the oats, almond milk, coconut water, peaches, mango chunks, and vanilla bean seeds and pod. Stir well. 2. Close and lock the lid of the pressure cooker. Set the valve to sealing. 3. Cook on high pressure for 5 minutes. 4. When the cooking is complete, allow the pressure to release naturally for 10 minutes, then quick release any remaining pressure. Hit Cancel. 5. Once the pin drops, unlock and remove the lid. 6. Discard the vanilla bean pod and stir well. 7. Spoon the oats into 4 bowls. Top each serving with a sprinkle of cinnamon and 1 tablespoon of the macadamia nuts.

Per Serving:
calories: 127 | fat: 7g | protein: 2g | carbs: 14g | sugars: 8g | fiber: 3g | sodium: 167mg

Sunrise Smoothie Bowl

Prep time: 5 minutes | Cook time: 0 minutes | Serves 1

½ cup (63 g) frozen raspberries	Greek yogurt
½ cup (72 g) frozen strawberries	Water, as needed
½ large banana	1 tbsp (5 g) unsweetened coconut flakes
½ cup (50 g) cauliflower florets	2 tbsp (14 g) coarsely chopped walnuts
½ cup (100 g) plain nonfat	

1. In a high-power blender, combine the raspberries, strawberries, banana, cauliflower, and yogurt. Blend the ingredients until they are smooth, adding water as needed to reach the desired consistency. 2. Pour the smoothie into a bowl and top it with the coconut flakes and walnuts.

Per Serving:
calorie: 336 | fat: 14g | protein: 17g | carbs: 44g | sugars: 21g | fiber: 12g | sodium: 69mg

Italian Frittata

Prep time: 10 minutes | Cook time: 30 minutes | Serves 6

2 tablespoons extra-virgin olive oil	bell peppers)
2 medium yellow onions, sliced thinly	2 teaspoons garlic, minced
6 large eggs, beaten until foamy	1 bunch fresh basil, finely chopped
2 cups mixed steamed vegetables (try chopped broccoli, asparagus, and red	½ teaspoon freshly ground black pepper
	¼ cup freshly grated Parmigiano-Reggiano cheese, for garnish

1. Preheat the oven to 350 degrees. Add the oil to a large, wide, ovenproof skillet and heat over medium heat. 2. Add the onions and sauté until lightly golden, approximately 5–10 minutes. 3. In a large bowl, combine the remaining ingredients (except the cheese), and add to the skillet. 4. Place the skillet in the oven and bake the frittata for 14–17 minutes until set. Remove from the oven and loosen the edges with a spatula. Sprinkle with grated cheese, cut into wedges, and serve.

Per Serving:
calories: 160 | fat: 11g | protein: g9 | carbs: 8g | sugars: 3g | fiber: 2g | sodium: 159mg

Mini Breakfast Quiches

Prep time: 10 minutes | Cook time: 20 minutes | Serves 6

4 ounces diced green chilies	½ teaspoon cumin
¼ cup diced pimiento	1 bunch fresh cilantro or Italian parsley, finely chopped
1 small eggplant, cubed	1 cup shredded reduced-fat cheddar cheese, divided
3 cups precooked brown rice	
½ cup egg whites	
⅓ cup fat-free milk	

1. Preheat the oven to 400 degrees. Spray a 12-cup muffin tin with nonstick cooking spray. 2. In a large mixing bowl, combine all the ingredients except ½ cup of the cheese. 3. Add a dash of salt and pepper, if desired. 4. Spoon the mixture evenly into muffin cups, and sprinkle with the remaining cheese. Bake for 12–15 minutes or until set. Carefully remove the quiches from the pan, arrange on a platter, and serve.

Per Serving:
calories: 189 | fat: 3g | protein: 11g | carbs: 31g | sugars: 6g | fiber: 5g | sodium: 214mg

BLT Breakfast Wrap

Prep time: 5 minutes | Cook time: 10 minutes | Serves 4

8 ounces (227 g) reduced-sodium bacon	4 Roma tomatoes, sliced
8 tablespoons mayonnaise	Salt and freshly ground black pepper, to taste
8 large romaine lettuce leaves	

1. Arrange the bacon in a single layer in the air fryer basket. (It's OK if the bacon sits a bit on the sides.) Set the air fryer to 350ºF (177ºC) and air fry for 10 minutes. Check for crispiness and air fry for 2 to 3 minutes longer if needed. Cook in batches, if necessary, and drain the grease in between batches. 2. Spread 1 tablespoon of mayonnaise on each of the lettuce leaves and top with the tomatoes and cooked bacon. Season to taste with salt and freshly ground black pepper. Roll the lettuce leaves as you would a burrito, securing with a toothpick if desired.

Per Serving:
calories: 343 | fat: 32g | protein: 10g | carbs: 5g | net carbs: 4g | fiber: 1g

Bran Apple Muffins

Prep time: 10 minutes | Cook time: 20 minutes | Makes 18 muffins

2 cups whole-wheat flour	2 eggs
1 cup wheat bran	1½ cups skim milk, at room temperature
⅓ cup granulated sweetener	½ cup melted coconut oil
1 tablespoon baking powder	2 teaspoons pure vanilla extract
2 teaspoons ground cinnamon	2 apples, peeled, cored, and diced
½ teaspoon ground ginger	
¼ teaspoon ground nutmeg	
Pinch sea salt	

1. Preheat the oven to 350°F. 2. Line 18 muffin cups with paper liners and set the tray aside. 3. In a large bowl, stir together the flour, bran, sweetener, baking powder, cinnamon, ginger, nutmeg, and salt. 4. In a small bowl, whisk the eggs, milk, coconut oil, and vanilla until blended. 5. Add the wet ingredients to the dry ingredients, stirring until just blended. 6. Stir in the apples and spoon equal amounts of batter into each muffin cup. 7. Bake the muffins until a toothpick inserted in the center of a muffin comes out clean, about 20 minutes. 8. Cool the muffins completely and serve. 9. Store leftover muffins in a sealed container in the refrigerator for up to 3 days or in the freezer for up to 1 month.

Per Serving:
calories: 145 | fat: 7g | protein: 4g | carbs: 19g | sugars: 6g | fiber: 4g | sodium: 17mg

Ginger Blackberry Bliss Smoothie Bowl

Prep time: 5 minutes | Cook time: 0 minutes | Serves 2

½ cup frozen blackberries	milk
1 cup plain Greek yogurt	½ teaspoon peeled and grated fresh ginger
1 cup baby spinach	
½ cup unsweetened almond	¼ cup chopped pecans

1. In a blender or food processor, combine the blackberries, yogurt, spinach, almond milk, and ginger. Blend until smooth. 2. Spoon the mixture into two bowls. 3. Top each bowl with 2 tablespoons of chopped pecans and serve.

Per Serving:
calories: 211 | fat: 11g | protein: 10g | carbs: 18g | sugars: 13g | fiber: 4g | sodium: 149mg

Mandarin Orange–Millet Breakfast Bowl

Prep time: 5 minutes | Cook time: 30 minutes | Serves 2

⅓ cup millet	Pinch salt
1 cup nonfat milk	Stevia, for sweetening
½ cup water	½ cup canned mandarin oranges, drained
¼ teaspoon cinnamon	
¼ teaspoon ground cardamom	2 tablespoons sliced almonds
1 teaspoon vanilla extract	

1. In a small saucepan set over medium-high heat, stir together the millet, milk, water, cinnamon, cardamom, vanilla, salt, and stevia. Bring to a boil. Reduce the heat to low. Cover and simmer for 25 minutes, without stirring. If the liquid is not completely absorbed, cook for 3 to 5 minutes longer, partially covered. 2. Stir in the oranges. Remove from the heat. 3. Top with the sliced almonds and serve.

Per Serving:
calories: 254 | fat: 7g | protein: 10g | carbs: 38g | sugars: 12g | fiber: 5g | sodium: 73mg

Smoked Salmon and Asparagus Quiche Cups

Prep time: 15 minutes | Cook time: 15 minutes | Serves 2

Nonstick cooking spray	salmon (skinless and boneless), chopped
4 asparagus spears, cut into ½-inch pieces	
2 tablespoons finely chopped onion	3 large eggs
	2 tablespoons 2% milk
3 ounces (85 g) smoked	¼ teaspoon dried dill
	Pinch ground white pepper

1. Pour 1½ cups of water into the electric pressure cooker and insert a wire rack or trivet. 2. Lightly spray the bottom and sides of the ramekins with nonstick cooking spray. Divide the asparagus, onion, and salmon between the ramekins. 3. In a measuring cup with a spout, whisk together the eggs, milk, dill, and white pepper. Pour half of the egg mixture into each ramekin. Loosely cover the ramekins with aluminum foil. 4. Carefully place the ramekins inside the pot on the rack. 5. Close and lock the lid of the pressure cooker. Set the valve to sealing. 6. Cook on high pressure for 15 minutes. 7. When the cooking is complete, hit Cancel and quick release the pressure. 8. Once the pin drops, unlock and remove the lid. 9. Carefully remove the ramekins from the pot. Cool, covered, for 5 minutes. 10. Run a small silicone spatula or a knife around the edge of each ramekin. Invert each quiche onto a small plate and serve.

Per Serving:
calories: 180 | fat: 9g | protein: 20g | carbs: 3g | sugars: 1g | fiber: 1g | sodium: 646mg

Cinnamon Wisp Pancakes

Prep time: 5 minutes | Cook time: 10 minutes | Serves 4

2 cups oat flour	Pinch of sea salt
2 tablespoons chia seeds	1½ teaspoons vanilla extract
1 tablespoon baking powder	1¾ cups + ¼ cup vanilla low-fat nondairy milk
2 teaspoons cinnamon	

1. In a large bowl, combine the oat flour, chia seeds, baking powder, cinnamon, and salt. Stir to combine. Add the vanilla and 1¾ cups of the milk, and whisk through the dry mixture until combined. Let the batter sit for a few minutes to thicken. 2. Lightly coat a large nonstick skillet with cooking spray. Heat the pan over medium-high heat for a few minutes until hot, then reduce the heat to medium or medium-low and let it rest for a minute. Using a ladle, scoop ¼ to ⅓ cup of the batter into the pan for each pancake. Depending on the size of pan, cook 2 or 3 pancakes at a time. Cook for several minutes, until small bubbles form on the outer edges and in the centers and the pancakes start to look dry on the top. (Wait until those bubbles form, or the pancakes will be tricky to flip.) Once ready, flip the pancakes to lightly cook the other side for about a minute. Repeat until the batter is all used, adding the extra milk, 1 tablespoon at a time, if needed to thin the batter as you go.

Per Serving:
calorie: 312 | fat: 6g | protein: 11g | carbs: 54g | sugars: 5g | fiber: 9g | sodium: 483mg

Orange Muffins

Prep time: 15 minutes | Cook time: 15 minutes | Serves 9

2½ cups finely ground almond flour	coconut oil
	2 large eggs
¾ teaspoon ground cinnamon	Grated zest and juice of 1 medium orange
½ teaspoon baking powder	
½ teaspoon ground cardamom	1 tablespoon raw honey or 100% pure maple syrup
¼ teaspoon salt	
4 tablespoons avocado or	¼ teaspoon vanilla extract

1. Preheat the oven to 375ºF. 2. In a large bowl, whisk together the almond flour, cinnamon, baking powder, cardamom, and salt. Set aside. 3. In a medium bowl, whisk together the oil, eggs, zest, juice, honey, and vanilla. Add this mixture to the dry ingredients, and stir until well combined. 4. In a nonstick muffin tin, fill each muffin cup until nearly full. 5. Bake for 15 minutes, or until the top center is firm.

Per Serving:
calories: 208 | fat: 17g | protein: 6g | carbs: 8g | sugars: 4g | fiber: 3g | sodium: 81mg

Carrot Pear Smoothie

Prep time: 10 minutes | Cook time: 0 minutes | Serves 2

2 carrots, peeled and grated	Juice and zest of 1 lime
1 ripe pear, unpeeled, cored and chopped	1 cup water
	½ teaspoon ground cinnamon
2 teaspoons grated fresh ginger	¼ teaspoon ground nutmeg

1. Put the carrots, pear, ginger, lime juice, lime zest, water, cinnamon, and nutmeg in a blender and blend until smooth. 2. Pour into two glasses and serve.

Per Serving:
calories: 61 | fat: 0g | protein: 1g | carbs: 15g | sugars: 7g | fiber: 4g | sodium: 45mg

Pizza Eggs

Prep time: 5 minutes | Cook time: 10 minutes | Serves 2

1 cup shredded Mozzarella cheese	¼ teaspoon dried oregano
	¼ teaspoon dried parsley
7 slices pepperoni, chopped	¼ teaspoon garlic powder
1 large egg, whisked	¼ teaspoon salt

1. Place Mozzarella in a single layer on the bottom of an ungreased round nonstick baking dish. Scatter pepperoni over cheese, then pour egg evenly around baking dish. 2. Sprinkle with remaining ingredients and place into air fryer basket. Adjust the temperature to 330°F (166°C) and bake for 10 minutes. When cheese is brown and egg is set, dish will be done. 3. Let cool in dish 5 minutes before serving.

Per Serving:
calories: 240 | fat: 18g | protein: 17g | carbs: 2g | net carbs: 2g | fiber: 0g

Crustless Potato, Spinach, and Mushroom Quiche

Prep time: 10 minutes | Cook time: 40 minutes | Serves 4

8 oz (227 g) yellow potatoes, thinly sliced	1 tsp balsamic vinegar
	2 cups (60 g) baby spinach
1 tbsp (15 ml) olive oil	6 large eggs
2 tsp (2 g) dried thyme, divided	2 cups (480 ml) 1% milk
1 tsp dried rosemary	2 oz (57 g) goat cheese, crumbled
10 oz (283 g) button mushrooms, coarsely chopped	½ cup (28 g) julienned sun-dried tomatoes (see Tip)

1. Preheat the oven to 375°F (191°C). 2. In a large bowl, toss the potatoes with the oil, 1 teaspoon of the thyme, and rosemary. Arrange the potatoes on the bottom of a large oven-safe skillet or baking dish. Bake the potatoes for 10 to 15 minutes, or until they soften and start to crisp. Do not turn off the oven. 3. Meanwhile, combine the remaining 1 teaspoon of thyme and the mushrooms in a large skillet over medium-high heat. Cook the mushrooms for about 5 minutes, or until the mushrooms are brown and most of their liquid has evaporated. Stir in the vinegar. Add the spinach and cook it for 3 to 4 minutes, stirring constantly, until it is wilted. Remove the mushrooms and spinach from the heat and set them aside. 4. In a large bowl, whisk together the eggs and milk. Add the mushroom and spinach mixture, goat cheese, and sun-dried tomatoes. Pour the mixture into the potato-lined skillet and bake the quiche for 25 minutes, or until the eggs are set and no longer runny in the center.

Per Serving:
calorie: 322 | fat: 16g | protein: 22g | carbs: 25g | sugars: 12g | fiber: 3g | sodium: 218mg

Cinnamon-Almond Green Smoothie

Prep time: 4 minutes | Cook time: 0 minutes | Serves 2

1½ cups nonfat milk	1 small apple, peeled, cored, and finely chopped
2 tablespoons finely ground flaxseed	1 teaspoon vanilla extract
1 tablespoon almond butter	1 teaspoon cinnamon
1 (8-ounce) container plain nonfat Greek yogurt	Stevia, for sweetening
1 cup frozen spinach	4 to 6 ice cubes (optional)

1. In a blender, combine the milk, flaxseed, and almond butter. Blend for 10 seconds on medium. 2. Add the yogurt, spinach, apple, vanilla, cinnamon, stevia, and ice cubes (if using). Blend for about 1 minute, or until smooth and creamy. 3. Pour into 2 glasses and sip to your health!

Per Serving:
calories: 292 | fat: 9g | protein: 24g | carbs: 32g | sugars: 18g | fiber: 8g | sodium: 200mg

Potato-Bacon Gratin

Prep time: 20 minutes | Cook time: 40 minutes | Serves 8

1 tablespoon olive oil	slices, divided
6-ounces bag fresh spinach	5-ounces reduced-fat grated Swiss cheddar, divided
1 clove garlic, minced	
4 large potatoes, peeled or unpeeled, divided	1 cup lower-sodium, lower-fat chicken broth
6-ounces Canadian bacon	

1. Set the Instant Pot to Sauté and pour in the olive oil. Cook the spinach and garlic in olive oil just until spinach is wilted (5 minutes or less). Turn off the instant pot. 2. Cut potatoes into thin slices about ¼" thick. 3. In a springform pan that will fit into the inner pot of your Instant Pot, spray it with nonstick spray then layer ⅓ the potatoes, half the bacon, ⅓ the cheese, and half the wilted spinach. 4. Repeat layers ending with potatoes. Reserve ⅓ cheese for later. 5. Pour chicken broth over all. 6. Wipe the bottom of your Instant Pot to soak up any remaining oil, then add in 2 cups of water and the steaming rack. Place the springform pan on top. 7. Close the lid and secure to the locking position. Be sure the vent is turned to sealing. Set for 35 minutes on Manual at high pressure. 8. Perform a quick release. 9. Top with the remaining cheese, then allow to stand 10 minutes before removing from the Instant Pot, cutting and serving.

Per Serving:
calories: 220 | fat: 7g | protein: 14g | carbs: 28g | sugars: 2g | fiber: 3g | sodium: 415mg

Oat and Walnut Granola

Prep time: 10 minutes | Cook time: 30 minutes | Serves 16

4 cups rolled oats	1 teaspoon ground ginger
1 cup walnut pieces	½ cup coconut oil, melted
½ cup pepitas	½ cup unsweetened applesauce
¼ teaspoon salt	1 teaspoon vanilla extract
1 teaspoon ground cinnamon	½ cup dried cherries

1. Preheat the oven to 350°F. Line a baking sheet with parchment paper. 2. In a large bowl, toss the oats, walnuts, pepitas, salt, cinnamon, and ginger. 3. In a large measuring cup, combine the coconut oil, applesauce, and vanilla. Pour over the dry mixture and mix well. 4. Transfer the mixture to the prepared baking sheet. Cook for 30 minutes, stirring about halfway through. Remove from the oven and let the granola sit undisturbed until completely cool. Break the granola into pieces, and stir in the dried cherries. 5. Transfer to an airtight container, and store at room temperature for up to 2 weeks.

Per Serving:
calories: 224| fat: 15g | protein: 5g | carbs: 20g | sugars: 5g | fiber: 3g | sodium: 30mg

Fresh Blueberry Pancakes

Prep time: 5 minutes | Cook time: 10 minutes | Serves 8

1 cup whole-wheat flour	¾ cup low-fat buttermilk
1½ teaspoon baking powder	¼ cup fat-free vanilla yogurt
Zest of 1 lemon	1 tablespoon canola oil
1 teaspoon cinnamon	½ cup fresh blueberries, washed and drained
1 egg white	

1. In a medium bowl, combine the flour, baking powder, lemon zest, and cinnamon; set aside. 2. In a small bowl, combine the egg white, buttermilk, yogurt, and oil, and mix well. Add the wet mixture to the dry ingredients, stirring until moistened. Then gently fold in the blueberries. 3. Coat a griddle or skillet with cooking spray. Pour 2 tablespoons of batter for each pancake onto a hot griddle. Turn the pancakes when the tops are covered with tiny bubbles and the edges are golden brown.

Per Serving:
calories: 92 | fat: 2g | protein: 4g | carbs: 15g | sugars: 3g | fiber: 2g | sodium: 57mg

Sweet Potato Toasts

Prep time: 10 minutes | Cook time: 2 minutes | Serves 1

2 slices sprouted grain bread	Freshly ground black pepper (optional)
½ cup mashed cooked sweet potato, peel removed	2 tablespoons cubed avocado or 1 tablespoon sliced black olives
½–1 teaspoon lemon juice	
A couple pinches of sea salt	

1. Toast the bread. In a small bowl, mash the sweet potato with the lemon juice (adjusting to taste), salt, and pepper (if using). Distribute the mashed sweet potato between the slices of toast, and top with either the cubed avocado or the black olives. Serve!

Per Serving:
calorie: 312 | fat: 5g | protein: 8g | carbs: 59g | sugars: 11g | fiber: 8g | sodium: 1018mg

Lentil, Squash, and Tomato Omelet

Prep time: 5 minutes | Cook time: 45 minutes | Serves 2

1 cup water	½ cup grape tomatoes, coarsely chopped
⅓ cup dried lentils, picked over, rinsed, and drained	1 garlic clove, chopped
Extra-virgin olive oil cooking spray	2 tablespoons chopped fresh chives
1 medium zucchini, thinly sliced	2 large eggs
	2 tablespoons nonfat milk

1. Preheat the oven to 350°F. 2. In a small saucepan set over high heat, heat the water until it boils. 3. Add the lentils. Reduce the heat to low. Simmer for about 15 minutes, or until most of the liquid has been absorbed. In a colander, drain and set aside. 4. Lightly coat an 8- or 9-inch nonstick skillet with cooking spray. Place the skillet over medium-high heat. 5. Add the zucchini, tomatoes, garlic, and chives. Sauté for 5 to 10 minutes, stirring frequently, or until soft. 6. Add the lentils to the skillet. 7. In a medium bowl, beat together the eggs and milk with a fork. 8. Lightly coat a small casserole or baking dish with cooking spray. 9. In the bottom of the prepared dish, spread the vegetable mixture. 10. Pour the egg mixture over. Use a fork to distribute evenly. 11. Place the dish in the preheated oven. Bake for 15 to 20 minutes, or until the dish is set in the middle. 12. Slice in half and enjoy!

Per Serving:
calories: 209 | fat: 6g | protein: 16g | carbs: 25g | sugars: 4g | fiber: 5g | sodium: 90mg

Goji Berry Muesli

Prep time: 30 minutes | Cook time: 0 minutes | Serves 2

½ cup old-fashioned rolled oats	½ cup fresh blueberries, divided
½ cup plain nonfat Greek yogurt	3 teaspoons pumpkin seeds, divided
2 tablespoons dried goji berries, or dried blueberries, cherries, or cranberries	3 teaspoons finely ground flaxseed, divided
1 teaspoon liquid stevia	½ cup unsweetened vanilla almond milk, divided
½ teaspoon vanilla extract	

1. In a medium bowl, stir together the oats, yogurt, goji berries, stevia, and vanilla. 2. Evenly divide the mixture between 2 small bowls. Cover and refrigerate overnight. 3. The next morning, top each serving with ¼ cup of blueberries, 1½ teaspoons of pumpkin seeds, and 1½ teaspoons of flaxseed. Stir to combine. Let sit for 5 to 10 minutes. 4. Top each with ¼ cup of vanilla almond milk and enjoy cold!

Per Serving:
calories: 180 | fat: 6g | protein: 10g | carbs: 27g | sugars: 11g | fiber: 6g | sodium: 88mg

Asparagus and Bell Pepper Strata

Prep time: 10 minutes | Cook time: 14 to 20 minutes | Serves 4

8 large asparagus spears, trimmed and cut into 2-inch pieces	wheat bread, cut into ½-inch cubes
⅓ cup shredded carrot	3 egg whites
½ cup chopped red bell pepper	1 egg
2 slices low-sodium whole-	3 tablespoons 1% milk
	½ teaspoon dried thyme

1. In a baking pan, combine the asparagus, carrot, red bell pepper, and 1 tablespoon of water. Bake in the air fryer at 330°F (166°C) for 3 to 5 minutes, or until crisp-tender. Drain well. 2. Add the bread cubes to the vegetables and gently toss. 3. In a medium bowl, whisk the egg whites, egg, milk, and thyme until frothy. 4. Pour the egg mixture into the pan. Bake for 11 to 15 minutes, or until the strata is slightly puffy and set and the top starts to brown. Serve.

Per Serving:
calories: 92 | fat: 2g | protein: 8g | carbs: 11g | sugars: 3g | fiber: 3g | sodium: 142mg

Breakfast Farro with Berries and Walnuts

Prep time: 8 minutes | Cook time: 10 minutes | Serves 6

1 cup farro, rinsed and drained	1 tablespoon pure maple syrup
1 cup unsweetened almond milk	1½ cups fresh blueberries, raspberries, or strawberries (or a combination)
¼ teaspoon kosher salt	6 tablespoons chopped walnuts
½ teaspoon pure vanilla extract	
1 teaspoon ground cinnamon	

1. In the electric pressure cooker, combine the farro, almond milk, 1 cup of water, salt, vanilla, cinnamon, and maple syrup. 2. Close and lock the lid. Set the valve to sealing. 3. Cook on high pressure for 10 minutes. 4. When the cooking is complete, allow the pressure to release naturally for 10 minutes, then quick release any remaining pressure. Hit Cancel. 5. Once the pin drops, unlock and remove the lid. 6. Stir the farro. Spoon into bowls and top each serving with ¼ cup of berries and 1 tablespoon of walnuts.

Per Serving:
calorie: 189 | fat: 5g | protein: 5g | carbs: 32g | sugars: 6g | fiber: 3g | sodium: 111mg

Harvest Blackberry Quinoa Bowl

Prep time: 5 minutes | Cook time: 20 minutes | Serves 2

1½ cups water	1 cup halved blackberries
Pinch kosher salt	Ground cinnamon, for garnish
¾ cup quinoa, rinsed	

1. In a medium saucepan, bring the water and salt to a boil over high heat, reduce the heat to low, and add the quinoa. 2. Cook until you see the grains are tender and the liquid is absorbed, about 15 minutes. 3. Remove the quinoa from the heat. If you prefer your quinoa to be fluffy, then cover with a lid for a few minutes and allow it to rest. Once the quinoa is rested, use a fork to fluff it up, top it with the blackberries and a sprinkle of cinnamon, and serve. 4. If you like your grains creamier, serve immediately topped with blackberries and cinnamon.

Per Serving:
calories: 266 | fat: 4g | protein: 10g | carbs: 48g | sugars: 4g | fiber: 8g | sodium: 7mg

Lentil, Squash, and Tomato Omelet

Prep time: 5 minutes | Cook time: 45 minutes | Serves 2

1 cup water	½ cup grape tomatoes, coarsely chopped
⅓ cup dried lentils, picked over, rinsed, and drained	1 garlic clove, chopped
Extra-virgin olive oil cooking spray	2 tablespoons chopped fresh chives
1 medium zucchini, thinly sliced	2 large eggs
	2 tablespoons nonfat milk

1. Preheat the oven to 350°F. 2. In a small saucepan set over high heat, heat the water until it boils. 3. Add the lentils. Reduce the heat to low. Simmer for about 15 minutes, or until most of the liquid has been absorbed. In a colander, drain and set aside. 4. Lightly coat an 8- or 9-inch nonstick skillet with cooking spray. Place the skillet over medium-high heat. 5. Add the zucchini, tomatoes, garlic, and chives. Sauté for 5 to 10 minutes, stirring frequently, or until soft. 6. Add the lentils to the skillet. 7. In a medium bowl, beat together the eggs and milk with a fork. 8. Lightly coat a small casserole or baking dish with cooking spray. 9. In the bottom of the prepared dish, spread the vegetable mixture. 10. Pour the egg mixture over. Use a fork to distribute evenly. 11. Place the dish in the preheated oven. Bake for 15 to 20 minutes, or until the dish is set in the middle. 12. Slice in half and enjoy!

Per Serving:
calories: 209 | fat: 6g | protein: 16g | carbs: 25g | sugars: 4g | fiber: 5g | sodium: 90mg

Veggie-Loaded All-American Breakfast

Prep time: 10 minutes | Cook time: 15 minutes | Serves 1

1 tsp cooking oil	chicken sausage
½ small sweet potato, cut into small cubes	2 large eggs
1 cup (67 g) coarsely chopped kale leaves, stems removed	1 cup (125 g) fresh berries of choice
2 oz (57 g) cooked low-sodium	1 slice whole-grain bread
	2 tbsp (22 g) mashed avocado

1. Heat the oil in a large skillet over medium heat. Tilt and turn the skillet to coat the bottom with the oil. 2. Add the sweet potato, kale, and chicken sausage to the skillet. Sauté them for 10 to 15 minutes, or until the sweet potato is tender and the kale is soft. 3. Transfer the veggie mixture to a plate and return the skillet to the heat. Crack the eggs into the skillet and prepare them as desired to your preferred doneness. Once they are cooked, serve them with the veggie mixture, berries, bread, and avocado.

Per Serving:
calorie: 561 | fat: 25g | protein: 29g | carbs: 10g | sugars: 21g | fiber: 10g | sodium: 820mg

Bacon and Spinach Egg Muffins

Prep time: 7 minutes | Cook time: 12 to 14 minutes | Serves 6

6 large eggs	¾ cup frozen chopped spinach, thawed and drained
¼ cup heavy (whipping) cream	
½ teaspoon sea salt	4 strips cooked bacon, crumbled
¼ teaspoon freshly ground black pepper	
¼ teaspoon cayenne pepper (optional)	2 ounces (57 g) shredded Cheddar cheese

1. In a large bowl (with a spout if you have one), whisk together the eggs, heavy cream, salt, black pepper, and cayenne pepper (if using). 2. Divide the spinach and bacon among 6 silicone muffin cups. Place the muffin cups in your air fryer basket. 3. Divide the egg mixture among the muffin cups. Top with the cheese. 4. Set the air fryer to 300ºF (149ºC). Bake for 12 to 14 minutes, until the eggs are set and cooked through.

Per Serving:
calories: 168 | fat: 13g | protein: 12g | carbs: 2g | net carbs: 1g | fiber: 1g

Spinach and Mushroom Mini Quiche

Prep time: 10 minutes | Cook time: 15 minutes | Serves 4

1 teaspoon olive oil, plus more for spraying	½ cup shredded Cheddar cheese
1 cup coarsely chopped mushrooms	½ cup shredded Mozzarella cheese
1 cup fresh baby spinach, shredded	¼ teaspoon salt
4 eggs, beaten	¼ teaspoon black pepper

1. Spray 4 silicone baking cups with olive oil and set aside. 2. In a medium sauté pan over medium heat, warm 1 teaspoon of olive oil. Add the mushrooms and sauté until soft, 3 to 4 minutes. 3. Add the spinach and cook until wilted, 1 to 2 minutes. Set aside. 4. In a medium bowl, whisk together the eggs, Cheddar cheese, Mozzarella cheese, salt, and pepper. 5. Gently fold the mushrooms and spinach into the egg mixture. 6. Pour ¼ of the mixture into each silicone baking cup. 7. Place the baking cups into the air fryer basket and air fry at 350ºF (177ºC) for 5 minutes. Stir the mixture in each ramekin slightly and air fry until the egg has set, an additional 3 to 5 minutes.

Per Serving:
calories: 156 | fat: 10g | protein: 14g | carbs: 2g | fiber: 1g | sodium: 411mg

Cranberry Almond Grits

Prep time: 10 minutes | Cook time: 10 minutes | Serves 5

¾ cup stone-ground grits or polenta (not instant)	1 tablespoon unsalted butter or ghee (optional)
½ cup unsweetened dried cranberries	1 tablespoon half-and-half
Pinch kosher salt	¼ cup sliced almonds, toasted

1. In the electric pressure cooker, stir together the grits, cranberries, salt, and 3 cups of water. 2. Close and lock the lid. Set the valve to sealing. 3. Cook on high pressure for 10 minutes. 4. When the cooking is complete, hit Cancel and quick release the pressure. 5. Once the pin drops, unlock and remove the lid. 6. Add the butter (if using) and half-and-half. Stir until the mixture is creamy, adding more half-and-half if necessary. 7. Spoon into serving bowls and sprinkle with almonds.

Per Serving:
calories: 218 | fat: 10g | protein: 5g | carbs: 32g | sugars: 7g | fiber: 4g | sodium: 28mg

Rice Breakfast Bake

Prep time: 10 minutes | Cook time: 20 minutes | Serves 4

1¼ cups vanilla low-fat nondairy milk	(optional)
1 tablespoon ground chia seeds	1 teaspoon cinnamon
2½ cups cooked short-grain brown rice	½ teaspoon pure vanilla extract
2 cups sliced ripe (but not overripe) banana (2–2½ medium bananas)	¼ teaspoon freshly grated nutmeg (optional)
	Rounded ⅛ teaspoon sea salt
1 cup chopped apple	2 tablespoons almond meal (or 1 tablespoon tigernut flour, for nut-free option)
2–3 tablespoons raisins	2 tablespoons coconut sugar

1. Preheat the oven to 400°F. 2. In a blender or food processor, combine the milk, ground chia, and 1 cup of the rice. Puree until fairly smooth. In a large bowl, combine the blended mixture, bananas, apple, raisins (if using), cinnamon, vanilla, nutmeg (if using), salt, and the remaining 1½ cups rice. Stir to fully combine. Transfer the mixture to a baking dish (8" x 8" or similar size). In a small bowl, combine the almond meal and sugar, and sprinkle it over the rice mixture. Cover with foil and bake for 15 minutes, then remove the foil and bake for another 5 minutes. Remove, let cool for 5 to 10 minutes, then serve.

Per Serving:
calorie: 334 | fat: 5g | protein: 7g | carbs: 69g | sugars: 22g | fiber: 7g | sodium: 145mg

Very Cherry Overnight Oatmeal in a Jar

Prep time: 30 minutes | Cook time: 0 minutes | Serves 2

½ cup uncooked old-fashioned rolled oats	2 tablespoons chia seeds
	1 teaspoon liquid stevia
½ cup nonfat milk	1 teaspoon cinnamon
½ cup plain nonfat Greek yogurt	½ teaspoon vanilla extract
	½ cup frozen cherries, divided

1. In a small bowl, mix together the oats, milk, yogurt, chia seeds, stevia, cinnamon, and vanilla. 2. Evenly divide the oat mixture between 2 mason jars or individual containers. Cover tightly and shake until well combined. 3. To each jar, stir in ¼ cup of cherries. 4. Seal the containers and refrigerate overnight. 5. The next day, enjoy chilled or heated.

Per Serving:
calories: 247 | fat: 4g | protein: 13g | carbs: 41g | sugars: 11g | fiber: 7g | sodium: 81mg

Bunless Breakfast Turkey Burgers

Prep time: 5 minutes | Cook time: 15 minutes | Serves 4

1 pound (454 g) ground turkey breakfast sausage	¼ cup seeded and chopped green bell pepper
½ teaspoon salt	2 tablespoons mayonnaise
¼ teaspoon ground black pepper	1 medium avocado, peeled, pitted, and sliced

1. In a large bowl, mix sausage with salt, black pepper, bell pepper, and mayonnaise. Form meat into four patties. 2. Place patties into ungreased air fryer basket. Adjust the temperature to 370°F (188°C) and air fry for 15 minutes, turning patties halfway through cooking. Burgers will be done when dark brown and they have an internal temperature of at least 165°F (74°C). 3. Serve burgers topped with avocado slices on four medium plates.

Per Serving:
calories: 283 | fat: 18g | protein: 23g | carbs: 6g | sugars: 1g | fiber: 4g | sodium: 620mg

Three-Berry Dutch Pancake

Prep time: 10 minutes | Cook time: 12 to 16 minutes | Serves 4

2 egg whites	1 tablespoon unsalted butter, melted
1 egg	1 cup sliced fresh strawberries
½ cup whole-wheat pastry flour	½ cup fresh blueberries
½ cup 2% milk	½ cup fresh raspberries
1 teaspoon pure vanilla extract	

1. In a medium bowl, use an eggbeater or hand mixer to quickly mix the egg whites, egg, pastry flour, milk, and vanilla until well combined. 2. Use a pastry brush to grease the bottom of a baking pan with the melted butter. Immediately pour in the batter and put the basket back in the fryer. Bake at 330°F (166°C) for 12 to 16 minutes, or until the pancake is puffed and golden brown. 3. Remove the pan from the air fryer; the pancake will fall. Top with the strawberries, blueberries, and raspberries. Serve immediately.

Per Serving:
calories: 151 | fat: 5g | protein: 7g | carbs: 20g | sugars: 6g | fiber: 4g | sodium: 59mg

Southwestern Egg Casserole

Prep time: 10 minutes | Cook time: 20 minutes | Serves 12

1 cup water	1½ cups shredded 75%-less-fat sharp cheddar cheese
2½ cups egg substitute	¼ cup no-trans-fat tub margarine, melted
½ cup flour	
1 teaspoon baking powder	2 (4-ounce) cans chopped green chilies
⅛ teaspoon salt	
⅛ teaspoon pepper	
2 cups fat-free cottage cheese	

1. Place the steaming rack into the bottom of the inner pot and pour in 1 cup of water. 2. Grease a round springform pan that will fit into the inner pot of the Instant Pot. 3. Combine the egg substitute, flour, baking powder, salt and pepper in a mixing bowl. It will be lumpy. 4. Stir in the cheese, margarine, and green chilies then pour into the springform pan. 5. Place the springform pan onto the steaming rack, close the lid, and secure to the locking position. Be sure the vent is turned to sealing. Set for 20 minutes on Manual at high pressure. 6. Let the pressure release naturally. 7. Carefully remove the springform pan with the handles of the steaming rack and allow to stand 10 minutes before cutting and serving.

Per Serving:
calories: 130 | fat: 4g | protein: 14g | carbs: 9g | sugars: 1g | fiber: 1g | sodium: 450mg

Gluten-Free Carrot and Oat Pancakes

Prep time: 10 minutes | Cook time: 20 minutes | Serves 4

1 cup rolled oats	½ teaspoon ground cinnamon
1 cup shredded carrots	2 tablespoons ground flaxseed
1 cup low-fat cottage cheese	¼ cup plain nonfat Greek yogurt
2 eggs	
½ cup unsweetened plain almond milk	1 tablespoon pure maple syrup
1 teaspoon baking powder	2 teaspoons canola oil, divided

1. In a blender jar, process the oats until they resemble flour. Add the carrots, cottage cheese, eggs, almond milk, baking powder, cinnamon, and flaxseed to the jar. Process until smooth. 2. In a small bowl, combine the yogurt and maple syrup and stir well. Set aside. 3. In a large skillet, heat 1 teaspoon of oil over medium heat. Using a measuring cup, add ¼ cup of batter per pancake to the skillet. Cook for 1 to 2 minutes until bubbles form on the surface, and flip the pancakes. Cook for another minute until the pancakes are browned and cooked through. Repeat with the remaining 1 teaspoon of oil and remaining batter. 4. Serve warm topped with the maple yogurt.

Per Serving:
calories: 226 | fat: 8g | protein: 15g | carbs: 24g | sugars: 7g | fiber: 4g | sodium: 403mg

Sausage, Sweet Potato, and Kale Hash

Prep time: 10 minutes | Cook time: 15 minutes | Serves 4

Avocado oil cooking spray	(about 2 bunches)
1⅓ cups peeled and diced sweet potatoes	4 links chicken or turkey breakfast sausage
8 cups roughly chopped kale, stemmed and loosely packed	4 large eggs
	4 lemon wedges

1. Heat a large skillet over medium heat. When hot, coat the cooking surface with cooking spray. Cook the sweet potatoes for 4 minutes, stirring once halfway through. 2. Reduce the heat to medium-low and move the potatoes to one side of the skillet. Arrange the kale and sausage in a single layer. Cover and cook for 3 minutes. 3. Stir the vegetables and sausage together, then push them to one side of the skillet to create space for the eggs. Add the eggs and cook them to your liking. Cover the skillet and cook for 3 minutes. 4. Divide the sausage and vegetables into four equal portions and top with an egg and a squeeze of lemon.

Per Serving:
calories: 160 | fat: 8g | protein: 11g | carbs: 13g | sugars: 3g | fiber: 3g | sodium: 197mg

Breakfast Tacos

Prep time: 5 minutes | Cook time: 10 minutes | Serves 4

For the Taco Filling: Avocado oil cooking spray 1 medium green bell pepper, chopped 8 large eggs ¼ cup shredded sharp Cheddar cheese 4 (6-inch) whole-wheat tortillas 1 cup fresh spinach leaves ½ cup Pico de Gallo Scallions, chopped, for garnish (optional)	Avocado slices, for garnish (optional) For the Pico De Gallo: 1 tomato, diced ½ large white onion, diced 2 tablespoons chopped fresh cilantro ½ jalapeño pepper, stemmed, seeded, and diced 1 tablespoon freshly squeezed lime juice ⅛ teaspoon salt

To make the taco filling 1. Heat a medium skillet over medium-low heat. When hot, coat the cooking surface with cooking spray and put the pepper in the skillet. Cook for 4 minutes. 2. Meanwhile, whisk the eggs in a medium bowl, then add the cheese and whisk to combine. Pour the eggs and cheese into the skillet with the green peppers and scramble until the eggs are fully cooked, about 5 minutes. 3. Microwave the tortillas very briefly, about 8 seconds. 4. For each serving, top a tortilla with one-quarter of the spinach, eggs, and pico de gallo. Garnish with scallions and avocado slices (if using). To make the pico de gallo 5. In a medium bowl, combine the tomato, onion, cilantro, pepper, lime juice, and salt. Mix well and serve.

Per Serving:
calories: 316 | fat: 16g | protein: 19g | carbs: 24g | sugars: 4g | fiber: 5g | sodium: 554mg

Potato, Egg and Sausage Frittata

Prep time: 30 minutes | Cook time: 20 minutes | Serves 4

4 frozen soy-protein breakfast sausage links (from 8-oz box), thawed 1 teaspoon olive oil 2 cups frozen country-style shredded hash brown potatoes (from 30-oz bag) 4 eggs or 8 egg whites ¼ cup fat-free (skim) milk ¼ teaspoon salt ⅛ teaspoon dried basil leaves	⅛ teaspoon dried oregano leaves 1½ cups chopped plum (Roma) tomatoes ½ cup shredded mozzarella and Asiago cheese blend with garlic (2 oz) Pepper, if desired Chopped green onion, if desired

1 Cut each sausage link into 8 pieces. Coat 10-inch nonstick skillet with oil; heat over medium heat. Add sausage and potatoes; cook 6 to 8 minutes, stirring occasionally, until potatoes are golden brown. 2 In small bowl, beat eggs and milk with fork or whisk until well blended. Pour egg mixture over potato mixture. Cook uncovered over medium-low heat about 5 minutes; as mixture begins to set on bottom and side, gently lift cooked portions with spatula so that thin, uncooked portion can flow to bottom. Cook until eggs are thickened throughout but still moist; avoid constant stirring. 3 Sprinkle salt, basil, oregano, tomatoes and cheese over eggs. Reduce heat to low; cover and cook about 5 minutes or until center is set and cheese is melted. Sprinkle with pepper and green onion.

Per Serving:
1 Panini: calorie: 280 | fat: 12g | protein: 17g | carbs: 26g | sugars: 5g | fiber: 3g | sodium: 590mg

Broccoli Cheese Breakfast Casserole

Prep time: 10 minutes | Cook time: 40 minutes | Serves 4

2 tablespoons extra-virgin olive oil 1 cup sliced button mushrooms ½ sweet onion, chopped 1 teaspoon minced garlic 1 cup chopped broccoli 8 large eggs	¼ cup skim milk 1 tablespoon chopped fresh basil 1 cup shredded fat-free Cheddar cheese Sea salt Freshly ground black pepper

1. Preheat the oven to 375°F. 2. Place a large ovenproof skillet over medium-high heat and add the olive oil. 3. Sauté the mushrooms, onion, and garlic until tender, about 5 minutes. 4. Add the broccoli and sauté for 5 minutes. 5. In a small bowl, whisk together the eggs, milk, and basil. 6. Remove the skillet from the heat and pour the egg mixture evenly over the vegetables. 7. Sprinkle the cheese over the casserole and bake, uncovered, until the eggs are puffy, about 30 minutes. 8. Season with salt and pepper. Serve hot or cold.

Per Serving:
calories: 255 | fat: 16g | protein: 21g | carbs: 6g | sugars: 4g | fiber: 1g | sodium: 338mg

Gouda Egg Casserole with Canadian Bacon

Prep time: 12 minutes | Cook time: 20 minutes | Serves 4

Nonstick cooking spray 1 slice whole grain bread, toasted ½ cup shredded smoked Gouda cheese 3 slices Canadian bacon, chopped	6 large eggs ¼ cup half-and-half ¼ teaspoon kosher salt ¼ teaspoon freshly ground black pepper ¼ teaspoon dry mustard

1. Spray a 6-inch cake pan with cooking spray, or if the pan is nonstick, skip this step. If you don't have a 6-inch cake pan, any bowl or pan that fits inside your pressure cooker should work. 2. Crumble the toast into the bottom of the pan. Sprinkle with the cheese and Canadian bacon. 3. In a medium bowl, whisk together the eggs, half-and-half, salt, pepper, and dry mustard. 4. Pour the egg mixture into the pan. Loosely cover the pan with aluminum foil. 5. Pour 1½ cups water into the electric pressure cooker and insert a wire rack or trivet. Place the covered pan on top of the rack. 6. Close and lock the lid of the pressure cooker. Set the valve to sealing. 7. Cook on high pressure for 20 minutes. 8. When the cooking is complete, hit Cancel and quick release the pressure. 9. Once the pin drops, unlock and remove the lid. 10. Carefully transfer the pan from the pressure cooker to a cooling rack and let it sit for 5 minutes. 11. Cut into 4 wedges and serve.

Per Serving:
calories: 247 | fat: 15g | protein: 20g | carbs: 8g | sugars: 1g | fiber: 1g | sodium: 717mg

Western Omelet

Prep time: 5 minutes | Cook time: 10 minutes | Serves 2

1½ teaspoons canola oil	2 tablespoons minced green bell pepper
¾ cup egg whites	2 tablespoons minced onion
¼ cup minced lean ham	⅛ teaspoon freshly ground black pepper

1. In a medium nonstick skillet over medium-low heat, heat the oil. 2. In a small mixing bowl, beat the egg whites slightly, and add the remaining ingredients along with a dash of salt, if desired. Pour the egg mixture into the heated skillet. 3. When the omelet begins to set, gently lift the edges of the omelet with a spatula, and tilt the skillet to allow the uncooked portion to flow underneath. Continue cooking until the eggs are firm. Then transfer to a serving platter.

Per Serving:
calories: 107 | fat: 4g | protein: 14g | carbs: 2g | sugars: 1g | fiber: 0g | sodium: 367mg

Chocolate-Zucchini Muffins

Prep time: 15 minutes | Cook time: 20 minutes | Serves 12

1½ cups grated zucchini	1 teaspoon vanilla extract
1½ cups rolled oats	¼ cup coconut oil, melted
1 teaspoon ground cinnamon	½ cup unsweetened applesauce
2 teaspoons baking powder	¼ cup honey
¼ teaspoon salt	¼ cup dark chocolate chips
1 large egg	

1. Preheat the oven to 350°F. Grease the cups of a 12-cup muffin tin or line with paper baking liners. Set aside. 2. Place the zucchini in a colander over the sink to drain. 3. In a blender jar, process the oats until they resemble flour. Transfer to a medium mixing bowl and add the cinnamon, baking powder, and salt. Mix well. 4. In another large mixing bowl, combine the egg, vanilla, coconut oil, applesauce, and honey. Stir to combine. 5. Press the zucchini into the colander, draining any liquids, and add to the wet mixture. 6. Stir the dry mixture into the wet mixture, and mix until no dry spots remain. Fold in the chocolate chips. 7. Transfer the batter to the muffin tin, filling each cup a little over halfway. Cook for 16 to 18 minutes until the muffins are lightly browned and a toothpick inserted in the center comes out clean. 8. Store in an airtight container, refrigerated, for up to 5 days.

Per Serving:
calories: 121 | fat: 7g | protein: 2g | carbs: 16g | sugars: 7g | fiber: 2g | sodium: 106mg

Chapter 2 Beans and Grains

Italian Bean Burgers

Prep time: 10 minutes | Cook time: 20 minutes | Makes 9 burgers

2 cans (14 or 15 ounces each) chickpeas, drained and rinsed	Scant ½ teaspoon sea salt
1 medium–large clove garlic, cut in half	2 tablespoons chopped fresh oregano
2 tablespoons tomato paste	⅓ cup roughly chopped fresh basil leaves
1½ tablespoons red wine vinegar (can substitute apple cider vinegar)	1 cup rolled oats
1 tablespoon tahini	⅓ cup chopped sun-dried tomatoes (not packed in oil)
1 teaspoon Dijon mustard	½ cup roughly chopped kalamata or green olives
½ teaspoon onion powder	

1. In a food processor, combine the chickpeas, garlic, tomato paste, vinegar, tahini, mustard, onion powder, and salt. Puree until fully combined. Add the oregano, basil, and oats, and pulse briefly. (You want to combine the ingredients but retain some of the basil's texture.) Finally, pulse in the sun-dried tomatoes and olives, again maintaining some texture. Transfer the mixture to a bowl and refrigerate, covered, for 30 minutes or longer. 2. Preheat the oven to 400°F. Line a baking sheet with parchment paper. Use an ice cream scoop to scoop the mixture onto the prepared baking sheet, flattening to shape into patties. Bake for about 20 minutes, flipping the burgers halfway through. Alternatively, you can cook the burgers in a nonstick skillet over medium heat for 6 to 8 minutes per side, or until golden brown. Serve.

Per Serving:
calorie: 148 | fat: 4g | protein: 6g | carbs: 23g | sugars: 4g | fiber: 6g | sodium: 387mg

Tex-Mex Rice 'N' Beans

Prep time: 10 minutes | Cook time: 25 minutes | Serves 4

1½ cups chopped bell pepper	instant pot)
1–1½ cups chopped onion	½ cup dried red lentils
1 tablespoon dried oregano	1 cup uncooked brown rice (can substitute quinoa)
2 teaspoons chili powder	2 cans (15 ounces each) black beans, rinsed and drained
½ tablespoon paprika	
½ tablespoon ground cumin	
1 teaspoon garlic powder	¼ cup tomato paste
½ teaspoon cinnamon	1 bay leaf
Rounded ½ teaspoon sea salt	2 tablespoons lime juice
2 tablespoons water + 2½ cups water (boiled, if using an	Hot sauce to taste (optional)

1. In an instant pot, combine the bell pepper, onion, oregano, chili powder, paprika, cumin, garlic powder, cinnamon, salt, and 2 tablespoons of the water, and set to the sauté function. Cook for 3 to 4 minutes, stirring frequently. Turn off the sauté function and add the lentils, rice, beans, tomato paste, bay leaf, and the remaining 2½ cups water. Stir, cover the instant pot, and set to high pressure for 20 minutes. After 20 minutes, you can manually release the pressure or let it naturally release. Stir in the lime juice, taste, and season as desired. Add the hot sauce (if using), and serve.

Per Serving:
calorie: 525 | fat: 3g | protein: 24g | carbs: 103g | sugars: 7g | fiber: 25g | sodium: 898mg

Farmers' Market Barley Risotto

Prep time: 30 minutes | Cook time: 15 minutes | Serves 4

1 tablespoon olive oil	chicken broth
1 medium onion, chopped (½ cup)	2 cups reduced-sodium chicken broth
1 medium bell pepper, coarsely chopped (1 cup)	3 cups water
2 cups chopped fresh mushrooms (4 oz)	1½ cups grape tomatoes, cut in half (if large, cut into quarters)
1 cup frozen whole-kernel corn	⅔ cup shredded Parmesan cheese
1 cup uncooked medium pearled barley	3 tablespoons chopped fresh or 1 teaspoon dried basil leaves
¼ cup dry white wine or	½ teaspoon pepper

1 In 4-quart Dutch oven or saucepan, heat oil over medium heat. Cook onion, bell pepper, mushrooms and corn in oil about 5 minutes, stirring frequently, until onion is crisp-tender. Add barley, stirring about 1 minute to coat. 2 Stir in wine and ½ cup of the broth. Cook 5 minutes, stirring frequently, until liquid is almost absorbed. Repeat with remaining broth and 3 cups water, adding ½ to ¾ cup of broth or water at a time and stirring frequently, until absorbed. 3 Stir in tomatoes, ¼ cup of the cheese, the basil and pepper. Cook until thoroughly heated. Sprinkle with remaining ¼ cup cheese.

Per Serving:
calorie: 370 | fat: 8g | protein: 15g | carbs: 55g | sugars: 6g | fiber: 11g | sodium: 520mg

Gingered Red Lentils with Millet

Prep time: 10 minutes | Cook time: 20 minutes | Serves 4

3 cups water	3-inch piece ginger, grated (or minced)
1 cup millet, rinsed	
½ cup red lentils, rinsed	4 cups cherry tomatoes, diced
3 tablespoons extra-virgin olive oil, divided	3 tablespoons unsalted peanuts, chopped
Pinch kosher salt	2 limes, quartered
1 onion, diced	1 bunch mint leaves

1. In a medium saucepan over medium heat, stir together the water, millet, lentils, 1 tablespoon of extra-virgin olive oil, and the salt. Bring to a boil, reduce the heat to low, cover, and simmer until tender, about 15 minutes. Remove the saucepan from the heat and let the grains sit for a few minutes. 2. Meanwhile, in a small saucepan, heat the remaining 2 tablespoons of extra-virgin olive oil. Sauté the onion until translucent, about 3 minutes. Add the ginger, tomatoes, and peanuts. Cook for about 5 minutes, adjust the seasonings as desired, and allow to sit until the millet and lentils are finished. 3. Divide the millet and lentils among four bowls, and top them with the gingered onion mixture. Garnish with lime wedges and mint leaves. 4. Serve, and store any leftovers in an airtight container in the refrigerator for up to 3 days.

Per Serving:
calorie: 454 | fat: 17g | protein: 15g | carbs: 65g | sugars: 6g | fiber: 11g | sodium: 18mg

Red Beans

Prep time: 10 minutes | Cook time: 45 minutes | Serves 8

1 cup crushed tomatoes	1 cup roughly chopped green beans
1 medium yellow onion, chopped	4 cups store-bought low-sodium vegetable broth
2 garlic cloves, minced	1 teaspoon smoked paprika
2 cups dried red kidney beans	

1. Select the Sauté setting on an electric pressure cooker, and combine the tomatoes, onion, and garlic. Cook for 3 to 5 minutes, or until softened. 2. Add the kidney beans, green beans, broth, and paprika. Stir to combine. 3. Close and lock the lid, and set the pressure valve to sealing. 4. Change to the Manual/Pressure Cook setting, and cook for 35 minutes. 5. Once cooking is complete, quick-release the pressure. Carefully remove the lid. 6. Serve.

Per Serving:
calorie: 73 | fat: 0g | protein: 4g | carbs: 14g | sugars: 4g | fiber: 4g | sodium: 167mg

Curried Rice with Pineapple

Prep time: 5 minutes | Cook time: 35 minutes | Serves 8

1 onion, chopped	1 teaspoon curry powder
1½ cups water	1 teaspoon ground turmeric
1¼ cups low-sodium chicken broth	1 teaspoon ground ginger
1 cup uncooked brown basmati rice, soaked in water 20 minutes and drained before cooking	2 garlic cloves, minced
	One 8-ounce can pineapple chunks packed in juice, drained
2 red bell peppers, minced	¼ cup sliced almonds, toasted

1. In a medium saucepan, combine the onion, water, and chicken broth. Bring to a boil, and add the rice, peppers, curry powder, turmeric, ginger, and garlic. Cover, placing a paper towel in between the pot and the lid, and reduce the heat. Simmer for 25 minutes. 2. Add the pineapple, and continue to simmer 5–7 minutes more until rice is tender and water is absorbed. Taste and add salt, if desired. Transfer to a serving bowl, and garnish with almonds to serve.

Per Serving:
calorie: 144 | fat: 3g | protein: 4g | carbs: 27g | sugars: 6g | fiber: 3g | sodium: 16mg

Easy Lentil Burgers

Prep time: 10 minutes | Cook time: 20 minutes | Serves 5

1 medium-large clove garlic	2 teaspoons onion powder
2 tablespoons tamari	¼ teaspoon sea salt
2 tablespoons tomato paste	Few pinches freshly ground black pepper
1 tablespoon red wine vinegar	3 cups cooked brown lentils
1½ tablespoons tahini	1 cup toasted breadcrumbs
2 tablespoons fresh thyme or oregano	½ cup rolled oats

1. In a food processor, combine the garlic, tamari, tomato paste, vinegar, tahini, thyme or oregano, onion powder, salt, pepper, and 1½ cups of the lentils. Puree until fairly smooth. Add the breadcrumbs, rolled oats, and the remaining 1½ cups of lentils. Pulse a few times. At this stage you're looking for a sticky texture that will hold together when pressed. If the mixture is still a little crumbly, pulse a few more times. 2. Preheat the oven to 400°F. Line a baking sheet with parchment paper. 3. Use an ice cream scoop to scoop the mixture onto the prepared baking sheet, flattening to shape into patties. Bake for about 20 minutes, flipping the burgers halfway through. Alternatively, you can cook the burgers in a nonstick skillet over medium heat for 4 to 5 minutes Per side, or until golden brown.

Per Serving:
calorie: 148 | fat: 2g | protein: 8g | carbs: 24g | sugars: 1g | fiber: 5g | sodium: 369mg

Coconut-Ginger Rice

Prep time: 10 minutes | Cook time: 20 minutes | Serves 8

2½ cups reduced-sodium chicken broth	long-grain white rice
⅔ cup reduced-fat (lite) coconut milk (not cream of coconut)	1 teaspoon grated lime peel
	3 medium green onions, chopped (3 tablespoons)
1 tablespoon grated gingerroot	3 tablespoons flaked coconut, toasted*
½ teaspoon salt	Lime slices
1⅓ cups uncooked regular	

1 In 3-quart saucepan, heat broth, coconut milk, gingerroot and salt to boiling over medium-high heat. Stir in rice. Return to boiling. Reduce heat; cover and simmer about 15 minutes or until rice is tender and liquid is absorbed. Remove from heat. 2 Add lime peel and onions; fluff rice mixture lightly with fork to mix. Garnish with coconut and lime slices.

Per Serving:
calorie: 150 | fat: 2g | protein: 3g | carbs: 30g | sugars: 1g | fiber: 0g | sodium: 340mg

Thai Red Lentils

Prep time: 5 minutes | Cook time: 25 minutes | Serves 4

2 cups dried red lentils	less if using more curry paste)
1 can (13½ ounces) lite coconut milk	2–2¼ cups water
2 tablespoons red or yellow Thai curry paste	⅓ cup finely chopped fresh basil
¼–½ teaspoon sea salt (use	3–4 tablespoons lime juice

1. In a large saucepan over high heat, combine the lentils, coconut milk, curry paste, salt, and 2 cups of the water. Stir and bring to a boil. Reduce the heat to low, cover, and cook for 20 minutes, or until the lentils are fully softened. Add the basil and 3 tablespoons of the lime juice, and stir. Season to taste with more salt and the remaining 1 tablespoon lime juice, if desired. Add the remaining ¼ cup water to thin, if desired.

Per Serving:
calorie: 389 | fat: 8g | protein: 25g | carbs: 58g | sugars: 4g | fiber: 16g | sodium: 441mg

Brown Rice–Stuffed Butternut Squash

Prep time: 30 minutes | Cook time: 50 minutes | Serves 4

2 small butternut squash (about 2 lb each)	2 links (3 oz each) sweet Italian turkey sausage, casings removed
4 teaspoons olive oil	1 small onion, chopped (⅓ cup)
¼ teaspoon salt	1 cup sliced cremini mushrooms
½ teaspoon freshly ground pepper	1 cup fresh baby spinach leaves
⅓ cup uncooked brown basmati rice	1 teaspoon chopped fresh or ¼ teaspoon dried sage leaves
1¼ cups reduced-sodium chicken broth	
1 thyme sprig	
1 bay leaf	

1 Heat oven to 375°F. Cut each squash lengthwise in half; remove seeds and fibers. Drizzle cut sides with 3 teaspoons of the olive oil; sprinkle with salt and pepper. On cookie sheet, place squash, cut side down. Bake 35 to 40 minutes, until squash is tender at thickest portion when pierced with fork. When cool enough to handle, cut off long ends of squash to within ½ inch edge of cavities (peel and refrigerate ends for another use). 2 Meanwhile, in 1-quart saucepan, heat remaining 1 teaspoon oil over medium heat. Add rice to oil, stirring well to coat. Stir in chicken broth, thyme and bay leaf. Heat to boiling; reduce heat. Cover and simmer 30 to 35 minutes, until all liquid is absorbed and rice is tender. Remove from heat; discard thyme sprig and bay leaf. 3 In 10-inch nonstick skillet, cook sausage and onion over medium-high heat 8 to 10 minutes, stirring frequently, until sausage is thoroughly cooked. Add mushrooms. Cook 4 minutes or until mushrooms are tender. Stir in cooked rice, spinach and sage; cook about 3 minutes or until spinach is wilted and mixture is hot. Divide sausage-rice mixture between squash halves, pressing down on filling so it forms a slight mound over cavity.

Per Serving:
calorie: 350 | fat: 10g | protein: 14g | carbs: 50g | sugars: 14g | fiber: 5g | sodium: 670mg

Lentil Bolognese

Prep time: 10 minutes | Cook time: 30 minutes | Serves 4

⅓ cup red wine	green lentils
1 cup diced onion	¼ cup chopped sun-dried tomatoes
½ cup minced carrot	1 can (28 ounces) diced tomatoes (use fire-roasted, if you'd like a spicy kick)
1 tablespoon dried oregano leaves	
1 teaspoon vegan Worcestershire sauce	2–3 tablespoons minced dates
¾ teaspoon smoked paprika	1 pound dry pasta
½ teaspoon sea salt	½ cup almond meal (toast until lightly golden if you want extra flavor)
¼ teaspoon ground nutmeg	
1½ cups cooked brown or	

1. In a large pot over high heat, combine the wine, onion, carrot, oregano, Worcestershire sauce, paprika, salt, and nutmeg. Cook for 5 minutes, stirring frequently. Add the lentils, sun-dried tomatoes, diced tomatoes, and dates, and bring to a boil. Reduce the heat to low, cover, and cook for 20 to 25 minutes. 2. While the sauce is simmering, prepare the pasta according to package directions. Once the pasta is almost cooked (still having some "bite," not mushy), drain and return it to the cooking pot. 3. Add the almond meal to the sauce, stir to incorporate, and cook for a couple of minutes. Taste, season as desired, and toss with the pasta before serving.

Per Serving:
calorie: 754 | fat: 11g | protein: 31g | carbs: 132g | sugars: 14g | fiber: 17g | sodium: 622mg

Baked Vegetable Macaroni Pie

Prep time: 15 minutes | Cook time: 35 minutes | Serves 6

1 (16-ounce) package whole-wheat macaroni	1 cup fat-free milk
1 small yellow onion, chopped	2 cups grated reduced-fat sharp Cheddar cheese
2 garlic cloves, minced	2 large zucchini, finely grated and squeezed dry
2 celery stalks, thinly sliced	2 roasted red peppers, chopped into ¼-inch pieces
¼ teaspoon freshly ground black pepper	
2 tablespoons chickpea flour	

1. Preheat the oven to 350°F. 2. Bring a large pot of water to a boil. 3. Add the macaroni and cook for 2 to 5 minutes, or until al dente. 4. Drain the macaroni, reserving 1 cup of the pasta water for the cheese sauce. Rinse under cold running water, and transfer to a large bowl. 5. In a large cast iron skillet, warm the pasta water over medium heat. 6. Add the onion, garlic, celery, and pepper. Cook for 3 to 5 minutes, or until the onion is translucent. 7. Add the chickpea flour slowly, mixing often. 8. Stir in the milk and cheese until a thick liquid is formed. It should be about the consistency of a smoothie. 9. Add the pasta to the cheese mixture along with the zucchini and red peppers. Mix thoroughly so the ingredients are evenly dispersed. 10. Cover the skillet tightly with aluminum foil, transfer to the oven, and bake for 15 to 20 minutes, or until the cheese is well melted. 11. Uncover and bake for 5 minutes, or until golden brown.

Per Serving:
calorie: 382 | fat: 4g | protein: 24g | carbs: 67g | sugars: 6g | fiber: 8g | sodium: 373mg

Sage and Garlic Vegetable Bake

Prep time: 30 minutes | Cook time: 1 hour 15 minutes | Serves 6

1 medium butternut squash, peeled, cut into 1-inch pieces (3 cups)	1 medium onion, coarsely chopped (½ cup)
2 medium parsnips, peeled, cut into 1-inch pieces (2 cups)	½ cup uncooked quick-cooking barley
2 cans (14.5 oz each) stewed tomatoes, undrained	½ cup water
2 cups frozen cut green beans	1 teaspoon dried sage leaves
	½ teaspoon seasoned salt
	2 cloves garlic, finely chopped

1 Heat oven to 375°F. In ungreased 3-quart casserole, mix all ingredients, breaking up large pieces of tomatoes. 2 Cover; bake 1 hour to 1 hour 15 minutes or until vegetables and barley are tender.

Per Serving:
calorie: 170 | fat: 0g | protein: 4g | carbs: 37g | sugars: 9g | fiber: 8g | sodium: 410mg

Colorful Rice Casserole

Prep time: 5 minutes | **Cook time:** 20 minutes | **Serves 12**

1 tablespoon extra-virgin olive oil	added chopped tomatoes, undrained
1½ pounds zucchini, thinly sliced	¼ cup chopped parsley
¾ cup chopped scallions	1 teaspoon oregano
2 cups corn kernels (frozen or fresh; if frozen, defrost)	3 cups cooked brown (or white) rice
One 14.5-ounce can no-salt-	⅛ teaspoon freshly ground black pepper

1. In a large skillet, heat the oil. Add the zucchini and scallions, and sauté for 5 minutes. 2. Add the remaining ingredients, cover, reduce heat, and simmer for 10–15 minutes or until the vegetables are heated through. Season with salt, if desired, and pepper. Transfer to a bowl, and serve.

Per Serving:
calorie: 109 | fat: 2g | protein: 3g | carbs: 21g | sugars: 4g | fiber: 3g | sodium: 14mg

Veggies and Kasha with Balsamic Vinaigrette

Prep time: 15 minutes | **Cook time:** 8 minutes | **Serves 4**

Salad	seeded, chopped (1¼ cups)
1 cup water	Vinaigrette
½ cup uncooked buckwheat kernels or groats (kasha)	2 tablespoons balsamic or red wine vinegar
4 medium green onions, thinly sliced (¼ cup)	1 tablespoon olive oil
2 medium tomatoes, seeded, coarsely chopped (1½ cups)	2 teaspoons sugar
	½ teaspoon salt
	¼ teaspoon pepper
1 medium unpeeled cucumber,	1 clove garlic, finely chopped

1 In 8-inch skillet, heat water to boiling. Add kasha; cook over medium-high heat 7 to 8 minutes, stirring occasionally, until tender. Drain if necessary. 2 In large bowl, mix kasha and remaining salad ingredients. 3 In tightly covered container, shake vinaigrette ingredients until blended. Pour vinaigrette over kasha mixture; toss. Cover; refrigerate 1 to 2 hours to blend flavors.

Per Serving:
calorie: 120 | fat: 4g | protein: 2g | carbs: 19g | sugars: 6g | fiber: 3g | sodium: 310mg

Texas Caviar

Prep time: 10 minutes | **Cook time:** 0 minutes | **Serves 6**

1 cup cooked black-eyed peas	½ red onion, chopped
1 cup cooked lima beans	3 tablespoons apple cider vinegar
1 ear fresh corn, kernels removed	2 tablespoons extra-virgin olive oil
2 celery stalks, chopped	
1 red bell pepper, chopped	1 teaspoon paprika

1. In a large bowl, combine the black-eyed peas, lima beans, corn, celery, bell pepper, and onion. 2. In a small bowl, to make the dressing, whisk the vinegar, oil, and paprika together. 3. Pour the dressing over the bean mixture, and gently mix. Set aside for 15 to 30 minutes, allowing the flavors to come together.

Per Serving:
calorie: 142 | fat: 5g | protein: 6g | carbs: 19g | sugars: 3g | fiber: 6g | sodium: 10mg

Veggie Unfried Rice

Prep time: 15 minutes | **Cook time:** 25 minutes | **Serves 4**

1 tablespoon extra-virgin olive oil	matchsticks
	1 red onion, thinly sliced
1 bunch collard greens, stemmed and cut into chiffonade	1 garlic clove, minced
	2 tablespoons coconut aminos
	1 cup cooked brown rice
½ cup store-bought low-sodium vegetable broth	1 large egg
	1 teaspoon red pepper flakes
1 carrot, cut into 2-inch	1 teaspoon paprika

1. In a large Dutch oven, heat the olive oil over medium heat. 2. Add the collard greens and cook for 3 to 5 minutes, or until the greens are wilted. 3. Add the broth, carrot, onion, garlic, and coconut aminos, then cover and cook for 5 to 7 minutes, or until the carrot softens and the onion and garlic are translucent. 4. Uncover, add the rice, and cook for 3 to 5 minutes, gently mixing all the ingredients together until well combined but not mushy. 5. Crack the egg over the pot and gently scramble the egg. Cook for 2 to 5 minutes, or until the eggs are no longer runny. 6. Remove from the heat and season with the red pepper flakes and paprika.

Per Serving:
calorie: 164 | fat: 4g | protein: 9g | carbs: 26g | sugars: 3g | fiber: 9g | sodium: 168mg

Spicy Couscous and Chickpea Salad

Prep time: 20 minutes | **Cook time:** 10 minutes | **Serves 4**

Salad	(green soybeans) or lima beans, thawed
½ cup uncooked whole wheat couscous	2 tablespoons chopped fresh cilantro
1½ cups water	
¼ teaspoon salt	Green bell peppers, halved, if desired
1 can (15 oz) chickpeas (garbanzo beans), drained, rinsed	Dressing
	2 tablespoons olive oil
1 can (14.5 oz) diced tomatoes with green chiles, undrained	1 teaspoon ground coriander
	½ teaspoon ground cumin
½ cup frozen shelled edamame	½ teaspoon ground cinnamon

1. Cook couscous in the water and salt as directed on package. 2. Meanwhile, in medium bowl, mix chickpeas, tomatoes, edamame and cilantro. In small bowl, mix dressing ingredients until well blended. 3. Add cooked couscous to salad; mix well. Pour dressing over salad; stir gently to mix. Spoon salad mixture into halved bell peppers. Serve immediately, or cover and refrigerate until serving time.

Per Serving:
calorie: 370 | fat: 11g | protein: 16g | carbs: 53g | sugars: 6g | fiber: 10g | sodium: 460mg

Green Chickpea Falafel

Prep time: 10 minutes | Cook time: 11 to 12 minutes | Serves 4

1 bag (14 ounces) green chickpeas, thawed (about 3½ cups)	2 medium-large cloves garlic
½ cup fresh flat-leaf parsley leaves	2 teaspoons ground cumin
½ cup fresh cilantro leaves	½ teaspoon turmeric
1½ tablespoons freshly squeezed lemon juice	1 teaspoon ground coriander
	1 teaspoon sea salt
	¼–½ teaspoon crushed red-pepper flakes
	1 cup rolled oats

1. In a food processor, combine the chickpeas, parsley, cilantro, lemon juice, garlic, cumin, turmeric, coriander, salt, and red-pepper flakes. (Use ¼ teaspoon if you like it mild and ½ teaspoon if you like it spicier.) Process until the mixture breaks down and begins to smooth out. Add the oats and pulse a few times to work them in. Refrigerate for 30 minutes, if possible. 2. Preheat the oven to 400°F. Line a baking sheet with parchment paper. 3. Use a cookie scoop to take small scoops of the mixture, 1 to 1½ tablespoons each. Place falafel balls on the prepared baking sheet. Bake for 11 to 12 minutes, until the falafel balls begin to firm (they will still be tender inside) and turn golden in spots.

Per Serving:
calorie: 253 | fat: 4g | protein: 12g | carbs: 43g | sugars: 5g | fiber: 10g | sodium: 601mg

Southwestern Quinoa Salad

Prep time: 15 minutes | Cook time: 25 minutes | Serves 6

Salad	chiles (from 4.5-oz can)
1 cup uncooked quinoa	1 tablespoon olive oil
1 large onion, chopped (1 cup)	1 can (15 oz) no-salt-added black beans, drained, rinsed
1½ cups reduced-sodium chicken broth	6 medium plum (Roma) tomatoes, chopped (2 cups)
1 cup packed fresh cilantro leaves	2 tablespoons lime juice
¼ cup raw unsalted hulled pumpkin seeds (pepitas)	Garnish
2 cloves garlic, sliced	1 avocado, pitted, peeled, thinly sliced
⅛ teaspoon ground cumin	4 small cilantro sprigs
2 tablespoons chopped green	

1 Rinse quinoa thoroughly by placing in a fine-mesh strainer and holding under cold running water until water runs clear; drain well. 2 Spray 3-quart saucepan with cooking spray. Heat over medium heat. Add onion to pan; cook 6 to 8 minutes, stirring occasionally, until golden brown. Stir in quinoa and chicken broth. Heat to boiling; reduce heat. Cover and simmer 10 to 15 minutes or until all liquid is absorbed; remove from heat. 3 Meanwhile, in small food processor*, place cilantro, pumpkin seeds, garlic and cumin. Cover; process 5 to 10 seconds, using quick on-and-off motions; scrape side. Add chiles and oil. Cover; process, using quick on-and-off motions, until paste forms. 4 To cooked quinoa, add pesto mixture and the remaining salad ingredients. Refrigerate at least 30 minutes to blend flavors. 5 To serve, divide salad evenly among 4 plates; top each serving with 3 or 4 slices avocado and 1 sprig cilantro.

Per Serving:
calorie: 310 | fat: 12g | protein: 13g | carbs: 38g | sugars: 5g | fiber: 9g | sodium: 170mg

Sunshine Burgers

Prep time: 10 minutes | Cook time: 18 to 20 minutes | Makes 10 burgers

2 cups sliced raw carrots	1 teaspoon red wine vinegar or apple cider vinegar
1 large clove garlic, sliced or quartered	1 teaspoon smoked paprika
2 cans (15 ounces each) chickpeas, rinsed and drained	½ teaspoon dried rosemary
¼ cup sliced dry-packed sun-dried tomatoes	½ teaspoon ground cumin
2 tablespoons tahini	½ teaspoon sea salt
	1 cup rolled oats

1. In a food processor, combine the carrots and garlic. Pulse several times to mince. Add the chickpeas, tomatoes, tahini, vinegar, paprika, rosemary, cumin, and salt. Puree until well combined, scraping down the sides of the bowl once or twice. Add the oats, and pulse briefly to combine. Refrigerate the mixture for 30 minutes, if possible. 2. Preheat the oven to 400°F. Line a baking sheet with parchment paper. 3. Use an ice cream scoop to scoop the mixture onto the prepared baking sheet, flattening to shape it into patties. Bake for 18 to 20 minutes, flipping the burgers halfway through. Alternatively, you can cook the burgers in a nonstick skillet over medium heat for 6 to 8 minutes Per side, or until golden brown. Serve.

Per Serving:
calorie: 137 | fat: 4 | protein: 6g | carbs: 21g | sugars: 4g | fiber: 6g | sodium: 278mg

BBQ Bean Burgers

Prep time: 10 minutes | Cook time: 20 minutes | Makes 8 burgers

2 cups sliced carrots	½ tablespoon vegan Worcestershire sauce
1 medium-large clove garlic, quartered	½ tablespoon Dijon mustard
1 can (15 ounces) kidney beans, rinsed and drained	Scant ½ teaspoon sea salt
1 cup cooked, cooled brown rice	¼–½ teaspoon smoked paprika
¼ cup barbecue sauce	1 tablespoon chopped fresh thyme
	1¼ cups rolled oats

1. In a food processor, combine the carrots and garlic. Pulse until minced. Add the beans, rice, barbecue sauce, Worcestershire sauce, mustard, salt, paprika, and thyme. Puree until well combined. Once the mixture is fairly smooth, add the oats and pulse to combine. Chill the mixture for 30 minutes, if possible. 2. Preheat the oven to 400°F. Line a baking sheet with parchment paper. 3. Use an ice cream scoop to scoop the mixture onto the prepared baking sheet, flattening to shape it into patties. Bake for about 20 minutes, flipping the burgers halfway through. Alternatively, you can cook the burgers in a nonstick skillet over medium heat for 6 to 8 minutes Per side, or until golden brown.

Per Serving:
calorie: 152 | fat: 2g | protein: 6g | carbs: 29g | sugars: 6 | fiber: 5g | sodium: 247mg

BBQ Lentils

Prep time: 10 minutes | Cook time: 55 minutes | Serves 5

- 2 cups dried green or brown lentils, rinsed
- 3 tablespoons balsamic vinegar
- 4½ cups water
- ½ cup tomato paste
- 2 tablespoons vegan Worcestershire sauce
- 2 teaspoons dried rosemary
- 1 teaspoon onion powder
- ½ teaspoon garlic powder
- ½ teaspoon allspice
- ¼ teaspoon sea salt
- 1 tablespoon coconut nectar or pure maple syrup

1. In a large saucepan over medium-high heat, combine the lentils with 2 tablespoons of the vinegar. Cook, stirring, for 5 to 7 minutes to lightly toast the lentils. Once the pan is getting dry, add the water, tomato paste, Worcestershire sauce, rosemary, onion powder, garlic powder, allspice, salt, nectar or syrup, and the remaining 1 tablespoon vinegar, and stir through. Bring to a boil, then reduce the heat to low, cover the pot, and cook for 37 to 40 minutes, or until the lentils are fully tender. Season to taste, and serve.

Per Serving:
calorie: 295 | fat: 1g | protein: 20g | carbs: 54g | sugars: 9g | fiber: 14g | sodium: 399mg

Dirty Forbidden Rice

Prep time: 15 minutes | Cook time: 35 minutes | Serves 10

- 1 pound 90 percent lean ground beef
- 1 small red onion, chopped
- 1 medium tomato, chopped
- 1 garlic clove, minced
- ½ large red bell pepper, chopped
- 2 large carrots, peeled and chopped
- 2⅔ cups (15-ounce) forbidden rice (black rice)
- 4¾ cups store-bought low-sodium chicken broth
- 1 tablespoon Creole seasoning

1. Heat a Dutch oven over medium heat. 2. Put the ground beef, onion, tomato, and garlic in the pot and cook for 5 minutes, or until the beef is browned. 3. Stir in the bell pepper, carrots, and rice. 4. Add the broth and Creole seasoning, cover, and cook over medium-low heat for 30 minutes, or until the rice is tender. 5. Serve with a plate of greens of your choice.

Per Serving:
calorie: 274 | fat: 4g | protein: 16g | carbs: 43g | sugars: 2g | fiber: 3g | sodium: 79mg

Chicken and Vegetables with Quinoa

Prep time: 25 minutes | Cook time: 25 minutes | Serves 4

- 1⅓ cups uncooked quinoa
- 2⅔ cups water
- ⅔ cup chicken broth
- 2 cups 1-inch pieces fresh green beans
- ½ cup ready-to-eat baby-cut carrots, cut in half lengthwise
- 1 tablespoon olive oil
- ½ lb boneless skinless chicken breasts, cut into bite-size pieces
- ½ cup bite-size strips red bell pepper
- ½ cup sliced fresh mushrooms
- ½ teaspoon dried rosemary leaves
- ¼ teaspoon salt
- 2 cloves garlic, finely chopped

1 Rinse quinoa thoroughly by placing in a fine-mesh strainer and holding under cold running water until water runs clear; drain well. 2 In 2-quart saucepan, heat water to boiling. Add quinoa; return to boiling. Reduce heat to low. Cover; cook 12 to 16 minutes or until liquid is absorbed. 3 Meanwhile, in 12-inch nonstick skillet, heat broth to boiling over high heat. Add green beans and carrots. Reduce heat to medium-high. Cover; cook 5 to 7 minutes or until vegetables are crisp-tender. 4 Stir oil, chicken, bell pepper, mushrooms, rosemary, salt and garlic into vegetables. Cook over medium-high heat 8 to 9 minutes, stirring frequently, until chicken is no longer pink in center. Serve over quinoa.

Per Serving:
calorie: 350 | fat: 9g | protein: 22g | carbs: 46g | sugars: 6g | fiber: 6g | sodium: 380mg

Chapter 3　Poultry

Baked Chicken Dijon

Prep time: 25 minutes | Cook time: 40 minutes | Serves 6

- 3 cups uncooked bow-tie (farfalle) pasta (6 oz)
- 2 cups frozen broccoli cuts (from 12-oz bag)
- 2 cups cubed cooked chicken
- ⅓ cup diced roasted red bell peppers (from 7-oz jar)
- 1 can (10.75 oz) condensed cream of chicken or cream of mushroom soup
- ⅓ cup reduced-sodium chicken broth (from 32-oz carton)
- 3 tablespoons Dijon mustard
- 1 tablespoon finely chopped onion
- ½ cup shredded Parmesan cheese

1 Heat oven to 375°F. Spray 2½-quart casserole with cooking spray. 2 Cook pasta as directed on package, adding broccoli for the last 2 minutes of cooking time; drain. In casserole, mix chicken and roasted peppers. In small bowl, mix soup, broth, mustard and onion; stir into chicken mixture. Stir in pasta and broccoli. Sprinkle with cheese. 3 Cover; bake about 30 minutes or until hot in center and cheese is melted.

Per Serving:

calories: 290 | fat: 9g | protein: 24g | carbs: 29g | sugars: 2g | fiber: 3g | sodium: 770mg

Lemon-Basil Turkey Breasts

Prep time: 30 minutes | Cook time: 58 minutes | Serves 4

- 2 tablespoons olive oil
- 2 pounds (907 g) turkey breasts, bone-in, skin-on
- Coarse sea salt and ground black pepper, to taste
- 1 teaspoon fresh basil leaves, chopped
- 2 tablespoons lemon zest, grated

1. Rub olive oil on all sides of the turkey breasts; sprinkle with salt, pepper, basil, and lemon zest. 2. Place the turkey breasts skin side up on the parchment-lined air fryer basket. 3. Cook in the preheated air fryer at 330°F (166°C) for 30 minutes. Now, turn them over and cook an additional 28 minutes. 4. Serve with lemon wedges, if desired. Bon appétit!

Per Serving:

calories: 417 | fat: 23g | protein: 50g | carbs: 0g | fiber: 0g | sodium: 134mg

Ginger Turmeric Chicken Thighs

Prep time: 5 minutes | Cook time: 25 minutes | Serves 4

- 4 (4-ounce / 113-g) boneless, skin-on chicken thighs
- 2 tablespoons coconut oil, melted
- ½ teaspoon ground turmeric
- ½ teaspoon salt
- ½ teaspoon garlic powder
- ½ teaspoon ground ginger
- ¼ teaspoon ground black pepper

1. Place chicken thighs in a large bowl and drizzle with coconut oil. Sprinkle with remaining ingredients and toss to coat both sides of thighs. 2. Place thighs skin side up into ungreased air fryer basket. Adjust the temperature to 400°F (204°C) and air fry for 25 minutes. After 10 minutes, turn thighs. When 5 minutes remain, flip thighs once more. Chicken will be done when skin is golden brown and the internal temperature is at least 165°F (74°C). Serve warm.

Per Serving:

calories: 392 | fat: 31g | protein: 25g | carbs: 1g | fiber: 0g | sodium: 412mg

Simply Terrific Turkey Meatballs

Prep time: 10 minutes | Cook time: 7 to 10 minutes | Serves 4

- 1 red bell pepper, seeded and coarsely chopped
- 2 cloves garlic, coarsely chopped
- ¼ cup chopped fresh parsley
- 1½ pounds (680 g) 85% lean ground turkey
- 1 egg, lightly beaten
- ½ cup grated Parmesan cheese
- 1 teaspoon salt
- ½ teaspoon freshly ground black pepper

1. Preheat the air fryer to 400°F (204°C). 2. In a food processor fitted with a metal blade, combine the bell pepper, garlic, and parsley. Pulse until finely chopped. Transfer the vegetables to a large mixing bowl. 3. Add the turkey, egg, Parmesan, salt, and black pepper. Mix gently until thoroughly combined. Shape the mixture into 1¼-inch meatballs. 4. Working in batches if necessary, arrange the meatballs in a single layer in the air fryer basket; coat lightly with olive oil spray. Pausing halfway through the cooking time to shake the basket, air fry for 7 to 10 minutes, until lightly browned and a thermometer inserted into the center of a meatball registers 165°F (74°C).

Per Serving:

calories: 388 | fat: 25g | protein: 34g | carbs: 5g | fiber: 1g | sodium: 527mg

Wine-Poached Chicken with Herbs and Vegetables

Prep time: 5 minutes | Cook time: 1 hour | Serves 8

- 4 quarts low-sodium chicken broth
- 2 cups dry white wine
- 4 large bay leaves
- 4 sprigs fresh thyme
- ¼ teaspoon freshly ground black pepper
- 4-pound chicken, giblets removed, washed and patted dry
- ½ pound carrots, peeled and julienned
- ½ pound turnips, peeled and julienned
- ½ pound parsnips, peeled and julienned
- 4 small leeks, washed and trimmed

1. In a large stockpot, combine the broth, wine, bay leaves, thyme, dash salt (optional), and pepper. Let simmer over medium heat while you prepare the chicken. 2. Stuff the cavity with ⅓ each of the carrots, turnips, and parsnips; then truss. Add the stuffed chicken to the stockpot, and poach, covered, over low heat for 30 minutes. 3. Add the remaining vegetables with the leeks, and continue to simmer for 25–30 minutes, or until juices run clear when the chicken is pierced with a fork. 4. Remove the chicken and vegetables to a serving platter. Carve the chicken, remove the skin, and surround the sliced meat with poached vegetables to serve.

Per Serving:

calorie: 476 | fat: 13g | protein: 57g | carbs: 24g | sugars: 6g | fiber: 4g | sodium: 387mg

Lemon Chicken

Prep time: 5 minutes | Cook time: 20 to 25 minutes | Serves 4

8 bone-in chicken thighs, skin on	½ teaspoon paprika
1 tablespoon olive oil	½ teaspoon garlic powder
1½ teaspoons lemon-pepper seasoning	¼ teaspoon freshly ground black pepper
	Juice of ½ lemon

1. Preheat the air fryer to 360°F (182°C). 2. Place the chicken in a large bowl and drizzle with the olive oil. Top with the lemon-pepper seasoning, paprika, garlic powder, and freshly ground black pepper. Toss until thoroughly coated. 3. Working in batches if necessary, arrange the chicken in a single layer in the basket of the air fryer. Pausing halfway through the cooking time to turn the chicken, air fry for 20 to 25 minutes, until a thermometer inserted into the thickest piece registers 165°F (74°C). 4. Transfer the chicken to a serving platter and squeeze the lemon juice over the top.

Per Serving:

calories: 399 | fat: 19g | protein: 56g | carbs: 1g | fiber: 0g | sodium: 367mg

One-Pot Roast Chicken Dinner

Prep time: 10 minutes | Cook time: 40 minutes | Serves 6

½ head cabbage, cut into 2-inch chunks	2 tablespoons extra-virgin olive oil, divided
1 sweet onion, peeled and cut into eighths	2 teaspoons minced fresh thyme
1 sweet potato, peeled and cut into 1-inch chunks	Sea salt
4 garlic cloves, peeled and lightly crushed	Freshly ground black pepper
	2½ pounds bone-in chicken thighs and drumsticks

1. Preheat the oven to 450°F. 2. Lightly grease a large roasting pan and arrange the cabbage, onion, sweet potato, and garlic in the bottom. Drizzle with 1 tablespoon of oil, sprinkle with the thyme, and season the vegetables lightly with salt and pepper. 3. Season the chicken with salt and pepper. 4. Place a large skillet over medium-high heat and brown the chicken on both sides in the remaining 1 tablespoon of oil, about 10 minutes in total. 5. Place the browned chicken on top of the vegetables in the roasting pan. Roast until the chicken is cooked through, about 30 minutes.

Per Serving:

calorie: 328 | fat: 13g | protein: 38g | carbs: 14g | sugars: 6g | fiber: 3g | sodium: 217mg

Smoky Chicken Leg Quarters

Prep time: 30 minutes | Cook time: 23 to 27 minutes | Serves 6

½ cup avocado oil	½ teaspoon dried thyme
2 teaspoons smoked paprika	½ teaspoon freshly ground black pepper
1 teaspoon sea salt	2 pounds (907 g) bone-in, skin-on chicken leg quarters
1 teaspoon garlic powder	
½ teaspoon dried rosemary	

1. In a blender or small bowl, combine the avocado oil, smoked paprika, salt, garlic powder, rosemary, thyme, and black pepper. 2. Place the chicken in a shallow dish or large zip-top bag. Pour the marinade over the chicken, making sure all the legs are coated. Cover and marinate for at least 2 hours or overnight. 3. Place the chicken in a single layer in the air fryer basket, working in batches if necessary. Set the air fryer to 400°F (204°C) and air fry for 15 minutes. Flip the chicken legs, then reduce the temperature to 350°F (177°C). Cook for 8 to 12 minutes more, until an instant-read thermometer reads 160°F (71°C) when inserted into the thickest piece of chicken. 4. Allow to rest for 5 to 10 minutes before serving.

Per Serving:

calories: 347 | fat: 25g | protein: 29g | carbs: 1g | fiber: 0g | sodium: 534mg

Coconut Chicken Curry

Prep time: 15 minutes | Cook time: 35 minutes | Serves 4

2 teaspoons extra-virgin olive oil	2 tablespoons curry powder
3 (5-ounce) boneless, skinless chicken breasts, cut into 1-inch chunks	2 cups low-sodium chicken broth
	1 cup canned coconut milk
1 tablespoon grated fresh ginger	1 carrot, peeled and diced
	1 sweet potato, diced
1 tablespoon minced garlic	2 tablespoons chopped fresh cilantro

1. Place a large saucepan over medium-high heat and add the oil. 2. Sauté the chicken until lightly browned and almost cooked through, about 10 minutes. 3. Add the ginger, garlic, and curry powder, and sauté until fragrant, about 3 minutes. 4. Stir in the chicken broth, coconut milk, carrot, and sweet potato and bring the mixture to a boil. 5. Reduce the heat to low and simmer, stirring occasionally, until the vegetables and chicken are tender, about 20 minutes. 6. Stir in the cilantro and serve.

Per Serving:

calorie: 327 | fat: 18g | protein: 29g | carbs: 14g | sugars: 2g | fiber: 3g | sodium: 122mg

Spicy Chicken Drumsticks

Prep time: 5 minutes | Cook time: 50 minutes | Serves 2

¼ cup plain low-fat yogurt	4 chicken drumsticks, skinned (about 1 pound)
2 tablespoons hot pepper sauce	¼ cup dried bread crumbs
Crushed red pepper flakes, to taste	

1. In a shallow dish, combine the yogurt, hot pepper sauce, and crushed red pepper flakes, mixing well. Add the drumsticks, turning to coat. Cover, and marinate in the refrigerator for 2–4 hours. 2. Preheat the oven to 350 degrees. 3. Remove the drumsticks from the marinade, dredge in the bread crumbs, and place in a baking dish. Bake at 350 degrees for 40–50 minutes. Transfer to a serving platter, and serve.

Per Serving:

calorie: 337 | fat: 10g | protein: 48g | carbs: 12g | sugars: 3g | fiber: 1g | sodium: 501mg

Chicken with Mushroom Cream Sauce

Prep time: 5 minutes | Cook time: 20 minutes | Serves 8

- 1 tablespoon extra-virgin olive oil
- Eight 3-ounce boneless, skinless chicken breast halves
- ½ cup sliced mushrooms
- 3 tablespoons flour
- ½ cup low-sodium chicken broth
- ¾ cup white wine
- 2 teaspoons lemon zest
- ½ teaspoons lemon pepper
- 1 cup plain fat-free Greek yogurt
- Parsley sprigs

1. In a large nonstick skillet, heat the oil; add the chicken and cook for 5 minutes on each side. Remove the chicken, and keep warm. Add the mushrooms to the skillet, and cook until tender. 2. In a small bowl, whisk the flour with the broth and wine. Stir the mixture into the skillet, and add the lemon zest and pepper. Cook until thickened and bubbly. 3. Return the chicken to the skillet, and cook until the chicken is no longer pink. Transfer the chicken to a platter. Stir the yogurt into the skillet and heat thoroughly. Pour the sauce over the chicken, and garnish with parsley.

Per Serving:
calorie: 166 | fat: 4g | protein: 22g | carbs: 6g | sugars: 3g | fiber: 0g | sodium: 68mg

Coconut Lime Chicken

Prep time: 5 minutes | Cook time: 15 minutes | Serves 4

- 1 tablespoon coconut oil
- 4 (4-ounce) boneless, skinless chicken breasts
- ½ teaspoon salt
- 1 red bell pepper, cut into ¼-inch-thick slices
- 16 asparagus spears, bottom ends trimmed
- 1 cup unsweetened coconut milk
- 2 tablespoons freshly squeezed lime juice
- ½ teaspoon garlic powder
- ¼ teaspoon red pepper flakes
- ¼ cup chopped fresh cilantro

1. In a large skillet, heat the oil over medium-low heat. When hot, add the chicken. 2. Season the chicken with the salt. Cook for 5 minutes, then flip. 3. Push the chicken to the side of the skillet, and add the bell pepper and asparagus. Cook, covered, for 5 minutes. 4. Meanwhile, in a small bowl, whisk together the coconut milk, lime juice, garlic powder, and red pepper flakes. 5. Add the coconut milk mixture to the skillet, and boil over high heat for 2 to 3 minutes. 6. Top with the cilantro.

Per Serving:
calorie: 319 | fat: 21g | protein: 28g | carbs: 7g | sugars: 4g | fiber: 2g | sodium: 353mg

Smoky Whole Chicken

Prep time: 20 minutes | Cook time: 21 minutes | Serves 6

- 2 tablespoons extra-virgin olive oil
- 1 tablespoon kosher salt
- 1½ teaspoons smoked paprika
- 1 teaspoon freshly ground black pepper
- ½ teaspoon herbes de Provence
- ¼ teaspoon cayenne pepper
- 1 (3½-pound) whole chicken, rinsed and patted dry, giblets removed
- 1 large lemon, halved
- 6 garlic cloves, peeled and crushed with the flat side of a knife
- 1 large onion, cut into 8 wedges, divided
- 1 cup Chicken Bone Broth, low-sodium store-bought chicken broth, or water
- 2 large carrots, each cut into 4 pieces
- 2 celery stalks, each cut into 4 pieces

1. In a small bowl, combine the olive oil, salt, paprika, pepper, herbes de Provence, and cayenne. 2. Place the chicken on a cutting board and rub the olive oil mixture under the skin and all over the outside. Stuff the cavity with the lemon halves, garlic cloves, and 3 to 4 wedges of onion. 3. Pour the broth into the electric pressure cooker. Add the remaining onion wedges, carrots, and celery. Insert a wire rack or trivet on top of the vegetables. 4. Place the chicken, breast-side up, on the rack. 5. Close and lock the lid of the pressure cooker. Set the valve to sealing. 6. Cook on high pressure for 21 minutes. 7. When the cooking is complete, hit Cancel and allow the pressure to release naturally for 15 minutes, then quick release any remaining pressure. 8. Once the pin drops, unlock and remove the lid. 9. Carefully remove the chicken to a clean cutting board. Remove the skin and cut the chicken into pieces or shred/chop the meat, and serve.

Per Serving:
calorie: 362 | fat: 9g | protein: 60g | carbs: 8g | sugars: 3g | fiber: 2g | sodium: 611mg

Asian Mushroom-Chicken Soup

Prep time: 30 minutes | Cook time: 15 minutes | Serves 6

- 1½ cups water
- 1 package (1 oz) dried portabella or shiitake mushrooms
- 1 tablespoon canola oil
- ¼ cup thinly sliced green onions (4 medium)
- 2 tablespoons gingerroot, peeled, minced
- 3 cloves garlic, minced
- 1 jalapeño chile, seeded, minced
- 1 cup fresh snow pea pods, sliced diagonally
- 3 cups reduced-sodium chicken broth
- 1 can (8 oz) sliced bamboo shoots, drained
- 2 tablespoons low-sodium soy sauce
- ½ teaspoon sriracha sauce
- 1 cup shredded cooked chicken breast
- 1 cup cooked brown rice
- 4 teaspoons lime juice
- ½ cup thinly sliced fresh basil leaves

1 In medium microwavable bowl, heat water uncovered on High 30 seconds or until hot. Add mushrooms; let stand 5 minutes or until tender. Drain mushrooms (reserve liquid). Slice any mushrooms that are large. Set aside. 2 In 4-quart saucepan, heat oil over medium heat. Add 2 tablespoons of the green onions, the gingerroot, garlic and chile to oil. Cook about 3 minutes, stirring occasionally, until vegetables are tender. Add snow pea pods; cook 2 minutes, stirring occasionally. Stir in mushrooms, reserved mushroom liquid and the remaining ingredients, except lime juice and basil. Heat to boiling; reduce heat. Cover and simmer 10 minutes or until hot. Stir in lime juice. 3 Divide soup evenly among 6 bowls. Top servings with basil and remaining green onions.

Per Serving:
calories: 150 | fat: 4g | protein: 11g | carbs: 16g | sugars: 3g | fiber: 3g | sodium: 490mg

Grilled Herb Chicken with Wine and Roasted Garlic

Prep time: 5 minutes | Cook time: 45 minutes | Serves 4

Four 3-ounce boneless, skinless chicken breast halves	5 garlic cloves, minced
2 tablespoons extra-virgin olive oil, divided	5 garlic cloves, whole and unpeeled
1 cup red wine	⅛ teaspoon freshly ground black pepper
3 sprigs fresh thyme	

1. In a plastic zippered bag, place chicken, 1 tablespoon of the oil, wine, thyme, and minced garlic. Marinate for 2–3 hours in the refrigerator. 2. Preheat the oven to 375 degrees. 3. Spread the whole garlic cloves on a cookie sheet, drizzle with the remaining oil, and sprinkle with pepper. Bake for 30 minutes, stirring occasionally, until soft. 4. When cool, squeeze the garlic paste from the cloves, and mash in a small bowl with a fork. 5. Remove the chicken from the marinade, and grill for 12–15 minutes, turning frequently and brushing with garlic paste. Transfer to a platter, and serve hot.

Per Serving:
calorie: 222 | fat: 9g | protein: 20g | carbs: 4g | sugars: 0g | fiber: 0g | sodium: 40mg

One-Pan Chicken Dinner

Prep time: 5 minutes | Cook time: 35 minutes | Serves 4

3 tablespoons extra-virgin olive oil	4 (4-ounce) boneless, skinless chicken breasts
1 tablespoon red wine vinegar or apple cider vinegar	2 cups cubed sweet potatoes
¼ teaspoon garlic powder	20 Brussels sprouts, halved lengthwise
3 tablespoons Italian seasoning	

1. Preheat the oven to 400°F. 2. In a large bowl, whisk together the oil, vinegar, garlic powder, and Italian seasoning. 3. Add the chicken, sweet potatoes, and Brussels sprouts, and coat thoroughly with the marinade. 4. Remove the ingredients from the marinade and arrange them on a baking sheet in a single layer. Roast for 15 minutes. 5. Remove the baking sheet from the oven, flip the chicken over, and bake for another 15 to 20 minutes.

Per Serving:
calorie: 346 | fat: 13g | protein: 30g | carbs: 26g | sugars: 6g | fiber: 7g | sodium: 575mg

Jerk Chicken Thighs

Prep time: 30 minutes | Cook time: 15 to 20 minutes | Serves 6

2 teaspoons ground coriander	½ teaspoon ground cinnamon
1 teaspoon ground allspice	½ teaspoon ground nutmeg
1 teaspoon cayenne pepper	2 pounds (907 g) boneless chicken thighs, skin on
1 teaspoon ground ginger	2 tablespoons olive oil
1 teaspoon salt	
1 teaspoon dried thyme	

1. In a small bowl, combine the coriander, allspice, cayenne, ginger, salt, thyme, cinnamon, and nutmeg. Stir until thoroughly combined. 2. Place the chicken in a baking dish and use paper towels to pat dry. Thoroughly coat both sides of the chicken with the spice mixture. Cover and refrigerate for at least 2 hours, preferably overnight. 3. Preheat the air fryer to 360°F (182°C). 4. Working in batches if necessary, arrange the chicken in a single layer in the air fryer basket and lightly coat with the olive oil. Pausing halfway through the cooking time to flip the chicken, air fry for 15 to 20 minutes, until a thermometer inserted into the thickest part registers 165°F (74°C).

Per Serving:
calories: 227 | fat: 11g | protein: 30g | carbs: 1g | fiber: 0g | sodium: 532mg

Jerk Chicken Kebabs

Prep time: 10 minutes | Cook time: 14 minutes | Serves 4

8 ounces (227 g) boneless, skinless chicken thighs, cut into 1-inch cubes	seeded and cut into 1-inch pieces
2 tablespoons jerk seasoning	¼ medium red onion, peeled and cut into 1-inch pieces
2 tablespoons coconut oil	½ teaspoon salt
½ medium red bell pepper,	

1. Place chicken in a medium bowl and sprinkle with jerk seasoning and coconut oil. Toss to coat on all sides. 2. Using eight (6-inch) skewers, build skewers by alternating chicken, pepper, and onion pieces, about three repetitions per skewer. 3. Sprinkle salt over skewers and place into ungreased air fryer basket. Adjust the temperature to 370°F (188°C) and air fry for 14 minutes, turning skewers halfway through cooking. Chicken will be golden and have an internal temperature of at least 165°F (74°C) when done. Serve warm.

Per Serving:
calories: 142 | fat: 9g | protein: 12g | carbs: 4g | fiber: 1g | sodium: 348mg

Pizza in a Pot

Prep time: 25 minutes | Cook time: 15 minutes | Serves 8

1 pound bulk lean sweet Italian turkey sausage, browned and drained	1 small green bell pepper, chopped
28-ounce can crushed tomatoes	2 garlic cloves, minced
15½-ounce can chili beans	¼ cup grated Parmesan cheese
2¼-ounce can sliced black olives, drained	1 tablespoon quick-cooking tapioca
1 medium onion, chopped	1 tablespoon dried basil
	1 bay leaf

1. Set the Instant Pot to Sauté, then add the turkey sausage. Sauté until browned. 2. Add the remaining ingredients into the Instant Pot and stir. 3. Secure the lid and make sure the vent is set to sealing. Cook on Manual for 15 minutes. 4. When cook time is up, let the pressure release naturally for 5 minutes then perform a quick release. Discard bay leaf.

Per Serving:
calorie: 251 | fat: 10g | protein: 18g | carbs: 23g | sugars: 8g | fiber: 3g | sodium: 936mg

Baked Chicken Stuffed with Collard Greens

Prep time: 10 minutes | Cook time: 30 minutes | Serves 4

For the gravy	For the chicken
2½ cups store-bought low-sodium chicken broth, divided	2 boneless, skinless chicken breasts
4 tablespoons whole-wheat flour, divided	Juice of 1 lime
1 medium yellow onion, chopped	1 teaspoon sweet paprika
	½ teaspoon onion powder
½ bunch fresh thyme, roughly chopped	½ teaspoon garlic powder
	2 medium tomatoes, chopped
2 garlic cloves, minced	1 bunch collard greens, center stem removed, cut into 1-inch ribbons
1 bay leaf	
½ teaspoon celery seeds	¼ cup chicken broth (optional)
1 teaspoon Worcestershire sauce	Generous pinch red pepper flakes
Freshly ground black pepper	

To make the gravy 1. In a shallow stockpot, combine ½ cup of broth and 1 tablespoon of flour and cook over medium-low heat, whisking until the flour is dissolved. Continue to add 1 cup of broth and the remaining 3 tablespoons of flour in increments until a thick sauce is formed. 2. Add the onion, thyme, garlic, bay leaf, and ½ cup of broth, stirring well. To make the chicken 1. Cut a slit in each chicken breast deep enough for stuffing along its entire length. 2. In a small mixing bowl, massage the chicken all over with the lime juice, paprika, onion powder, and garlic powder. 3. In an electric pressure cooker, combine the tomatoes and collard greens. If the mixture looks dry, add the chicken broth. 4. Close and lock the lid, and set the pressure valve to sealing. 5. Select the Manual/Pressure Cook setting, and cook for 2 minutes. 6. Once cooking is complete, quick-release the pressure. Carefully remove the lid. 7. Using tongs or a slotted spoon, remove the greens while leaving the tomatoes behind. 8. Stuff the chicken breasts with the greens. Lay on the bed of tomatoes in the pressure cooker, with the side with greens facing up. 9. Spoon half of the gravy over the stuffed chicken. 10. Close and lock the lid, and set the pressure valve to sealing. 11. Select the Manual/Pressure Cook setting, and cook for 10 minutes. 12. Once cooking is complete, quick-release the pressure. Carefully remove the lid. 13. Remove the chicken and tomatoes from pressure cooker, and transfer to a serving dish. Season with the red pepper flakes.
Per Serving:
calorie: 301 | fat: 6g | protein: 41g | carbs: 24g | sugars: 4g | fiber: 9g | sodium: 155mg

Mexican Turkey Tenderloin

Prep time: 5 minutes | Cook time: 8 minutes | Serves 6

1 cup Low-Sodium Salsa or bottled salsa	tenderloin or boneless turkey breast, cut into 6 pieces
1 teaspoon chili powder	Freshly ground black pepper
½ teaspoon ground cumin	½ cup shredded Monterey Jack cheese or Mexican cheese blend
¼ teaspoon dried oregano	
1½ pounds unseasoned turkey	

1. In a small bowl or measuring cup, combine the salsa, chili powder, cumin, and oregano. Pour half of the mixture into the electric pressure cooker. 2. Nestle the turkey into the sauce. Grind some pepper onto each piece of turkey. Pour the remaining salsa mixture on top. 3. Close and lock the lid of the pressure cooker. Set the valve to sealing. 4. Cook on high pressure for 8 minutes. 5. When the cooking is complete, hit Cancel. Allow the pressure to release naturally for 10 minutes, then quick release any remaining pressure. 6. Once the pin drops, unlock and remove the lid. 7. Sprinkle the cheese on top, and put the lid back on for a few minutes to let the cheese melt. 8. Serve immediately.
Per Serving:
calorie: 156 | fat: 4g | protein: 28g | carbs: 4g | sugars: 2g | fiber: 1g | sodium: 525mg

Ann's Chicken Cacciatore

Prep time: 25 minutes | Cook time: 3 to 9 minutes | Serves 8

1 large onion, thinly sliced	¼ teaspoons pepper
3 pound chicken, cut up, skin removed, trimmed of fat	1–2 garlic cloves, minced
	1–2 teaspoons dried oregano
2 6-ounce cans tomato paste	½ teaspoon dried basil
4-ounce can sliced mushrooms, drained	½ teaspoon celery seed, optional
1 teaspoon salt	1 bay leaf
¼ cup dry white wine	

1. In the inner pot of the Instant Pot, place the onion and chicken. 2. Combine remaining ingredients and pour over the chicken. 3. Secure the lid and make sure vent is at sealing. Cook on Slow Cook mode, low 7–9 hours, or high 3–4 hours.
Per Serving:
calories: 161 | fat: 4g | protein: 19g | carbs: 12g | sugars: 3g | fiber: 3g | sodium: 405mg

Easy Chicken Cacciatore

Prep time: 5 minutes | Cook time: 20 minutes | Serves 2

Extra-virgin olive oil cooking spray	1 cup sliced cremini mushrooms
1 garlic clove, chopped	½ cup chopped tomatoes, with juice
½ cup chopped red onion	
¾ cup chopped green bell pepper	1 cup green beans
	1 teaspoon dried oregano
2 (6-ounce) boneless skinless chicken breasts, cubed	1 teaspoon dried rosemary

1. Coat a skillet with cooking spray. Place it over medium heat. 2. Add the garlic. Sauté for about 1 minute, or until browned. 3. Add the red onion, green bell pepper, and chicken. Cook for about 6 minutes, or until the chicken is slightly browned, tossing to cook all sides. 4. Stir in the mushrooms, tomatoes, green beans, oregano, and rosemary. Reduce the heat to medium-low. Simmer for 8 to 10 minutes, stirring constantly. 5. Remove from the heat and serve hot. 6. Enjoy!
Per Serving:
calorie: 265 | fat: 5g | protein: 42g | carbs: 13g | sugars: 6g | fiber: 4g | sodium: 91mg

Ground Turkey Tetrazzini

Prep time: 5 minutes | Cook time: 20 minutes | Serves 6

1 tablespoon extra-virgin olive oil	wheat elbow pasta
2 garlic cloves, minced	2 cups low-sodium chicken broth
1 yellow onion, diced	1½ cups frozen green peas, thawed
8 ounces cremini or button mushrooms, sliced	3 cups baby spinach
½ teaspoon fine sea salt	Three ¾-ounce wedges Laughing Cow creamy light Swiss cheese, or 2 tablespoons Neufchâtel cheese, at room temperature
¼ teaspoon freshly ground black pepper	
1 pound 93 percent lean ground turkey	
1 teaspoon poultry seasoning	⅓ cup grated Parmesan cheese
6 ounces whole-grain extra-broad egg-white pasta (such as No Yolks brand) or whole-	1 tablespoon chopped fresh flat-leaf parsley

1. Select the Sauté setting on the Instant Pot and heat the oil and garlic for 2 minutes, until the garlic is bubbling but not browned. Add the onion, mushrooms, salt, and pepper and sauté for about 5 minutes, until the mushrooms have wilted and begun to give up their liquid. Add the turkey and poultry seasoning and sauté, using a wooden spoon or spatula to break up the meat as it cooks, for about 4 minutes more, until cooked through and no streaks of pink remain. 2. Stir in the pasta. Pour in the broth and use the spoon or spatula to nudge the pasta into the liquid as much as possible. It's fine if some pieces are not completely submerged. 3. Secure the lid and set the Pressure Release to Sealing. Press the Cancel button to reset the cooking program, then select the Pressure Cook or Manual setting and set the cooking time for 5 minutes at high pressure. (The pot will take about 5 minutes to come up to pressure before the cooking program begins.) 4. When the cooking program ends, let the pressure release naturally for 5 minutes, then move the Pressure Release to Venting to release any remaining steam. Open the pot and stir in the peas, spinach, Laughing Cow cheese, and Parmesan. Let stand for 2 minutes, then stir the mixture once more. 5. Ladle into bowls or onto plates and sprinkle with the parsley. Serve right away.

Per Serving:
calories: 321 | fat: 11g | protein: 26g | carbs: 35g | sugars: 4g | fiber: 5g | sodium: 488mg

Garlic Galore Rotisserie Chicken

Prep time: 5 minutes | Cook time: 3 minutes | Serves 4

3-pound whole chicken	stock, broth, or water
2 tablespoons olive oil, divided	2 tablespoons garlic powder
Salt to taste	2 teaspoons onion powder
Pepper to taste	½ teaspoon basil
20–30 cloves fresh garlic, peeled and left whole	½ teaspoon cumin
1 cup low-sodium chicken	½ teaspoon chili powder

1. Rub chicken with one tablespoon of the olive oil and sprinkle with salt and pepper. 2. Place the garlic cloves inside the chicken. Use butcher's twine to secure the legs. 3. Press the Sauté button on the Instant Pot, then add the rest of the olive oil to the inner pot. 4. When the pot is hot, place the chicken inside. You are just trying to sear it, so leave it for about 4 minutes on each side. 5. Remove the chicken and set aside. Place the trivet at the bottom of the inner pot and pour in the chicken stock. 6. Mix together the remaining seasonings and rub them all over the entire chicken. 7. Place the chicken back inside the inner pot, breast-side up, on top of the trivet and secure the lid to the sealing position. 8. Press the Manual button and use the +/- to set it for 25 minutes. 9. When the timer beeps, allow the pressure to release naturally for 15 minutes. If the lid will not open at this point, quick release the remaining pressure and remove the chicken. 10. Let the chicken rest for 5–10 minutes before serving.

Per Serving:
calories: 333 | fat: 23g | protein: 24g | carbs: 9g | sugars: 0g | fiber: 1g | sodium: 110mg

Turkey Cabbage Soup

Prep time: 15 minutes | Cook time: 30 minutes | Serves 4

1 tablespoon extra-virgin olive oil	
1 sweet onion, chopped	8 cups chicken or turkey broth
2 celery stalks, chopped	2 bay leaves
2 teaspoons minced fresh garlic	1 cup chopped cooked turkey
4 cups finely shredded green cabbage	2 teaspoons chopped fresh thyme
	Sea salt
1 sweet potato, peeled, diced	Freshly ground black pepper

1. Place a large saucepan over medium-high heat and add the olive oil. 2. Sauté the onion, celery, and garlic until softened and translucent, about 3 minutes. 3. Add the cabbage and sweet potato and sauté for 3 minutes. 4. Stir in the chicken broth and bay leaves and bring the soup to a boil. 5. Reduce the heat to low and simmer until the vegetables are tender, about 20 minutes. 6. Add the turkey and thyme and simmer until the turkey is heated through, about 4 minutes. 7. Remove the bay leaves and season the soup with salt and pepper.

Per Serving:
calorie: 444 | fat: 14g | protein: 38g | carbs: 46g | sugars: 17g | fiber: 7g | sodium: 427mg

Greek Chicken

Prep time: 25 minutes | Cook time: 20 minutes | Serves 6

4 potatoes, unpeeled, quartered	3 teaspoons dried oregano
2 pounds chicken pieces, trimmed of skin and fat	¾ teaspoons salt
	½ teaspoons pepper
2 large onions, quartered	1 tablespoon olive oil
1 whole bulb garlic, cloves minced	1 cup water

1. Place potatoes, chicken, onions, and garlic into the inner pot of the Instant Pot, then sprinkle with seasonings. Top with oil and water. 2. Secure the lid and make sure vent is set to sealing. Cook on Manual mode for 20 minutes. 3. When cook time is over, let the pressure release naturally for 5 minutes, then release the rest manually.

Per Serving:

calorie: 278 | fat: 6g | protein: 27g | carbs: 29g | sugars: 9g | fiber: 4g | sodium: 358mg

Herb-Roasted Turkey and Vegetables

Prep time: 20 minutes | Cook time: 2 hours | Serves 6

2 teaspoons minced garlic	Sea salt
1 tablespoon chopped fresh parsley	Freshly ground black pepper
1 teaspoon chopped fresh thyme	2 sweet potatoes, peeled and cut into 2-inch chunks
1 teaspoon chopped fresh rosemary	2 carrots, peeled and cut into 2-inch chunks
2 pounds boneless, skinless whole turkey breast	2 parsnips, peeled and cut into 2-inch chunks
3 teaspoons extra-virgin olive oil, divided	1 sweet onion, peeled and cut into eighths

1. Preheat the oven to 350°F. 2. Line a large roasting pan with aluminum foil and set it aside. 3. In a small bowl, mix together the garlic, parsley, thyme, and rosemary. 4. Place the turkey breast in the roasting pan and rub it all over with 1 teaspoon of olive oil. 5. Rub the garlic-herb mixture all over the turkey and season lightly with salt and pepper. 6. Place the turkey in the oven and roast for 30 minutes. 7. While the turkey is roasting, toss the sweet potatoes, carrots, parsnips, onion, and the remaining 2 teaspoons of olive oil in a large bowl. 8. Remove the turkey from the oven and arrange the vegetables around it. 9. Roast until the turkey is cooked through (170°F internal temperature) and the vegetables are lightly caramelized, about 1 ½ hours.

Per Serving:
calorie: 267 | fat: 4g | protein: 35g | carbs: 25g | sugars: 8g | fiber: 5g | sodium: 379mg

Pulled BBQ Chicken and Texas-Style Cabbage Slaw

Prep time: 5 minutes | Cook time: 20 minutes | Serves 6

Chicken	cut into narrow strips
1 cup water	2 carrots, julienned
¼ teaspoon fine sea salt	1 large Fuji or Gala apple, julienned
3 garlic cloves, peeled	½ cup chopped fresh cilantro
2 bay leaves	3 tablespoons fresh lime juice
2 pounds boneless, skinless chicken thighs (see Note)	3 tablespoons extra-virgin olive oil
Cabbage Slaw	½ teaspoon ground cumin
½ head red or green cabbage, thinly sliced	¼ teaspoon fine sea salt
1 red bell pepper, seeded and thinly sliced	¾ cup low-sugar or unsweetened barbecue sauce
2 jalapeño chiles, seeded and	Cornbread, for serving

1. To make the chicken: Combine the water, salt, garlic, bay leaves, and chicken thighs in the Instant Pot, arranging the chicken in a single layer. 2. Secure the lid and set the Pressure Release to Sealing. Select the Poultry, Pressure Cook, or Manual setting and set the cooking time for 10 minutes at high pressure. (The pot will take about 10 minutes to come up to pressure before the cooking program begins.) 3. To make the slaw: While the chicken is cooking, in a large bowl, combine the cabbage, bell pepper, jalapeños, carrots, apple, cilantro, lime juice, oil, cumin, and salt and toss together until the vegetables and apples are evenly coated. 4. When the cooking program ends, perform a quick pressure release by moving the Pressure Release to Venting, or let the pressure release naturally. Open the pot and, using tongs, transfer the chicken to a cutting board. Using two forks, shred the chicken into bite-size pieces. Wearing heat-resistant mitts, lift out the inner pot and discard the cooking liquid. Return the inner pot to the housing. 5. Return the chicken to the pot and stir in the barbecue sauce. You can serve it right away or heat it for a minute or two on the Sauté setting, then return the pot to its Keep Warm setting until ready to serve. 6. Divide the chicken and slaw evenly among six plates. Serve with wedges of cornbread on the side.

Per Serving:
calories: 320 | fat: 14g | protein: 32g | carbs: 18g | sugars: 7g | fiber: 4g | sodium: 386mg

BBQ Turkey Meat Loaf

Prep time: 5 minutes | Cook time: 40 minutes | Serves 6

1 pound 93 percent lean ground turkey	½ small yellow onion, finely diced
⅓ cup low-sugar or unsweetened barbecue sauce, plus 2 tablespoons	1 garlic clove, minced
	½ teaspoon fine sea salt
⅓ cup gluten-free panko (Japanese bread crumbs)	½ teaspoon freshly ground black pepper
1 large egg	Cooked cauliflower "rice" or brown rice for serving

1. Pour 1 cup water into the Instant Pot. Lightly grease a 7 by 3-inch round cake pan or a 5½ by 3-inch loaf pan with olive oil or coat with nonstick cooking spray. 2. In a medium bowl, combine the turkey, ⅓ cup barbecue sauce, panko, egg, onion, garlic, salt, and pepper and mix well with your hands until all of the ingredients are evenly distributed. Transfer the mixture to the prepared pan, pressing it into an even layer. Cover the pan tightly with aluminum foil. Place the pan on a long-handled silicone steam rack, then, holding the handles of the steam rack, lower it into the pot. (If you don't have the long-handled rack, use the wire metal steam rack and a homemade sling) 3. Secure the lid and set the Pressure Release to Sealing. Select the Pressure Cook or Manual setting and set the cooking time for 25 minutes at high pressure if using a 7-inch round cake pan, or for 35 minutes at high pressure if using a 5½ by 3-inch loaf pan. (The pot will take about 10 minutes to come up to pressure before the cooking program begins.) 4. Preheat a toaster oven or position an oven rack 4 to 6 inches below the heat source and preheat the broiler. 5. When the cooking program ends, perform a quick pressure release by moving the Pressure Release to Venting. Open the pot and, wearing heat-resistant mitts, grasp the handles of the steam rack and lift it out of the pot. Uncover the pan, taking care not to get burned by the steam or to drip condensation onto the meat loaf. Brush the remaining 2 tablespoons barbecue sauce on top of the meat loaf. 6. Broil the meat loaf for a few minutes, just until the glaze becomes bubbly and browned. Cut the meat loaf into slices and serve hot, with the cauliflower "rice" alongside.

Per Serving:
calories: 236 | fat: 11g | protein: 25g | carbs: 10g | sugars: 2g | fiber: 3g | sodium: 800mg

Mushroom-Sage Stuffed Turkey Breast

Prep time: 10 minutes | Cook time: 1 hour 5 minutes | Serves 8

2 tablespoons extra-virgin olive oil, divided	black pepper, divided
8 ounces brown mushrooms, finely chopped	2 tablespoons chopped fresh sage
2 garlic cloves, minced	1 boneless, skinless turkey breast (about 3 pounds), butterflied
½ teaspoon salt, divided	
¼ teaspoon freshly ground	

1. Preheat the oven to 375°F. 2. In a large skillet, heat 1 tablespoon of oil over medium heat. Add the mushrooms and cook for 4 to 5 minutes, stirring regularly, until most of the liquid has evaporated from the pan. Add the garlic, ¼ teaspoon of salt, and ⅛ teaspoon of pepper, and continue to cook for an additional minute. Add the sage to the pan, cook for 1 minute, and remove the pan from the heat. 3. On a clean work surface, lay the turkey breast flat. Use a kitchen mallet to pound the breast to an even 1-inch thickness throughout. 4. Spread the mushroom-sage mixture on the turkey breast, leaving a 1-inch border around the edges. Roll the breast tightly into a log. 5. Using kitchen twine, tie the breast two or three times around to hold it together. Rub the remaining 1 tablespoon of oil over the turkey breast. Season with the remaining ¼ teaspoon of salt and ⅛ teaspoon of pepper. 6. Transfer to a roasting pan and roast for 50 to 60 minutes, until the juices run clear, the meat is cooked through, and the internal temperature reaches 180°F. 7. Let rest for 5 minutes. Cut off the twine, slice, and serve.

Per Serving:
calories: 232 | fat: 6g | protein: 41g | carbs: 2g | sugars: 0g | fiber: 0g | sodium: 320mg

Roast Chicken with Pine Nuts and Fennel

Prep time: 20 minutes | Cook time: 30 minutes | Serves 2

For the herb paste	drumsticks
2 tablespoons fresh rosemary leaves	2 teaspoons extra-virgin olive oil
1 tablespoon freshly grated lemon zest	For the vegetables
2 garlic cloves, quartered	1 large fennel bulb, cored and chopped (about 3 cups)
½ teaspoon freshly ground black pepper	1 cup sliced fresh mushrooms
¼ teaspoon salt	½ cup sliced carrots
1 teaspoon extra-virgin olive oil	¼ cup chopped sweet onion
For the chicken	2 teaspoons extra-virgin olive oil
4 (6-ounce) skinless chicken	2 tablespoons pine nuts
	2 teaspoons white wine vinegar

To make the vegetables 1. Preheat the oven to 450°F. 2. In a 9-by-13-inch baking dish, toss together the fennel, mushrooms, carrots, onion, and olive oil. Place the dish in the preheated oven. Bake for 10 minutes. 3. Stir in the pine nuts. 4. Top with the browned drumsticks. Return the dish to the oven. Bake for 15 to 20 minutes more, or until the fennel is golden and an instant-read thermometer inserted into the thickest part of a drumstick without touching the bone registers 165°F. 5. Remove the chicken from the pan. 6. Stir the white wine vinegar into the pan. Toss the vegetables to coat, scraping up any browned bits. 7. Serve the chicken with the vegetables and enjoy!

Per Serving:
calorie: 316 | fat: 15g | protein: 35g | carbs: 10g | sugars: 4g | fiber: 3g | sodium: 384mg

Herbed Whole Turkey Breast

Prep time: 10 minutes | Cook time: 30 minutes | Serves 12

3 tablespoons extra-virgin olive oil	1 tablespoon kosher salt
1½ tablespoons herbes de Provence or poultry seasoning	1½ teaspoons freshly ground black pepper
2 teaspoons minced garlic	1 (6-pound) bone-in, skin-on whole turkey breast, rinsed and patted dry
1 teaspoon lemon zest (from 1 small lemon)	

1. In a small bowl, whisk together the olive oil, herbes de Provence, garlic, lemon zest, salt, and pepper. 2. Rub the outside of the turkey and under the skin with the olive oil mixture. 3. Pour 1 cup of water into the electric pressure cooker and insert a wire rack or trivet. 4. Place the turkey on the rack, skin-side up. 5. Close and lock the lid of the pressure cooker. Set the valve to sealing. 6. Cook on high pressure for 30 minutes. 7. When the cooking is complete, hit Cancel. Allow the pressure to release naturally for 20 minutes, then quick release any remaining pressure. 8. Once the pin drops, unlock and remove the lid. 9. Carefully transfer the turkey to a cutting board. Remove the skin, slice, and serve.

Per Serving:
calorie: 389 | fat: 19g | protein: 50g | carbs: 1g | sugars: 0g | fiber: 0g | sodium: 582mg

Creamy Garlic Chicken with Broccoli

Prep time: 5 minutes | Cook time: 15 minutes | Serves 4

½ cup uncooked brown rice or quinoa	1 teaspoon garlic powder, divided
4 (4-ounce) boneless, skinless chicken breasts	Avocado oil cooking spray
¼ teaspoon salt	3 cups fresh or frozen broccoli florets
¼ teaspoon freshly ground black pepper	1 cup half-and-half

1. Cook the rice according to the package instructions. 2. Meanwhile, season both sides of the chicken breasts with the salt, pepper, and ½ teaspoon of garlic powder. 3. Heat a large skillet over medium-low heat. When hot, coat the cooking surface with cooking spray and add the chicken and broccoli in a single layer. 4. Cook for 4 minutes, then flip the chicken breasts over and cover. Cook for 5 minutes more. 5. Add the half-and-half and remaining ½ teaspoon of garlic powder to the skillet and stir. Increase the heat to high and simmer for 2 minutes. 6. Divide the rice into four equal portions. Top each portion with 1 chicken breast and one-quarter of the broccoli and cream sauce.

Per Serving:
calorie: 274 | fat: 5g | protein: 31g | carbs: 27g | sugars: 3g | fiber: 1g | sodium: 271mg

Teriyaki Turkey Meatballs

Prep time: 20 minutes | Cook time: 20 minutes | Serves 6

1 pound lean ground turkey	1 teaspoon grated fresh ginger
¼ cup finely chopped scallions, both white and green parts	2 tablespoons reduced-sodium tamari or gluten-free soy sauce
1 egg	1 tablespoon honey
2 garlic cloves, minced	2 teaspoons mirin
	1 teaspoon toasted sesame oil

1. Preheat the oven to 400°F. Line a baking sheet with parchment paper. 2. In a large mixing bowl, combine the turkey, scallions, egg, garlic, ginger, tamari, honey, mirin, and sesame oil. Mix well. 3. Using your hands, form the meat mixture into balls about the size of a tablespoon. Arrange on the prepared baking sheet. 4. Bake for 10 minutes, flip with a spatula, and continue baking for an additional 10 minutes until the meatballs are cooked through.

Per Serving:
calories: 153 | fat: 8g | protein: 16g | carbs: 5g | sugars: 4g | fiber: 0g | sodium: 270mg

Chicken Nuggets

Prep time: 10 minutes | Cook time: 15 minutes | Serves 4

1 pound (454 g) ground chicken thighs	1 large egg, whisked
½ cup shredded Mozzarella cheese	½ teaspoon salt
	¼ teaspoon dried oregano
	¼ teaspoon garlic powder

1. In a large bowl, combine all ingredients. Form mixture into twenty nugget shapes, about 2 tablespoons each. 2. Place nuggets into ungreased air fryer basket, working in batches if needed. Adjust the temperature to 375°F (191°C) and air fry for 15 minutes, turning nuggets halfway through cooking. Let cool 5 minutes before serving.

Per Serving:
calories: 195 | fat: 8g | protein: 28g | carbs: 1g | fiber: 0g | sodium: 419mg

Chicken in Mushroom Gravy

Prep time: 10 minutes | Cook time: 10 minutes | Serves 6

6 (5 ounces each) boneless, skinless chicken-breast halves	10¾-ounce can 98% fat-free, reduced-sodium cream of mushroom soup
Salt and pepper to taste	4 ounces sliced mushrooms
¼ cup dry white wine or low-sodium chicken broth	

1. Place chicken in the inner pot of the Instant Pot. Season with salt and pepper. 2. Combine wine and soup in a bowl, then pour over the chicken. Top with the mushrooms. 3. Secure the lid and make sure the vent is set to sealing. Set on Manual mode for 10 minutes. 4. When cooking time is up, let the pressure release naturally.

Per Serving:
calories: 204 | fat: 4g | protein: 34g | carbs: 6g | sugars: 1g | fiber: 1g | sodium: 320mg

Chicken Patties

Prep time: 15 minutes | Cook time: 12 minutes | Serves 4

1 pound (454 g) ground chicken thigh meat	½ teaspoon garlic powder
½ cup shredded Mozzarella cheese	¼ teaspoon onion powder
1 teaspoon dried parsley	1 large egg
	2 ounces (57 g) pork rinds, finely ground

1. In a large bowl, mix ground chicken, Mozzarella, parsley, garlic powder, and onion powder. Form into four patties. 2. Place patties in the freezer for 15 to 20 minutes until they begin to firm up. 3. Whisk egg in a medium bowl. Place the ground pork rinds into a large bowl. 4. Dip each chicken patty into the egg and then press into pork rinds to fully coat. Place patties into the air fryer basket. 5. Adjust the temperature to 360°F (182°C) and air fry for 12 minutes. 6. Patties will be firm and cooked to an internal temperature of 165°F (74°C) when done. Serve immediately.

Per Serving:
calories: 265 | fat: 15g | protein: 29g | carbs: 1g | fiber: 0g | sodium: 285mg

Orange Chicken Thighs with Bell Peppers

Prep time: 15 to 20 minutes | Cook time: 7 minutes | Serves 4 to 6

6 boneless skinless chicken thighs, cut into bite-sized pieces	3 cloves garlic, minced or chopped
2 packets crystallized True Orange flavoring	½ teaspoon pink salt
½ teaspoon True Orange Orange Ginger seasoning	½ teaspoon black pepper
½ teaspoon coconut aminos	1 teaspoon garlic powder
¼ teaspoon Worcestershire sauce	1 teaspoon ground ginger
Olive oil or cooking spray	¼–½ teaspoon red pepper flakes
2 cups bell pepper strips, any color combination (I used red)	2 tablespoons tomato paste
1 onion, chopped	½ cup chicken bone broth or water
1 tablespoon green onion, chopped fine	1 tablespoon brown sugar substitute (I use Sukrin Gold)
	½ cup Seville orange spread (I use Crofter's brand)

1. Combine the chicken with the 2 packets of crystallized orange flavor, the orange ginger seasoning, the coconut aminos, and the Worcestershire sauce. Set aside. 2. Turn the Instant Pot to Sauté and add a touch of olive oil or cooking spray to the inner pot. Add in the orange ginger marinated chicken thighs. 3. Sauté until lightly browned. Add in the peppers, onion, green onion, garlic, and seasonings. Mix well. 4. Add the remaining ingredients; mix to combine. 5. Lock the lid, set the vent to sealing, set to 7 minutes. 6. Let the pressure release naturally for 2 minutes, then manually release the rest when cook time is up.

Per Serving:
calories: 120 | fat: 2g | protein: 12g | carbs: 8g | sugars: 10g | fiber: 1.6g | sodium: 315mg

Turkey Chili

Prep time: 15 minutes | Cook time: 30 minutes | Serves 6

- 1 tablespoon extra-virgin olive oil
- 1 pound lean ground turkey
- 1 large onion, diced
- 3 garlic cloves, minced
- 1 red bell pepper, seeded and diced
- 1 cup chopped celery
- 2 tablespoons chili powder
- 1 tablespoon ground cumin
- 1 (28-ounce) can reduced-salt diced tomatoes
- 1 (15-ounce) can low-sodium kidney beans, drained and rinsed
- 2 cups low-sodium chicken broth
- ½ teaspoon salt
- Shredded cheddar cheese, for serving (optional)

1. In a large pot, heat the oil over medium heat. Add the turkey, onion, and garlic, and cook, stirring regularly, until the turkey is cooked through. 2. Add the bell pepper, celery, chili powder, and cumin. Stir well and continue to cook for 1 minute. 3. Add the tomatoes with their liquid, kidney beans, and chicken broth. Bring to a boil, reduce the heat to low, and simmer for 20 minutes. 4. Season with the salt and serve topped with cheese (if using).

Per Serving:
calorie: 276 | fat: 10g | protein: 23g | carbs: 27g | sugars: 7g | fiber: 8g | sodium: 556mg

Chapter 4 Beef, Pork, and Lamb

Steak Gyro Platter

Prep time: 30 minutes | Cook time: 8 to 10 minutes | Serves 4

1 pound (454 g) flank steak	½ cup crumbled feta cheese
1 teaspoon garlic powder	½ cup peeled and diced cucumber
1 teaspoon ground cumin	⅓ cup sliced red onion
½ teaspoon sea salt	¼ cup seeded and diced tomato
½ teaspoon freshly ground black pepper	2 tablespoons pitted and sliced black olives
5 ounces (142 g) shredded romaine lettuce	Tzatziki sauce, for serving

1. Pat the steak dry with paper towels. In a small bowl, combine the garlic powder, cumin, salt, and pepper. Sprinkle this mixture all over the steak, and allow the steak to rest at room temperature for 45 minutes. 2. Preheat the air fryer to 400ºF (204ºC). Place the steak in the air fryer basket and air fry for 4 minutes. Flip the steak and cook 4 to 6 minutes more, until an instant-read thermometer reads 120ºF (49ºC) at the thickest point for medium-rare (or as desired). Remove the steak from the air fryer and let it rest for 5 minutes. 3. Divide the romaine among plates. Top with the feta, cucumber, red onion, tomato, and olives.

Per Serving:
calories: 229 | fat: 10g | protein: 28g | carbs: 5g | fiber: 2g | sodium: 559mg

Steak with Bell Pepper

Prep time: 30 minutes | Cook time: 20 to 23 minutes | Serves 6

¼ cup avocado oil	steak or flank steak, thinly sliced against the grain
¼ cup freshly squeezed lime juice	1 red bell pepper, cored, seeded, and cut into ½-inch slices
2 teaspoons minced garlic	
1 tablespoon chili powder	
½ teaspoon ground cumin	1 green bell pepper, cored, seeded, and cut into ½-inch slices
Sea salt and freshly ground black pepper, to taste	
1 pound (454 g) top sirloin	1 large onion, sliced

1. In a small bowl or blender, combine the avocado oil, lime juice, garlic, chili powder, cumin, and salt and pepper to taste. 2. Place the sliced steak in a zip-top bag or shallow dish. Place the bell peppers and onion in a separate zip-top bag or dish. Pour half the marinade over the steak and the other half over the vegetables. Seal both bags and let the steak and vegetables marinate in the refrigerator for at least 1 hour or up to 4 hours. 3. Line the air fryer basket with an air fryer liner or aluminum foil. Remove the vegetables from their bag or dish and shake off any excess marinade. Set the air fryer to 400ºF (204ºC). Place the vegetables in the air fryer basket and cook for 13 minutes. 4. Remove the steak from its bag or dish and shake off any excess marinade. Place the steak on top of the vegetables in the air fryer, and cook for 7 to 10 minutes or until an instant-read thermometer reads 120ºF (49ºC) for medium-rare (or cook to your desired doneness). 5. Serve with desired fixings, such as keto tortillas, lettuce, sour cream, avocado slices, shredded Cheddar cheese, and cilantro.

Per Serving:
calories: 252 | fat: 18g | protein: 17g | carbs: 6g | fiber: 2g | sodium: 81mg

Creole Braised Sirloin

Prep time: 15 minutes | Cook time: 40 minutes | Serves 4

1 pound beef round sirloin tip, cut into 4 strips	coarsely chopped
	2 garlic cloves, minced
¼ teaspoon freshly ground black pepper	4 medium tomatoes, coarsely chopped
2 cups store-bought low-sodium chicken broth, divided	1 bunch mustard greens including stems, coarsely chopped
1 medium onion, chopped	
1 celery stalk, coarsely chopped	1 tablespoon Creole seasoning
	¼ teaspoon red pepper flakes
1 medium green bell pepper,	2 bay leaves

1. Preheat the oven to 450ºF. 2. Massage the beef all over with black pepper. 3. In a Dutch oven, bring 1 cup of broth to a simmer over medium heat. 4. Add the onion, celery, bell pepper, and garlic and cook, stirring often, for 5 minutes, or until the vegetables are softened. 5. Add the tomatoes, mustard greens, Creole seasoning, and red pepper flakes and cook for 3 to 5 minutes, or until the greens are wilted. 6. Add the bay leaves, beef, and remaining 1 cup of broth. 7. Cover the pot, transfer to the oven, and cook for 30 minutes, or until the juices run clear when you pierce the beef. 8. Remove the beef from the oven, and let rest for 5 to 7 minutes. Discard the bay leaves. 9. Thinly slice the beef and serve.

Per Serving:
calorie: 215 | fat: 6g | protein: 29g | carbs: 11g | sugars: 5g | fiber: 3g | sodium: 121mg

Beef and Pepper Fajita Bowls

Prep time: 10 minutes | Cook time: 15 minutes | Serves 4

4 tablespoons extra-virgin olive oil, divided	sliced
	1 onion, thinly sliced
1 head cauliflower, riced	2 garlic cloves, minced
1 pound sirloin steak, cut into ¼-inch-thick strips	Juice of 2 limes
	1 teaspoon chili powder
1 red bell pepper, seeded and	

1. In a large skillet over medium-high heat, heat 2 tablespoons of olive oil until it shimmers. Add the cauliflower. Cook, stirring occasionally, until it softens, about 3 minutes. Set aside. 2. Wipe out the skillet with a paper towel. Add the remaining 2 tablespoons of oil to the skillet, and heat it on medium-high until it shimmers. Add the steak and cook, stirring occasionally, until it browns, about 3 minutes. Use a slotted spoon to remove the steak from the oil in the pan and set aside. 3. Add the bell pepper and onion to the pan. Cook, stirring occasionally, until they start to brown, about 5 minutes. 4. Add the garlic and cook, stirring constantly, for 30 seconds. 5. Return the beef along with any juices that have collected and the cauliflower to the pan. Add the lime juice and chili powder. Cook, stirring, until everything is warmed through, 2 to 3 minutes.

Per Serving:
calorie: 390 | fat: 27g | protein: 27g | carbs: 12g | sugars: 5g | fiber: 4g | sodium: 126mg

Bacon-Wrapped Vegetable Kebabs

Prep time: 10 minutes | Cook time: 10 to 12 minutes | Serves 4

4 ounces (113 g) mushrooms, sliced	halved
1 small zucchini, sliced	Avocado oil spray
12 grape tomatoes	Sea salt and freshly ground black pepper, to taste
4 ounces (113 g) sliced bacon,	

1. Stack 3 mushroom slices, 1 zucchini slice, and 1 grape tomato. Wrap a bacon strip around the vegetables and thread them onto a skewer. Repeat with the remaining vegetables and bacon. Spray with oil and sprinkle with salt and pepper. 2. Set the air fryer to 400ºF (204ºC). Place the skewers in the air fryer basket in a single layer, working in batches if necessary, and air fry for 5 minutes. Flip the skewers and cook for 5 to 7 minutes more, until the bacon is crispy and the vegetables are tender. 3. Serve warm.

Per Serving:
calorie: 140 | fat: 11g | protein: 5g | carbs: 5g | sugars: 4g | fiber: 1g | sodium: 139mg

Pork and Apple Skillet

Prep time: 10 minutes | Cook time: 20 minutes | Serves 4

1 pound ground pork	2 garlic cloves, minced
1 red onion, thinly sliced	¼ cup apple cider vinegar
2 apples, peeled, cored, and thinly sliced	1 tablespoon Dijon mustard
2 cups shredded cabbage	½ teaspoon sea salt
1 teaspoon dried thyme	⅛ teaspoon freshly ground black pepper

1. In a large skillet over medium-high heat, cook the ground pork, crumbling it with a spoon, until browned, about 5 minutes. Use a slotted spoon to transfer the pork to a plate. 2. Add the onion, apples, cabbage, and thyme to the fat in the pan. Cook, stirring occasionally, until the vegetables are soft, about 5 minutes. 3. Add the garlic and cook, stirring constantly, for 5 minutes. 4. Return the pork to the pan. 5. In a small bowl, whisk together the vinegar, mustard, salt, and pepper. Add to the pan. Bring to a simmer. Cook, stirring, until the sauce thickens, about 2 minutes.

Per Serving:
calorie: 218 | fat: 5g | protein: 25g | carbs: 20g | sugars: 12g | fiber: 4g | sodium: 425mg

Beef Burgundy

Prep time: 30 minutes | Cook time: 30 minutes | Serves 6

2 tablespoons olive oil	1 teaspoon salt
2 pounds stewing meat, cubed, trimmed of fat	¼ teaspoon dried marjoram
2½ tablespoons flour	¼ teaspoon dried thyme
5 medium onions, thinly sliced	⅛ teaspoon pepper
½ pound fresh mushrooms, sliced	¾ cup beef broth
	1½ cups burgundy

1. Press Sauté on the Instant pot and add in the olive oil. 2. Dredge meat in flour, then brown in batches in the Instant Pot. Set aside the meat. Sauté the onions and mushrooms in the remaining oil and drippings for about 3–4 minutes, then add the meat back in. Press Cancel. 3. Add the salt, marjoram, thyme, pepper, broth, and wine to the Instant Pot. 4. Secure the lid and make sure the vent is set to sealing. Press the Manual button and set to 30 minutes. 5. When cook time is up, let the pressure release naturally for 15 minutes, then perform a quick release. 6. Serve over cooked noodles.

Per Serving:
calories: 358 | fat: 11g | protein: 37g | carbs: 15g | sugars: 5g | fiber: 2g | sodium: 472mg

Pot Roast with Gravy and Vegetables

Prep time: 30 minutes | Cook time: 1 hour 15 minutes | Serves 6

1 tablespoon olive oil	or gravy browning seasoning sauce
3–4 pound bottom round, rump, or arm roast, trimmed of fat	1 garlic clove, minced
¼ teaspoon salt	2 medium onions, cut in wedges
2–3 teaspoons pepper	4 medium potatoes, cubed, unpeeled
2 tablespoons flour	2 carrots, quartered
1 cup cold water	1 green bell pepper, sliced
1 teaspoon Kitchen Bouquet,	

1. Press the Sauté button on the Instant Pot and pour the oil inside, letting it heat up. Sprinkle each side of the roast with salt and pepper, then brown it for 5 minutes on each side inside the pot. 2. Mix together the flour, water and Kitchen Bouquet and spread over roast. 3. Add garlic, onions, potatoes, carrots, and green pepper. 4. Secure the lid and make sure the vent is set to sealing. Press Manual and set the Instant Pot for 1 hour and 15 minutes. 5. When cook time is up, let the pressure release naturally.

Per Serving:
calories: 551 | fat: 30g | protein: 49g | carbs: 19g | sugars: 2g | fiber: 3g | sodium: 256mg

Spinach and Provolone Steak Rolls

Prep time: 10 minutes | Cook time: 12 minutes | Makes 8 rolls

1 (1-pound / 454-g) flank steak, butterflied	1 cup fresh spinach leaves
8 (1-ounce / 28-g, ¼-inch-thick) deli slices provolone cheese	½ teaspoon salt
	¼ teaspoon ground black pepper

1. Place steak on a large plate. Place provolone slices to cover steak, leaving 1-inch at the edges. Lay spinach leaves over cheese. Gently roll steak and tie with kitchen twine or secure with toothpicks. Carefully slice into eight pieces. Sprinkle each with salt and pepper. 2. Place rolls into ungreased air fryer basket, cut side up. Adjust the temperature to 400ºF (204ºC) and air fry for 12 minutes. Steak rolls will be browned and cheese will be melted when done and have an internal temperature of at least 150ºF (66ºC) for medium steak and 180ºF (82ºC) for well-done steak. Serve warm.

Per Serving:
calorie: 155 | fat: 8g | protein: 19g | carbs: 1g | sugars: 0g | fiber: 0g | sodium: 351mg

Spicy Beef Stew with Butternut Squash

Prep time: 15 minutes | Cook time: 30 minutes | Serves 8

1½ tablespoons smoked paprika	1 cup low-sodium beef or vegetable broth
2 teaspoons ground cinnamon	1 medium red onion, cut into wedges
1½ teaspoons kosher salt	8 garlic cloves, minced
1 teaspoon ground ginger	1 (28-ounce) carton or can no-salt-added diced tomatoes
1 teaspoon red pepper flakes	2 pounds butternut squash, peeled and cut into 1-inch pieces
½ teaspoon freshly ground black pepper	
2 pounds beef shoulder roast, cut into 1-inch cubes	
2 tablespoons avocado oil, divided	Chopped fresh cilantro or parsley, for serving

1. In a zip-top bag or medium bowl, combine the paprika, cinnamon, salt, ginger, red pepper, and black pepper. Add the beef and toss to coat. 2. Set the electric pressure cooker to the Sauté setting. When the pot is hot, pour in 1 tablespoon of avocado oil. 3. Add half of the beef to the pot and cook, stirring occasionally, for 3 to 5 minutes or until the beef is no longer pink. Transfer it to a plate, then add the remaining 1 tablespoon of avocado oil and brown the remaining beef. Transfer to the plate. Hit Cancel. 4. Stir in the broth and scrape up any brown bits from the bottom of the pot. Return the beef to the pot and add the onion, garlic, tomatoes and their juices, and squash. Stir well. 5. Close and lock lid of pressure cooker. Set the valve to sealing. 6. Cook on high pressure for 30 minutes. 7. When cooking is complete, hit Cancel. Allow the pressure to release naturally for 10 minutes, then quick release any remaining pressure. 8. Unlock and remove lid. 9. Spoon into serving bowls, sprinkle with cilantro or parsley, and serve.

Per Serving:
calorie: 275 | fat: 9g | protein: 28g | carbs: 24g | sugars: 7g | fiber: 6g | sodium: 512mg

Broiled Dijon Burgers

Prep time: 25 minutes | Cook time: 10 minutes | Makes 6 burgers

¼ cup fat-free egg product or 2 egg whites	1 cup soft bread crumbs (about 2 slices bread)
2 tablespoons fat-free (skim) milk	1 small onion, finely chopped (⅓ cup)
2 teaspoons Dijon mustard or horseradish sauce	1 lb extra-lean (at least 90%) ground beef
¼ teaspoon salt	6 whole-grain burger buns, split, toasted
⅛ teaspoon pepper	

1 Set oven control to broil. Spray broiler pan rack with cooking spray. 2 In medium bowl, mix egg product, milk, mustard, salt and pepper. Stir in bread crumbs and onion. Stir in beef. Shape mixture into 6 patties, each about ½ inch thick. Place patties on rack in broiler pan. 3 Broil with tops of patties about 5 inches from heat 6 minutes. Turn; broil until meat thermometer inserted in center of patties reads 160°F, 4 to 6 minutes longer. Serve patties in buns.

Per Serving:
calories: 250 | fat: 8g | protein: 22g | carbs: 23g | sugars: 5g | fiber: 3g | sodium: 450mg

Easy Pot Roast and Vegetables

Prep time: 20 minutes | Cook time: 35 minutes | Serves 6

3–4 pound chuck roast, trimmed of fat and cut into serving-sized chunks	4 medium carrots, sliced, or 1 pound baby carrots
4 medium potatoes, cubed, unpeeled	2 celery ribs, sliced thin
	1 envelope dry onion soup mix
	3 cups water

1. Place the pot roast chunks and vegetables into the Instant Pot along with the potatoes, carrots and celery. 2. Mix together the onion soup mix and water and pour over the contents of the Instant Pot. 3. Secure the lid and make sure the vent is set to sealing. Set the Instant Pot to Manual mode for 35 minutes. Let pressure release naturally when cook time is up.

Per Serving:
calorie: 325 | fat: 8g | protein: 35g | carbs: 26g | sugars: 6g | fiber: 4g | sodium: 560mg

Spice-Rubbed Pork Loin

Prep time: 5 minutes | Cook time: 20 minutes | Serves 6

1 teaspoon paprika	1 (1½-pound / 680-g) boneless pork loin
½ teaspoon ground cumin	½ teaspoon salt
½ teaspoon chili powder	¼ teaspoon ground black pepper
½ teaspoon garlic powder	
2 tablespoons coconut oil	

1. In a small bowl, mix paprika, cumin, chili powder, and garlic powder. 2. Drizzle coconut oil over pork. Sprinkle pork loin with salt and pepper, then rub spice mixture evenly on all sides. 3. Place pork loin into ungreased air fryer basket. Adjust the temperature to 400°F (204°C) and air fry for 20 minutes, turning pork halfway through cooking. Pork loin will be browned and have an internal temperature of at least 145°F (63°C) when done. Serve warm.

Per Serving:
calories: 192 | fat: 9g | protein: 26g | carbs: 1g | fiber: 0g | sodium: 257mg

Mexican-Style Shredded Beef

Prep time: 5 minutes | Cook time: 35 minutes | Serves 6

1 (2-pound / 907-g) beef chuck roast, cut into 2-inch cubes	pepper
1 teaspoon salt	½ cup no-sugar-added chipotle sauce
½ teaspoon ground black	

1. In a large bowl, sprinkle beef cubes with salt and pepper and toss to coat. Place beef into ungreased air fryer basket. Adjust the temperature to 400°F (204°C) and air fry for 30 minutes, shaking the basket halfway through cooking. Beef will be done when internal temperature is at least 160°F (71°C). 2. Place cooked beef into a large bowl and shred with two forks. Pour in chipotle sauce and toss to coat. 3. Return beef to air fryer basket for an additional 5 minutes at 400°F (204°C) to crisp with sauce. Serve warm.

Per Serving:
calories: 204 | fat: 9g | protein: 31g | carbs: 0g | fiber: 0g | sodium: 539mg

Italian Beef Kebabs

Prep time: 25 minutes | Cook time: 10 minutes | Serves 2

2 garlic cloves, finely chopped	1 (¾-pound, 1-inch-thick) beef bone-in sirloin, or round steak, fat removed, cut into 1-inch pieces
¼ cup balsamic vinegar	
¼ cup water	
2 tablespoons extra-virgin olive oil	1 medium yellow squash, sliced
1 tablespoon chopped fresh oregano leaves, or 1 teaspoon dried	1 medium green bell pepper, cut into 1-inch squares
1½ teaspoons chopped fresh marjoram leaves, or ½ teaspoon dried	6 whole fresh button mushrooms
1 teaspoon granulated stevia	1 small red onion, cut into 1-inch squares

1. In a medium glass bowl, mix together the garlic, balsamic vinegar, water, olive oil, oregano, marjoram, and stevia. 2. Add the beef. Stir until coated. Cover and refrigerate, stirring occasionally, for at least 1 hour but no longer than 12 hours. 3. Preheat the oven to broil. 4. Remove the beef from the marinade, reserving the marinade. 5. Using 10-inch metal skewers, thread on 1 piece of beef, 1 piece of yellow squash, 1 piece of bell pepper, 1 mushroom, and 1 piece of onion, leaving ½ inch of space between each piece. Repeat with the remaining ingredients until all are used. Brush the kebabs with the reserved marinade. 6. Place the kebabs on a rack in the broiler pan. Place the pan under the preheated broiler about 3 inches from the heat. Broil for 6 to 8 minutes for medium-rare to medium doneness, turning and brushing with the marinade after 3 minutes. Discard any remaining marinade. 7. Enjoy this delightful meal on a stick!

Per Serving:
calorie: 494 | fat: 28g | protein: 42g | carbs: 19g | sugars: 11g | fiber: 4g | sodium: 114mg

Creole Steak

Prep time: 5 minutes | Cook time: 1 hour 40 minutes | Serves 4

2 teaspoons extra-virgin olive oil	¼ teaspoon celery seed
¼ cup chopped onion	4 cloves garlic, finely chopped
¼ cup chopped green bell pepper	¼ teaspoon salt
1 cup canned crushed tomatoes	1 teaspoon cumin
½ teaspoon chili powder	1 pound lean boneless round steak

1 In a large skillet over medium heat, heat the oil. Add the onions and green pepper, and sauté until the onions are translucent (about 5 minutes). 2 Add the tomatoes, chili powder, celery seed, garlic, salt, and cumin; cover and let simmer over low heat for 20–25 minutes. This allows the flavors to blend. 3 Preheat the oven to 350 degrees. Trim all visible fat off the steak. 4 In a nonstick pan or a pan that has been sprayed with nonstick cooking spray, lightly brown the steak on each side. Transfer the steak to a 13-x-9-x-2-inch baking dish; pour the sauce over the steak, and cover. 5 Bake for 1¼ hours or until the steak is tender. Remove from the oven; slice the steak, and arrange on a serving platter. Spoon the sauce over the steak, and serve.

Per Serving:
calorie: 213 | fat: 10g | protein: 25g | carbs: 5g | sugars: 2g | fiber: 2g | sodium: 235mg

Cheese Pork Chops

Prep time: 15 minutes | Cook time: 9 to 14 minutes | Serves 4

2 large eggs	½ teaspoon dried oregano
½ cup finely grated Parmesan cheese	½ teaspoon garlic powder
½ cup finely ground blanched almond flour or finely crushed pork rinds	Salt and freshly ground black pepper, to taste
	1¼ pounds (567 g) (1-inch-thick) boneless pork chops
1 teaspoon paprika	Avocado oil spray

1. Beat the eggs in a shallow bowl. In a separate bowl, combine the Parmesan cheese, almond flour, paprika, oregano, garlic powder, and salt and pepper to taste. 2. Dip the pork chops into the eggs, then coat them with the Parmesan mixture, gently pressing the coating onto the meat. Spray the breaded pork chops with oil. 3. Set the air fryer to 400°F (204°C). Place the pork chops in the air fryer basket in a single layer, working in batches if necessary. Cook for 6 minutes. Flip the chops and spray them with more oil. Cook for another 3 to 8 minutes, until an instant-read thermometer reads 145°F (63°C). 4. Allow the pork chops to rest for at least 5 minutes, then serve.

Per Serving:
calories: 313 | fat: 14g | protein: 40g | carbs: 4g | net carbs: 3g | fiber: 1g

Garlic Beef Stroganoff

Prep time: 20 minutes | Cook time: 25 minutes | Serves 6

2 tablespoons canola oil	reserved
1½ pounds boneless round steak, cut into thin strips, trimmed of fat	10¾-ounce can 98% fat-free, lower-sodium cream of mushroom soup
2 teaspoons sodium-free beef bouillon powder	1 large onion, chopped
1 cup mushroom juice, with water added to make a full cup	3 garlic cloves, minced
	1 tablespoon Worcestershire sauce
2 (4½-ounce) jars sliced mushrooms, drained with juice	6-ounces fat-free cream cheese, cubed and softened

1. Press the Sauté button and put the oil into the Instant Pot inner pot. 2. Once the oil is heated, sauté the beef until it is lightly browned, about 2 minutes on each side. Set the beef aside for a moment. Press Cancel and wipe out the Instant Pot with some paper towel. 3. Press Sauté again and dissolve the bouillon in the mushroom juice and water in inner pot of the Instant Pot. Once dissolved, press Cancel. 4. Add the mushrooms, soup, onion, garlic, and Worcestershire sauce and stir. Add the beef back to the pot. 5. Secure the lid and make sure the vent is set to sealing. Press Manual and set for 15 minutes. 6. When cook time is up, let the pressure release naturally for 15 minutes, then perform a quick release. 7. Press Cancel and remove the lid. Press Sauté. Stir in cream cheese until smooth. 8. Serve over noodles.

Per Serving:
calories: 202 | fat: 8g | protein: 21g | carbs: 10g | sugars: 4g | fiber: 2g | sodium: 474mg

Parmesan-Crusted Pork Chops

Prep time: 5 minutes | Cook time: 12 minutes | Serves 4

1 large egg	½ teaspoon salt
½ cup grated Parmesan cheese	¼ teaspoon ground black pepper
4 (4-ounce / 113-g) boneless pork chops	

1. Whisk egg in a medium bowl and place Parmesan in a separate medium bowl. 2. Sprinkle pork chops on both sides with salt and pepper. Dip each pork chop into egg, then press both sides into Parmesan. 3. Place pork chops into ungreased air fryer basket. Adjust the temperature to 400ºF (204ºC) and air fry for 12 minutes, turning chops halfway through cooking. Pork chops will be golden and have an internal temperature of at least 145ºF (63ºC) when done. Serve warm.

Per Serving:
calories: 218 | fat: 9g | protein: 32g | carbs: 1g | fiber: 0g | sodium: 372mg

Meatloaf for Two

Prep time: 15 minutes | Cook time: 45 minutes | Serves 2

Extra-virgin olive oil cooking spray	oil, divided
1 large egg, beaten	Dash freshly ground black pepper
1 cup frozen spinach	½ pound (96 percent) extra-lean ground beef
⅓ cup almond meal	¼ cup tomato paste
¼ cup chopped onion	1 tablespoon granulated stevia
¼ cup nonfat milk	¼ teaspoon Worcestershire sauce
¼ teaspoon salt	
¼ teaspoon dried sage	
2 teaspoons extra-virgin olive	

1. Preheat the oven to 350°F. 2. Coat a shallow baking dish with cooking spray. 3. In a large bowl, combine the beaten egg, spinach, almond meal, onion, milk, salt, sage, 1 teaspoon of olive oil, and pepper. 4. Crumble the beef over the spinach mixture. Mix well to combine. Divide the meat mixture in half. Shape each half into a loaf. Place the loaves in the prepared dish. 5. In a small bowl, whisk together the tomato paste, stevia, Worcestershire sauce, and remaining 1 teaspoon of olive oil. Spoon half of the sauce over each meatloaf. 6. Place the dish in the preheated oven. Bake for 40 to 45 minutes, or until the meat is no longer pink and an instant-read thermometer inserted into the center reads 160°F. 7. Serve immediately and enjoy!

Per Serving:
calorie: 349 | fat: 18g | protein: 35g | carbs: 16g | sugars: 7g | fiber: 5g | sodium: 502mg

Beef Roast with Onions and Potatoes

Prep time: 30 minutes | Cook time: 9 to 10 hours | Serves 6

1 large sweet onion, cut in half, then cut into thin slices	fat
1 boneless beef bottom round roast (3 lb), trimmed of excess	3 baking potatoes, cut into 1½- to 2-inch cubes
	2 cloves garlic, finely chopped
1¾ cups beef-flavored broth	mix (from 2-oz box)
1 package (1 oz) onion soup	¼ cup all-purpose flour

1. Spray 5- to 6-quart slow cooker with cooking spray. In slow cooker, place onion. If beef roast comes in netting or is tied, remove netting or strings. Place beef on onion. Place potatoes and garlic around beef. In small bowl, mix 1¼ cups of the broth and the dry soup mix; pour over beef. (Refrigerate remaining broth.) 2. Cover; cook on Low heat setting 9 to 10 hours. 3. Remove beef and vegetables from slow cooker; place on serving platter. Cover to keep warm. 4. In small bowl, mix remaining ½ cup broth and the flour; gradually stir into juices in slow cooker. Increase heat setting to High. Cover; cook about 15 minutes, stirring occasionally, until sauce has thickened. Serve sauce over beef and vegetables.

Per Serving:
calorie: 416 | fat: 9g | protein: 54g | carbs: 27g | sugars: 4g | fiber: 3g | sodium: 428mg

Mustard Herb Pork Tenderloin

Prep time: 5 minutes | Cook time: 20 minutes | Serves 6

¼ cup mayonnaise	tenderloin
2 tablespoons Dijon mustard	½ teaspoon salt
½ teaspoon dried thyme	¼ teaspoon ground black pepper
¼ teaspoon dried rosemary	
1 (1-pound / 454-g) pork	

1. In a small bowl, mix mayonnaise, mustard, thyme, and rosemary. Brush tenderloin with mixture on all sides, then sprinkle with salt and pepper on all sides. 2. Place tenderloin into ungreased air fryer basket. Adjust the temperature to 400ºF (204ºC) and air fry for 20 minutes, turning tenderloin halfway through cooking. Tenderloin will be golden and have an internal temperature of at least 145ºF (63ºC) when done. Serve warm.

Per Serving:
calorie: 118 | fat: 5g | protein: 17g | carbs: 1g | sugars: 0g | fiber: 0g | sodium: 368mg

Steak Fajita Bake

Prep time: 10 minutes | Cook time: 15 minutes | Serves 4

1 green bell pepper	2 tablespoons avocado oil
1 yellow bell pepper	½ teaspoon ground cumin
1 red bell pepper	¼ teaspoon chili powder
1 small white onion	¼ teaspoon garlic powder
10 ounces sirloin steak, trimmed of visible fat	4 (6-inch) 100% whole-wheat tortillas

1. Preheat the oven to 400ºF. 2. Cut the green bell pepper, yellow bell pepper, red bell pepper, onion, and steak into ½-inch-thick slices, and put them on a large baking sheet. 3. In a small bowl, combine the oil, cumin, chili powder, and garlic powder, then drizzle the mixture over the meat and vegetables to fully coat them. 4. Arrange the steak and vegetables in a single layer, and bake for 10 to 15 minutes, or until the steak is cooked through. 5. Divide the steak and vegetables equally between the tortillas.

Per Serving:
calorie: 360 | fat: 19g | protein: 20g | carbs: 27g | sugars: 4g | fiber: 6g | sodium: 257mg

Flank Steak with Smoky Honey Mustard Sauce

Prep time: 30 minutes | Cook time: 17 to 20 minutes | Serves 6

Sauce	sauce (from 7-oz can), finely chopped
¼ cup fat-free honey mustard or honey Dijon dressing	Steak
1 tablespoon frozen (thawed) orange juice concentrate	1 beef flank steak (about 1½ lb)
1 tablespoon water	6 flour tortillas for burritos (8 inch), heated as directed on package
1 clove garlic, finely chopped	
1 chipotle chile in adobo	

1 Heat gas or charcoal grill. In small bowl, mix sauce ingredients. On both sides of beef, make cuts about ½ inch apart and 1/8 inch deep in diamond pattern. Brush 2 tablespoons of the sauce on both sides of beef. 2 Place beef on grill over medium heat. Cover grill; cook 17 to 20 minutes, turning once, until beef is of desired doneness. 3 Cut beef across grain into thin slices. Serve with tortillas and remaining sauce.

Per Serving:
calories: 310 | fat: 9g | protein: 36g | carbs: 22g | sugars: 2g | fiber: 0g | sodium: 380mg

Beef Stew

Prep time: 30 minutes | Cook time: 1 hour 20 minutes | Serves 2

4 cups low-sodium beef broth, divided	2 garlic cloves, minced
3 tablespoons freshly squeezed lemon juice	4 baby beets, tops removed, peeled, and cut into 1-inch cubes
2 teaspoons reduced-sodium soy sauce	1 cup chopped Brussels sprouts
2 teaspoons Worcestershire sauce	2 medium carrots, sliced into 1-inch pieces
½ pound cubed beef stew meat	1 cup sliced baby portobello mushrooms
2 teaspoons extra-virgin olive oil	2 fresh thyme sprigs
1 small onion, chopped	1/8 teaspoon cayenne pepper
	2 teaspoons cornstarch

1. In a large sealable plastic bag, combine 1 cup of beef broth, the lemon juice, soy sauce, and Worcestershire sauce. Add the beef. Seal the bag, turning to coat. Refrigerate for 8 hours, or overnight. 2. The next day, drain the beef and discard the marinade. 3. In a large saucepan set over medium heat, combine the olive oil and drained beef. Cook for 8 to 10 minutes, or until browned. Transfer the meat to a bowl and set aside. 4. To the same saucepan, add the onion. Sauté for 5 to 7 minutes, or until tender. 5. Add the garlic. Cook for 1 minute. 6. Add 2½ cups of beef broth. Return the meat to the pan. Increase the heat to high. Bring to a boil. Reduce the heat to low. Cover and simmer for 30 minutes. 7. Add the beets, Brussels sprouts, carrots, mushrooms, thyme, and cayenne pepper. Increase the heat to high. Return to a boil. Reduce the heat to low. Cover and simmer for 30 minutes, or until the vegetables and beef are tender. Remove and discard the thyme sprigs. 8. In a small bowl, whisk together the cornstarch and remaining ½ cup of beef broth until smooth. Gradually add to the stew, stirring to incorporate. Increase the heat to high. Bring to a boil again. Cook for 2 minutes, stirring, or until thickened.

Per Serving:
calorie: 428 | fat: 12g | protein: 40g | carbs: 44g | sugars: 18g | fiber: 10g | sodium: 499mg

Steak Stroganoff

Prep time: 15 minutes | Cook time: 30 minutes | Serves 6

1 tablespoon olive oil	mushroom soup
2 tablespoons flour	½ cup water
½ teaspoon garlic powder	1 envelope sodium-free dried onion soup mix
½ teaspoon pepper	9-ounces jar sliced mushrooms, drained
¼ teaspoon paprika	½ cup fat-free sour cream
1¾-pound boneless beef round steak, trimmed of fat, cut into 1½ × ½-inch strips.	1 tablespoon minced fresh parsley
10¾-ounce can reduced-sodium, 98% fat-free cream of	

1. Place the oil in the Instant Pot and press Sauté. 2. Combine flour, garlic powder, pepper, and paprika in a small bowl. Stir the steak pieces through the flour mixture until they are evenly coated. 3. Lightly brown the steak pieces in the oil in the Instant Pot, about 2 minutes each side. Press Cancel when done. 4. Stir the mushroom soup, water, and onion soup mix then pour over the steak. 5. Secure the lid and set the vent to sealing. Press the Manual button and set for 15 minutes. 6. When cook time is up, let the pressure release naturally for 15 minutes, then release the rest manually. 7. Remove the lid and press Cancel then Sauté. Stir in mushrooms, sour cream, and parsley. Let the sauce come to a boil and cook for about 10–15 minutes.

Per Serving:
calories: 248 | fat: 6g | protein: 33g | carbs: 12g | sugars: 2g | fiber: 2g | sodium: 563mg

Peppered Beef with Greens and Beans

Prep time: 10 minutes | Cook time: 20 minutes | Serves 2

1 (½-pound, ½-inch-thick) boneless beef sirloin, halved	1 teaspoon dried basil
2 teaspoons coarsely ground black pepper, divided	3 cups (1 bunch) chopped kale
¼ cup tomato sauce	1 cup chopped green beans
2 tablespoons red wine vinegar	¾ cup chopped red bell pepper, or yellow bell pepper
	¼ cup chopped onion

1. Rub each side of the steak halves with ½ teaspoon of coarsely ground pepper. 2. Heat a 10-inch nonstick skillet over medium heat. Add the beef. Cook for 8 to 12 minutes, turning once halfway through. 3. Add the tomato sauce, red wine vinegar, and basil. Stir to combine. 4. Add the kale, green beans, bell pepper, and onion. Stir to mix with the sauce. Reduce the heat to medium-low. Cook for about 5 minutes, uncovered, or until the vegetables are tender and beef is cooked medium doneness (160°F). 5. Serve immediately and enjoy!

Per Serving:
calorie: 277 | fat: 13g | protein: 27g | carbs: 13g | sugars: 6g | fiber: 5g | sodium: 80mg

Sage-Parmesan Pork Chops

Prep time: 30 minutes | Cook time: 25 minutes | Serves 2

Extra-virgin olive oil cooking spray	½ cup soy Parmesan cheese
2 tablespoons coconut flour	1½ teaspoons rubbed sage
¼ teaspoon salt	½ teaspoon grated lemon zest
Pinch freshly ground black pepper	2 (4-ounce) boneless pork chops
¼ cup almond meal	1 large egg, lightly beaten
½ cup finely ground flaxseed meal	1 tablespoon extra-virgin olive oil

1. Preheat the oven to 425°F. 2. Lightly coat a medium baking dish with cooking spray. 3. In a shallow dish, mix together the coconut flour, salt, and pepper. 4. In a second shallow dish, stir together the almond meal, flaxseed meal, soy Parmesan cheese, sage, and lemon zest. 5. Gently press one pork chop into the coconut flour mixture to coat. Shake off any excess. Dip into the beaten egg. Press into the almond meal mixture. Gently toss between your hands so any coating that hasn't stuck can fall away. Place the coated chop on a plate. Repeat the process with the remaining pork chop and coating ingredients. 6. In a large skillet set over medium heat, heat the olive oil. 7. Add the coated chops. Cook for about 4 minutes per side, or until browned. Transfer to the prepared baking dish. Place the dish in the preheated oven. Bake for 10 to 15 minutes, or until the juices run clear and an instant-read thermometer inserted into the middle of the pork reads 160°F.

Per Serving:

calorie: 520 | fat: 31g | protein: 45g | carbs: 14g | sugars: 1g | fiber: 6g | sodium: 403mg

Coffee-and-Herb-Marinated Steak

Prep time: 10 minutes | Cook time: 10 minutes | Serves 4

¼ cup whole coffee beans	black pepper
2 teaspoons minced garlic	2 tablespoons apple cider vinegar
2 teaspoons chopped fresh rosemary	2 tablespoons extra-virgin olive oil
2 teaspoons chopped fresh thyme	1 pound flank steak, trimmed of visible fat
1 teaspoon freshly ground	

1. Place the coffee beans, garlic, rosemary, thyme, and black pepper in a coffee grinder or food processor and pulse until coarsely ground. 2. Transfer the coffee mixture to a resealable plastic bag and add the vinegar and oil. Shake to combine. 3. Add the flank steak and squeeze the excess air out of the bag. Seal it. Marinate the steak in the refrigerator for at least 2 hours, occasionally turning the bag over. 4. Preheat the broiler. Line a baking sheet with aluminum foil. 5. Take the steak out of the bowl and discard the marinade. 6. Place the steak on the baking sheet and broil until it is done to your liking, about 5 minutes per side for medium. 7. Let the steak rest for 10 minutes before slicing it thinly on a bias. 8. Serve with a mixed green salad or your favorite side dish.

Per Serving:

calorie: 191 | fat: 9g | protein: 25g | carbs: 1g | sugars: 0g | fiber: 0g | sodium: 127mg

Short Ribs with Chimichurri

Prep time: 30 minutes | Cook time: 13 minutes | Serves 4

1 pound (454 g) boneless short ribs	1 tablespoon freshly squeezed lemon juice
1½ teaspoons sea salt, divided	½ teaspoon ground cumin
½ teaspoon freshly ground black pepper, divided	¼ teaspoon red pepper flakes
½ cup fresh parsley leaves	2 tablespoons extra-virgin olive oil
½ cup fresh cilantro leaves	Avocado oil spray
1 teaspoon minced garlic	

1. Pat the short ribs dry with paper towels. Sprinkle the ribs all over with 1 teaspoon salt and ¼ teaspoon black pepper. Let sit at room temperature for 45 minutes. 2. Meanwhile, place the parsley, cilantro, garlic, lemon juice, cumin, red pepper flakes, the remaining ½ teaspoon salt, and the remaining ¼ teaspoon black pepper in a blender or food processor. With the blender running, slowly drizzle in the olive oil. Blend for about 1 minute, until the mixture is smooth and well combined. 3. Set the air fryer to 400ºF (204ºC). Spray both sides of the ribs with oil. Place in the basket and air fry for 8 minutes. Flip and cook for another 5 minutes, until an instant-read thermometer reads 125ºF (52ºC) for medium-rare (or to your desired doneness). 4. Allow the meat to rest for 5 to 10 minutes, then slice. Serve warm with the chimichurri sauce.

Per Serving:

calories: 251 | fat: 17g | protein: 25g | carbs: 1g | fiber: 1g | sodium: 651mg

Bavarian Beef

Prep time: 35 minutes | Cook time: 1 hour 15 minutes | Serves 8

1 tablespoon canola oil	broth
3-pound boneless beef chuck roast, trimmed of fat	⅓ cup German-style mustard
3 cups sliced carrots	2 teaspoons coarsely ground black pepper
3 cups sliced onions	2 bay leaves
2 large kosher dill pickles, chopped	¼ teaspoon ground cloves
1 cup sliced celery	1 cup water
½ cup dry red wine or beef	⅓ cup flour

1. Press Sauté on the Instant Pot and add in the oil. Brown roast on both sides for about 5 minutes. Press Cancel. 2. Add all of the remaining ingredients, except for the flour, to the Instant Pot. 3. Secure the lid and make sure the vent is set to sealing. Press Manual and set the time to 1 hour and 15 minutes. Let the pressure release naturally. 4. Remove meat and vegetables to large platter. Cover to keep warm. 5. Remove 1 cup of the liquid from the Instant Pot and mix with the flour. Press Sauté on the Instant Pot and add the flour/broth mixture back in, whisking. Cook until the broth is smooth and thickened. 6. Serve over noodles or spaetzle.

Per Serving:

calories: 251 | fat: 8g | protein: 26g | carbs: 17g | sugars: 7g | fiber: 4g | sodium: 525mg

Pork Carnitas

Prep time: 10 minutes | Cook time: 20 minutes | Serves 8

1 teaspoon kosher salt	Juice and zest of 1 medium lime
2 teaspoons chili powder	6-inch gluten-free corn tortillas, warmed, for serving (optional)
2 teaspoons dried oregano	
½ teaspoon freshly ground black pepper	
1 (2½-pound) pork sirloin roast or boneless pork butt, cut into 1½-inch cubes	Chopped avocado, for serving (optional)
2 tablespoons avocado oil, divided	Roasted Tomatillo Salsa or salsa verde, for serving (optional)
3 garlic cloves, minced	Shredded cheddar cheese, for serving (optional)
Juice and zest of 1 large orange	

1. In a large bowl or gallon-size zip-top bag, combine the salt, chili powder, oregano, and pepper. Add the pork cubes and toss to coat. 2. Set the electric pressure cooker to the Sauté/More setting. When the pot is hot, pour in 1 tablespoon of avocado oil. 3. Add half of the pork to the pot and sear until the pork is browned on all sides, about 5 minutes. Transfer the pork to a plate, add the remaining 1 tablespoon of avocado oil to the pot, and sear the remaining pork. Hit Cancel. 4. Return all of the pork to the pot and add the garlic, orange zest and juice, and lime zest and juice to the pot. 5. Close and lock the lid of the pressure cooker. Set the valve to sealing. 6. Cook on high pressure for 20 minutes. 7. When the cooking is complete, hit Cancel. Allow the pressure to release naturally for 15 minutes then quick release any remaining pressure. 8. Once the pin drops, unlock and remove the lid. 9. Using two forks, shred the meat right in the pot. 10. (Optional) For more authentic carnitas, spread the shredded meat on a broiler-safe sheet pan. Preheat the broiler with the rack 6 inches from the heating element. Broil the pork for about 5 minutes or until it begins to crisp. (Watch carefully so you don't let the pork burn.) 11. Place the pork in a serving bowl. Top with some of the juices from the pot. Serve with tortillas, avocado, salsa, and Cheddar cheese (if using).

Per Serving:
calorie: 218 | fat: 7g | protein: 33g | carbs: 4g | sugars: 2g | fiber: 1g | sodium: 400mg

Homestyle Herb Meatballs

Prep time: 10 minutes | Cook time: 15 minutes | Serves 4

½ pound lean ground pork	2 teaspoons minced garlic
½ pound lean ground beef	1 egg
1 sweet onion, finely chopped	Pinch sea salt
¼ cup bread crumbs	Pinch freshly ground black pepper
2 tablespoons chopped fresh basil	

1. Preheat the oven to 350°F. 2. Line a baking tray with parchment paper and set it aside. 3. In a large bowl, mix together the pork, beef, onion, bread crumbs, basil, garlic, egg, salt, and pepper until very well mixed. 4. Roll the meat mixture into 2-inch meatballs. 5. Transfer the meatballs to the baking sheet and bake until they are browned and cooked through, about 15 minutes. 6. Serve the meatballs with your favorite marinara sauce and some steamed green beans.

Per Serving:
calorie: 214 | fat: 7g | protein: 27g | carbs: 12g | sugars: 5g | fiber: 1g | sodium: 147mg

Zoodles Carbonara

Prep time: 10 minutes | Cook time: 25 minutes | Serves 4

6 slices bacon, cut into pieces	3 large eggs, beaten
1 red onion, finely chopped	1 tablespoon heavy cream
3 zucchini, cut into noodles	Pinch red pepper flakes
1 cup peas	½ cup grated Parmesan cheese (optional, for garnish)
½ teaspoon sea salt	
3 garlic cloves, minced	

1. In a large skillet over medium-high heat, cook the bacon until browned, about 5 minutes. With a slotted spoon, transfer the bacon to a plate. 2. Add the onion to the bacon fat in the pan and cook, stirring, until soft, 3 to 5 minutes. Add the zucchini, peas, and salt. Cook, stirring, until the zucchini softens, about 3 minutes. Add the garlic and cook, stirring constantly, for 5 minutes. 3. In a small bowl, whisk together the eggs, cream, and red pepper flakes. Add to the vegetables. 4. Remove the pan from the stove top and stir for 3 minutes, allowing the heat of the pan to cook the eggs without setting them. 5. Return the bacon to the pan and stir to mix. 6. Serve topped with Parmesan cheese, if desired.

Per Serving:
calorie: 294 | fat: 21g | protein: 14g | carbs: 14g | sugars: 7g | fiber: 4g | sodium: 544mg

Teriyaki Rib-Eye Steaks

Prep time: 10 minutes | Cook time: 15 minutes | Serves 2

2 tablespoons water	½ teaspoon onion powder
1 tablespoon reduced-sodium soy sauce	¼ teaspoon garlic powder
	⅛ teaspoon ground
1½ teaspoons Worcestershire sauce	2 (6-ounce) lean beef rib-eye steaks
1¼ teaspoons distilled white vinegar	Extra-virgin olive oil cooking spray
1 teaspoon extra-virgin olive oil	2 cups sugar snap peas
	1 cup sliced carrots
½ teaspoon granulated stevia	1 red bell pepper, sliced

1. In a large bowl, whisk together the water, soy sauce, Worcestershire sauce, white vinegar, olive oil, stevia, onion powder, garlic powder, and ginger. 2. With a fork, pierce the steaks several times. Add to the marinade. Let marinate in the refrigerator for at least 2 hours. 3. Spray a large skillet with cooking spray. Place it over medium heat. 4. Add the steaks. Cook for 7 minutes. Turn the steaks. Add the sugar snap peas, carrots, and bell pepper to the skillet. Cook for 7 minutes more, or until an instant-read thermometer inserted into the center of the steak reads 140°F. 5. Serve and savor!

Per Serving:
calorie: 630 | fat: 40g | protein: 40g | carbs: 29g | sugars: 12g | fiber: 9g | sodium: 271mg

Sirloin Steaks with Cilantro Chimichurri

Prep time: 25 minutes | Cook time: 7 to 10 minutes | Serves 4

1 cup loosely packed fresh cilantro	2 teaspoons canola oil
1 small onion, cut into quarters	½ teaspoon salt
2 cloves garlic, cut in half	2 teaspoons ground cumin
1 jalapeño chile, cut in half, seeded	½ teaspoon pepper
2 teaspoons lime juice	4 beef sirloin steaks, 1 inch thick (about 1½ lb)

1. Heat gas or charcoal grill. In food processor, place cilantro, onion, garlic, chile, lime juice, oil and ¼ teaspoon of the salt. Cover; process until finely chopped. Blend in 2 to 3 teaspoons water to make sauce thinner, if desired. Transfer to small bowl; set aside until serving time. 2. In small bowl, mix cumin, pepper and remaining ¼ teaspoon salt; rub evenly over steaks. Place steaks on grill over medium heat. Cover grill; cook 7 to 10 minutes for medium-rare (145°F), turning once halfway through cooking. 3. Serve 2 tablespoons chimichurri over each steak.

Per Serving:
calorie: 266 | fat: 10g | protein: 38g | carbs: 3g | sugars: 1g | fiber: 1g | sodium: 392mg

Open-Faced Pulled Pork

Prep time: 15 minutes | Cook time: 1 hour 35 minutes | Serves 2

2 tablespoons hoisin sauce	1 teaspoon chile-garlic sauce
2 tablespoons tomato paste	¾ pound pork shoulder, trimmed of any visible fat, cut into 2-inch-square cubes
2 tablespoons rice vinegar	
1 tablespoon minced fresh ginger	
2 teaspoons minced garlic	4 large romaine lettuce leaves

1. Preheat the oven to 300°F. 2. In a medium ovenproof pot with a tight-fitting lid, stir together the hoisin sauce, tomato paste, rice vinegar, ginger, garlic, and chile-garlic sauce. 3. Add the pork. Toss to coat. 4. Place the pot over medium heat. Bring to a simmer. Cover and carefully transfer the ovenproof pot to the preheated oven. Cook for 90 minutes. 5. Check the meat for doneness by inserting a fork into one of the chunks. If it goes in easily and the pork falls apart, the meat is done. If not, cook for another 30 minutes or so, until the meat passes the fork test. 6. Using a coarse strainer, strain the cooked pork into a fat separator. Shred the meat. Set aside. If you don't have a fat separator, remove the meat from the sauce and set aside. Let the sauce cool until any fat has risen to the top. With a spoon, remove as much fat as possible or use paper towels to blot it off. 7. In a small saucepan set over high heat, pour the defatted sauce. Bring to a boil, stirring frequently to prevent scorching. Cook for 2 to 3 minutes, or until thickened. 8. Add the shredded meat. Toss to coat with the sauce. Cook for 1 minute to reheat the meat. 9. Spoon equal amounts of pork into the romaine lettuce leaves and enjoy!

Per Serving:
calorie: 289 | fat: 11g | protein: 33g | carbs: 13g | sugars: 7g | fiber: 1g | sodium: 391mg

Gingered-Pork Stir-Fry

Prep time: 10 minutes | Cook time: 20 minutes | Serves 2

2 tablespoons extra-virgin olive oil	1 teaspoon sesame oil
2 garlic cloves, minced	1 cup snow peas
1 (½-inch) piece fresh ginger, peeled, thinly sliced	1 medium red bell pepper, sliced
¼ pound lean pork, thinly sliced	6 whole fresh mushrooms, sliced
2 teaspoons low-sodium soy sauce	2 scallions, chopped
	1 tablespoon Chinese rice wine
1 teaspoon granulated stevia	2 tablespoons chopped cashews, divided

1. In a large skillet or wok set over medium-high heat, heat the olive oil. 2. Add the garlic and ginger. Sauté for 1 to 2 minutes, or until fragrant. 3. Add the pork, soy sauce, and stevia. Cook for 10 minutes, stirring occasionally. 4. Stir in the sesame oil, snow peas, bell pepper, mushrooms, scallions, and rice wine. Reduce the heat to low. Simmer for 4 to 8 minutes, or until the pork is tender. 5. Divide between 2 serving plates, sprinkle each serving with 1 tablespoon of cashews and enjoy!

Per Serving:
calorie: 365 | fat: 23g | protein: 21g | carbs: 22g | sugars: 8g | fiber: 6g | sodium: 203mg

Autumn Pork Chops with Red Cabbage and Apples

Prep time: 15 minutes | Cook time: 30 minutes | Serves 4

¼ cup apple cider vinegar	oil
2 tablespoons granulated sweetener	½ red cabbage, finely shredded
4 (4-ounce) pork chops, about 1 inch thick	1 sweet onion, thinly sliced
	1 apple, peeled, cored, and sliced
Sea salt	
Freshly ground black pepper	1 teaspoon chopped fresh thyme
1 tablespoon extra-virgin olive	

1. In a small bowl, whisk together the vinegar and sweetener. Set it aside. 2. Season the pork with salt and pepper. 3. Place a large skillet over medium-high heat and add the olive oil. 4. Cook the pork chops until no longer pink, turning once, about 8 minutes per side. 5. Transfer the chops to a plate and set aside. 6. Add the cabbage and onion to the skillet and sauté until the vegetables have softened, about 5 minutes. 7. Add the vinegar mixture and the apple slices to the skillet and bring the mixture to a boil. 8. Reduce the heat to low and simmer, covered, for 5 additional minutes. 9. Return the pork chops to the skillet, along with any accumulated juices and thyme, cover, and cook for 5 more minutes.

Per Serving:
calorie: 251 | fat: 8g | protein: 26g | carbs: 19g | sugars: 13g | fiber: 2g | sodium: 76mg

Chipotle Chili Pork Chops

Prep time: 5 minutes | Cook time: 20 minutes | Serves 4

Juice and zest of 1 lime
1 tablespoon extra-virgin olive oil
1 tablespoon chipotle chili powder
2 teaspoons minced garlic
1 teaspoon ground cinnamon
Pinch sea salt
4 (5-ounce) pork chops, about 1 inch thick
Lime wedges, for garnish

1. Combine the lime juice and zest, oil, chipotle chili powder, garlic, cinnamon, and salt in a resealable plastic bag. Add the pork chops. Remove as much air as possible and seal the bag. 2. Marinate the chops in the refrigerator for at least 4 hours, and up to 24 hours, turning them several times. 3. Preheat the oven to 400°F and set a rack on a baking sheet. Let the chops rest at room temperature for 15 minutes, then arrange them on the rack and discard the remaining marinade. 4. Roast the chops until cooked through, turning once, about 10 minutes per side. 5. Serve with lime wedges.

Per Serving:
calorie: 224 | fat: 9g | protein: 32g | carbs: 4g | sugars: 0g | fiber: 2g | sodium: 140mg

Chapter 5 Fish and Seafood

Crispy Fish Sticks

Prep time: 15 minutes | Cook time: 10 minutes | Serves 4

1 ounce (28 g) pork rinds, finely ground	1 tablespoon coconut oil
¼ cup blanched finely ground almond flour	1 large egg
½ teaspoon Old Bay seasoning	1 pound (454 g) cod fillet, cut into ¾-inch strips

1. Place ground pork rinds, almond flour, Old Bay seasoning, and coconut oil into a large bowl and mix together. In a medium bowl, whisk egg. 2. Dip each fish stick into the egg and then gently press into the flour mixture, coating as fully and evenly as possible. Place fish sticks into the air fryer basket. 3. Adjust the temperature to 400ºF (204ºC) and air fry for 10 minutes or until golden. 4. Serve immediately.

Per Serving:
calories: 223 | fat: 14g | protein: 21g | carbs: 2g | fiber: 1g | sodium: 390mg

Almond Pesto Salmon

Prep time: 5 minutes | Cook time: 12 minutes | Serves 2

¼ cup pesto	fillets (about 4 ounces / 113 g each)
¼ cup sliced almonds, roughly chopped	2 tablespoons unsalted butter, melted
2 (1½-inch-thick) salmon	

1. In a small bowl, mix pesto and almonds. Set aside. 2. Place fillets into a round baking dish. 3. Brush each fillet with butter and place half of the pesto mixture on the top of each fillet. Place dish into the air fryer basket. 4. Adjust the temperature to 390ºF (199ºC) and set the timer for 12 minutes. 5. Salmon will easily flake when fully cooked and reach an internal temperature of at least 145ºF (63ºC). Serve warm.

Per Serving:
calories: 478 | fat: 39g | protein: 29g | carbs: 4g | sugars: 1g | fiber: 2g | sodium: 366mg

Quinoa Pilaf with Salmon and Asparagus

Prep time: 30 minutes | Cook time: 15 minutes | Serves 4

1 cup uncooked quinoa	(¼ cup)
6 cups water	1 cup frozen sweet peas (from 1-lb bag), thawed
1 vegetable bouillon cube	½ cup halved grape tomatoes
1 lb salmon fillets	½ cup vegetable or chicken broth
2 teaspoons butter or margarine	1 teaspoon lemon-pepper seasoning
20 stalks fresh asparagus, cut diagonally into 2-inch pieces (2 cups)	2 teaspoons chopped fresh or ½ teaspoon dried dill weed
4 medium green onions, sliced	

1 Rinse quinoa thoroughly by placing in a fine-mesh strainer and holding under cold running water until water runs clear; drain well. 2 In 2-quart saucepan, heat 2 cups of the water to boiling over high heat. Add quinoa; reduce heat to low. Cover; simmer 10 to 12 minutes or until water is absorbed. 3 Meanwhile, in 12-inch skillet, heat remaining 4 cups water and the bouillon cube to boiling over high heat. Add salmon, skin side up; reduce heat to low. Cover; simmer 10 to 12 minutes or until fish flakes easily with fork. Transfer with slotted spoon to plate; let cool. Discard water. Remove skin from salmon; break into large pieces. 4 Meanwhile, rinse and dry skillet. Melt butter in skillet over medium heat. Add asparagus; cook 5 minutes, stirring frequently. Stir in onions; cook 1 minute, stirring frequently. Stir in peas, tomatoes and broth; cook 1 minute. 5 Gently stir quinoa, salmon, lemon-pepper seasoning and dill weed into asparagus mixture. Cover; cook about 2 minutes or until hot.

Per Serving:
calories: 380 | fat: 12g | protein: 32g | carbs: 37g | sugars: 7g | fiber: 6g | sodium: 600mg

Quick Shrimp Skewers

Prep time: 10 minutes | Cook time: 5 minutes | Serves 5

4 pounds (1.8 kg) shrimp, peeled	1 tablespoon avocado oil
1 tablespoon dried rosemary	1 teaspoon apple cider vinegar

1. Mix the shrimps with dried rosemary, avocado oil, and apple cider vinegar. 2. Then sting the shrimps into skewers and put in the air fryer. 3. Cook the shrimps at 400ºF (204ºC) for 5 minutes.

Per Serving:
calories: 336 | fat: 5g | protein: 73g | carbs: 0g | fiber: 0g | sodium: 432mg

Roasted Salmon with Salsa Verde

Prep time: 5 minutes | Cook time: 25 minutes | Serves 4

Nonstick cooking spray	oil
8 ounces tomatillos, husks removed	½ teaspoon salt, divided
½ onion, quartered	4 (4-ounce) wild-caught salmon fillets
1 jalapeño or serrano pepper, seeded	¼ teaspoon freshly ground black pepper
1 garlic clove, unpeeled	¼ cup chopped fresh cilantro
1 teaspoon extra-virgin olive	Juice of 1 lime

1. Preheat the oven to 425°F. Spray a baking sheet with nonstick cooking spray. 2. In a large bowl, toss the tomatillos, onion, jalapeño, garlic, olive oil, and ¼ teaspoon of salt to coat. Arrange in a single layer on the prepared baking sheet, and roast for about 10 minutes until just softened. Transfer to a dish or plate and set aside. 3. Arrange the salmon fillets skin-side down on the same baking sheet, and season with the remaining ¼ teaspoon of salt and the pepper. Bake for 12 to 15 minutes until the fish is firm and flakes easily. 4. Meanwhile, peel the roasted garlic and place it and the roasted vegetables in a blender or food processor. Add a scant ¼ cup of water to the jar, and process until smooth. 5. Add the cilantro and lime juice and process until smooth. Serve the salmon topped with the salsa verde.

Per Serving:
calories: 199 | fat: 9g | protein: 23g | carbs: 6g | sugars: 3g | fiber: 2g | sodium: 295mg

Tuna Steak

Prep time: 10 minutes | Cook time: 12 minutes | Serves 4

1 pound (454 g) tuna steaks, boneless and cubed	1 tablespoon avocado oil
1 tablespoon mustard	1 tablespoon apple cider vinegar

1. Mix avocado oil with mustard and apple cider vinegar. 2. Then brush tuna steaks with mustard mixture and put in the air fryer basket. 3. Cook the fish at 360°F (182°C) for 6 minutes per side.

Per Serving:
calories: 197 | fat: 9g | protein: 27g | carbs: 0g | fiber: 0g | sodium: 87mg

Citrus-Glazed Salmon

Prep time: 10 minutes | Cook time: 13 to 17 minutes | Serves 4

2 medium limes	2 tablespoons sliced green onions
1 small orange	1 lime slice, cut into 4 wedges
⅓ cup agave syrup	1 orange slice, cut into 4 wedges
1 teaspoon salt	Hot cooked orzo pasta or rice, if desired
1 teaspoon pepper	
4 cloves garlic, finely chopped	
1¼ lb salmon fillet, cut into 4 pieces	

1 Heat oven to 400°F. Line 15x10x1-inch pan with cooking parchment paper or foil. In small bowl, grate lime peel from limes. Squeeze enough lime juice to equal 2 tablespoons; add to peel in bowl. Grate orange peel from oranges into bowl. Squeeze enough orange juice to equal 2 tablespoons; add to peel mixture. Stir in agave syrup, salt, pepper and garlic. In small cup, measure ¼ cup citrus mixture for salmon (reserve remaining citrus mixture). 2 Place salmon fillets in pan, skin side down. Using ¼ cup citrus mixture, brush tops and sides of salmon. Bake 13 to 17 minutes or until fish flakes easily with fork. Lift salmon pieces from skin with metal spatula onto serving plate. Sprinkle with green onions. Top each fish fillet with lime and orange wedges. Serve each fillet with 3 tablespoons reserved sauce and rice.

Per Serving:
calories: 320 | fat: 8g | protein: 31g | carbs: 30g | sugars: 23g | fiber: 3g | sodium: 680mg

Poached Red Snapper

Prep time: 5 minutes | Cook time: 25 minutes | Serves 4

1 cup dry white wine	¼ teaspoon salt
1 medium lemon, sliced	1 cup water
6 parsley sprigs, plus additional for garnish	1 red snapper (about 1½–2 pounds), cleaned and scaled with head and tail left on
5 peppercorns	1 lemon, sliced
5 scallions, sliced	
2 bay leaves	

1. In a fish poacher or very large skillet, combine the wine, lemon slices, 6 parsley sprigs, peppercorns, scallions, bay leaves, salt, and water. Bring the mixture to a boil; add the snapper. 2. Cover the pan, lower the heat, and simmer the red snapper for 15–20 minutes until the fish flakes easily with a fork. 3. Carefully lift out the snapper, and transfer to a platter. Garnish with lemon slices and parsley.

Per Serving:
calories: 269 | fat: 3g | protein: 43g | carbs: 6g | sugars: 2g | fiber: 2g | sodium: 285mg

Avo-Tuna with Croutons

Prep time: 10 minutes | Cook time: 0 minutes | Serves 3

2 (5-ounce) cans chunk-light tuna, drained	black pepper
2 tablespoons low-fat mayonnaise	3 avocados, halved and pitted
½ teaspoon freshly ground	6 tablespoons packaged croutons

1. In a medium bowl, combine the tuna, mayonnaise, and pepper, and mix well. 2. Top the avocados with the tuna mixture and croutons.

Per Serving:
calories: 441 | fat: 32g | protein: 23g | carbs: 22g | sugars: 2g | fiber: 14g | sodium: 284mg

Herb-Crusted Halibut

Prep time: 10 minutes | Cook time: 20 minutes | Serves 4

4 (5-ounce) halibut fillets	1 teaspoon chopped fresh thyme
Extra-virgin olive oil, for brushing	1 teaspoon chopped fresh basil
½ cup coarsely ground unsalted pistachios	Pinch sea salt
1 tablespoon chopped fresh parsley	Pinch freshly ground black pepper

1. Preheat the oven to 350°F. 2. Line a baking sheet with parchment paper. 3. Pat the halibut fillets dry with a paper towel and place them on the baking sheet. 4. Brush the halibut generously with olive oil. 5. In a small bowl, stir together the pistachios, parsley, thyme, basil, salt, and pepper. 6. Spoon the nut and herb mixture evenly on the fish, spreading it out so the tops of the fillets are covered. 7. Bake the halibut until it flakes when pressed with a fork, about 20 minutes. 8. Serve immediately.

Per Serving:
calories: 351 | fat: 27g | protein: 24g | carbs: 4g | sugars: 1g | fiber: 2g | sodium: 214mg

Balsamic Tilapia

Prep time: 5 minutes | Cook time: 15 minutes | Serves 4

4 tilapia fillets, boneless	1 teaspoon avocado oil
2 tablespoons balsamic vinegar	1 teaspoon dried basil

1. Sprinkle the tilapia fillets with balsamic vinegar, avocado oil, and dried basil. 2. Then put the fillets in the air fryer basket and cook at 365°F (185°C) for 15 minutes.

Per Serving:
calories: 129 | fat: 3g | protein: 23g | carbs: 1g | fiber: 0g | sodium: 92mg

Salmon with Brussels Sprouts

Prep time: 5 minutes | Cook time: 20 minutes | Serves 4

2 tablespoons unsalted butter, divided	4 (4-ounce) skinless salmon fillets
20 Brussels sprouts, halved lengthwise	½ teaspoon salt
	¼ teaspoon garlic powder

1. Heat a medium skillet over medium-low heat. When hot, melt 1 tablespoon of butter in the skillet, then add the Brussels sprouts cut-side down. Cook for 10 minutes. 2. Season both sides of the salmon fillets with the salt and garlic powder. 3. Heat another medium skillet over medium-low heat. When hot, melt the remaining 1 tablespoon of butter in the skillet, then add the salmon. Cover and cook for 6 to 8 minutes, or until the salmon is opaque and flakes easily with a fork. 4. Meanwhile, flip the Brussels sprouts and cover. Cook for 10 minutes or until tender. 5. Divide the Brussels sprouts into four equal portions and add 1 salmon fillet to each portion.

Per Serving:
calories: 236 | fat: 11g | protein: 27g | carbs: 9g | sugars: 2g | fiber: 4g | sodium: 400mg

Charcuterie Dinner For One

Prep time: 5 minutes | Cook time: 10 to 12 minutes | Serves 1

1 (6-oz [170-g]) salmon fillet	cucumbers
Cooking oil spray, as needed	¼ cup (50 g) plain nonfat Greek yogurt
1 oz (28 g) fresh mozzarella cheese slices or balls	1 oz (28 g) grain-free or whole-grain crackers
½ cup (60 g) thinly sliced	

1. Preheat the oven to 400°F (204°C). Line a medium baking sheet with parchment paper. 2. Lightly spray the salmon fillet with the cooking oil spray and place the salmon on the prepared baking sheet. Bake the salmon for 10 to 12 minutes, or until it has browned slightly on top. 3. Meanwhile, assemble the mozzarella cheese, cucumbers, yogurt, and crackers on a plate. 4. Transfer the salmon to the plate and serve.

Per Serving:
calorie: 517 | fat: 29g | protein: 47g | carbs: 16g | sugars: 5g | fiber: 1g | sodium: 418mg

Haddock with Creamy Cucumber Sauce

Prep time: 10 minutes | Cook time: 10 minutes | Serves 4

¼ cup 2 percent plain Greek yogurt	mint
½ English cucumber, grated, liquid squeezed out	1 teaspoon honey
	Sea salt
½ scallion, white and green parts, finely chopped	4 (5-ounce) haddock fillets
	Freshly ground black pepper
2 teaspoons chopped fresh	Nonstick cooking spray

1. In a small bowl, stir together the yogurt, cucumber, scallion, mint, honey, and a pinch of salt. Set it aside. 2. Pat the fish fillets dry with paper towels and season them lightly with salt and pepper. 3. Place a large skillet over medium-high heat and spray lightly with cooking spray. 4. Cook the haddock, turning once, until it is just cooked through, about 5 minutes per side. 5. Remove the fish from the heat and transfer to plates. 6. Serve topped with the cucumber sauce.

Per Serving:
calories: 123 | fat: 1g | protein: 24g | carbs: 3g | sugars: 3g | fiber: 0g | sodium: 310mg

Chili Tilapia

Prep time: 5 minutes | Cook time: 20 minutes | Serves 4

4 tilapia fillets, boneless	1 tablespoon avocado oil
1 teaspoon chili flakes	1 teaspoon mustard
1 teaspoon dried oregano	

1. Rub the tilapia fillets with chili flakes, dried oregano, avocado oil, and mustard and put in the air fryer. 2. Cook it for 10 minutes per side at 360°F (182°C).

Per Serving:
calories: 146 | fat: 6g | protein: 23g | carbs: 1g | fiber: 0g | sodium: 94mg

Asian Salmon in a Packet

Prep time: 10 minutes | Cook time: 20 minutes | Serves 2

For the sauce	1 cup cooked brown rice, divided
1 tablespoon extra-virgin olive oil, divided	2 cups coarsely chopped bok choy, divided
1 teaspoon grated fresh ginger	
1 garlic clove, minced	1 small red bell pepper, sliced, divided
2 tablespoons low-sodium soy sauce	½ cup sliced shiitake mushrooms, divided
2 teaspoons dark sesame oil	
For the salmon packets	2 (6-ounce) salmon steaks, rinsed
1 teaspoon extra-virgin olive oil, divided	2 scallions, chopped, divided

To make the sauce In a small bowl, whisk together the olive oil, ginger, garlic, soy sauce, and sesame oil. Set aside. To make the salmon packets 1. Preheat the oven to 450°F. 2. Fold 2 (12-by-24-inch) aluminum foil sheets in half widthwise into 2 (12-by-12-inch) squares. 3. Brush ½ teaspoon of the olive oil in the center of each foil square. 4. Spread ½ cup of the rice in the center of each square. 5. Over the rice in each packet, layer 1 cup of bok choy, half of the red bell pepper slices, ¼ cup of mushrooms, 1 salmon steak, and half of the scallions. 6. Pour half of the sauce over each. 7. Fold and seal the foil into airtight packets. Place the packets in a baking dish and into the preheated oven. Bake for 20 minutes. 8. Carefully avoiding the steam that will be released, open a packet and check that the fish is cooked. It should be opaque and flake easily. To test for doneness, poke the tines of a fork into the thickest portion of the fish at a 45-degree angle. Gently twist the fork and pull up some of the fish. If the fish resists flaking, return it to the oven for another 2 minutes then test again. Fish cooks very quickly, so be careful not to overcook it. 9. Transfer the contents of the packets to serving plates or bowls. 10. Enjoy!

Per Serving:
calories: 491 | fat: 22g | protein: 41g | carbs: 31g | sugars: 4g | fiber: 5g | sodium: 595mg

Tarragon Cod in a Packet

Prep time: 10 minutes | Cook time: 20 minutes | Serves 2

1 tablespoon extra-virgin olive oil, divided	1 teaspoon dried tarragon
1 small zucchini, thinly sliced	Dash salt
1 cup sliced fresh mushrooms	Dash freshly ground black pepper
2 (6-ounce) cod fillets, rinsed	1 (6.5-ounce) jar marinated quartered artichoke hearts, drained
½ red onion, thinly sliced	
Juice of 1 lemon	
¼ cup low-sodium vegetable broth	6 black olives, halved and pitted

1. Preheat the oven to 450°F. 2. Fold 2 (12-by-24-inch) aluminum foil sheets in half widthwise into 2 (12-by-12-inch) squares. 3. Brush ½ teaspoon of olive oil in the center of each foil square. 4. In the middle of each square, layer, in this order, half of the zucchini slices, ½ cup of mushrooms, 1 cod fillet, and half of the onion slices. 5. Sprinkle each packet with 1 of the remaining 2 teaspoons of olive oil, half of the lemon juice, 2 tablespoons of vegetable broth, and ½ teaspoon of tarragon. Season with salt and pepper. 6. Top with half of the artichokes and 6 black olive halves. 7. Fold and seal the foil into airtight packets. Place the packets in a baking dish and into the preheated oven. Bake for 20 minutes. 8. Carefully avoiding the steam that will be released, open a packet and check that the fish is cooked. It should be opaque and flake easily. To test for doneness, poke the tines of a fork into the thickest portion of the fish at a 45-degree angle. Gently twist the fork and pull up some of the fish. If the fish resists flaking, return it to the oven for another 2 minutes then test again. Fish cooks very quickly, so be careful not to overcook it. 9. With a spatula, lift the fish and vegetables onto individual serving plates. Pour any liquid left in the foil over each serving. 10. Enjoy!

Per Serving:
calories: 296 | fat: 10g | protein: 35g | carbs: 19g | sugars: 5g | fiber: 10g | sodium: 428mg

Whole Veggie-Stuffed Trout

Prep time: 10 minutes | Cook time: 25 minutes | Serves 2

Nonstick cooking spray	½ red bell pepper, seeded and thinly sliced
2 (8-ounce) whole trout fillets, dressed (cleaned but with bones and skin intact)	1 small onion, thinly sliced
	2 or 3 shiitake mushrooms, sliced
1 tablespoon extra-virgin olive oil	
¼ teaspoon salt	1 poblano pepper, seeded and thinly sliced
⅛ teaspoon freshly ground black pepper	1 lemon, sliced

1. Preheat the oven to 425°F. Spray a baking sheet with nonstick cooking spray. 2. Rub both trout, inside and out, with the olive oil, then season with the salt and pepper. 3. In a large bowl, combine the bell pepper, onion, mushrooms, and poblano pepper. Stuff half of this mixture into the cavity of each fish. Top the mixture with 2 or 3 lemon slices inside each fish. 4. Arrange the fish on the prepared baking sheet side by side and roast for 25 minutes until the fish is cooked through and the vegetables are tender.

Per Serving:
calories: 452 | fat: 22g | protein: 49g | carbs: 14g | sugars: 2g | fiber: 3g | sodium: 357mg

Scallops in Lemon-Butter Sauce

Prep time: 10 minutes | Cook time: 6 minutes | Serves 2

8 large dry sea scallops (about ¾ pound / 340 g)	2 tablespoons chopped flat-leaf parsley
Salt and freshly ground black pepper, to taste	1 tablespoon fresh lemon juice
	2 teaspoons capers, drained and chopped
2 tablespoons olive oil	
2 tablespoons unsalted butter, melted	1 teaspoon grated lemon zest
	1 clove garlic, minced

1. Preheat the air fryer to 400°F (204°C). 2. Use a paper towel to pat the scallops dry. Sprinkle lightly with salt and pepper. Brush with the olive oil. Arrange the scallops in a single layer in the air fryer basket. Pausing halfway through the cooking time to turn the scallops, air fry for about 6 minutes until firm and opaque. 3. Meanwhile, in a small bowl, combine the oil, butter, parsley, lemon juice, capers, lemon zest, and garlic. Drizzle over the scallops just before serving.

Per Serving:
calories: 304 | fat: 22g | protein: 21g | carbs: 5g | net carbs: 4g | fiber: 1g

North Carolina Fish Stew

Prep time: 20 minutes | Cook time: 20 minutes | Serves 8

½ cup store-bought low-sodium seafood broth	3 bay leaves
	1 pound new potatoes, halved
2 large white onions, chopped	3 cups water
4 garlic cloves, minced	2 pounds fish fillets, such as rockfish, striped bass, or cod, cut into ½- to 1-inch dice
¼ cup tomato paste	
1 teaspoon red pepper flakes	
2 teaspoons smoked paprika	8 medium eggs

1. Select the Sauté setting on an electric pressure cooker, and combine the broth, onions, garlic, tomato paste, red pepper flakes, paprika, and bay leaves. Cook for 2 minutes, or until the onions and garlic are translucent. 2. Add the potatoes and 1 cup of water. 3. Close and lock the lid, and set the pressure valve to sealing. 4. Change to the Manual/Pressure Cook setting, and cook for 3 minutes. 5. Once cooking is complete, quick-release the pressure. Carefully remove the lid. 6. Add the fish and enough of the water just to cover the fish. 7. Close and lock the lid, and set the pressure valve to sealing. 8. Select the Manual/Pressure Cook setting, and cook for 3 more minutes. 9. Once cooking is complete, quick-release the pressure. Carefully remove the lid. 10. Carefully crack the eggs one by one into the stew, keeping the yolks intact. 11. Close and lock the lid, and set the pressure valve to sealing. 12. Select the Manual/Pressure Cook setting, and cook for 1 minute. 13. Once cooking is complete, quick-release the pressure. Carefully remove the lid, discard the bay leaves, and serve in bowls.

Per Serving:
calories: 228 | fat: 5g | protein: 28g | carbs: 16g | sugars: 3g | fiber: 3g | sodium: 184mg

Mediterranean-Style Cod

Prep time: 5 minutes | Cook time: 12 minutes | Serves 4

4 (6-ounce / 170-g) cod fillets	¼ teaspoon salt
3 tablespoons fresh lemon juice	6 cherry tomatoes, halved
1 tablespoon olive oil	¼ cup pitted and sliced kalamata olives

1. Place cod into an ungreased round nonstick baking dish. Pour lemon juice into dish and drizzle cod with olive oil. Sprinkle with salt. Place tomatoes and olives around baking dish in between fillets. 2. Place dish into air fryer basket. Adjust the temperature to 350°F (177°C) and bake for 12 minutes, carefully turning cod halfway through cooking. Fillets will be lightly browned, easily flake, and have an internal temperature of at least 145°F (63°C) when done. Serve warm.

Per Serving:
calories: 186 | fat: 5g | protein: 31g | carbs: 2g | fiber: 1g | sodium: 300mg

Oregano Tilapia Fingers

Prep time: 15 minutes | Cook time: 9 minutes | Serves 4

1 pound (454 g) tilapia fillet	½ teaspoon ground paprika
½ cup coconut flour	1 teaspoon dried oregano
2 eggs, beaten	1 teaspoon avocado oil

1. Cut the tilapia fillets into fingers and sprinkle with ground paprika and dried oregano. 2. Then dip the tilapia fingers in eggs and coat in the coconut flour. 3. Sprinkle fish fingers with avocado oil and cook in the air fryer at 370°F (188°C) for 9 minutes.

Per Serving:
calories: 187 | fat: 9g | protein: 26g | carbs: 2g | fiber: 1g | sodium: 92mg

Cobia with Lemon-Caper Sauce

Prep time: 25 minutes | Cook time: 10 minutes | Serves 4

⅓ cup all-purpose flour	½ cup reduced-sodium chicken broth
¼ teaspoon salt	2 tablespoons lemon juice
¼ teaspoon pepper	1 tablespoon capers, rinsed, drained
1¼ lb cobia or sea bass fillets, cut into 4 pieces	1 tablespoon chopped fresh parsley
2 tablespoons olive oil	
⅓ cup dry white wine	

1 In shallow dish, stir flour, salt and pepper. Coat cobia pieces in flour mixture (reserve remaining flour mixture). In 12-inch nonstick skillet, heat oil over medium-high heat. Place coated cobia in oil. Cook 8 to 10 minutes, turning halfway through cooking, until fish flakes easily with fork; remove from heat. Lift fish from skillet to serving platter with slotted spatula (do not discard drippings); keep warm. 2 Heat skillet (with drippings) over medium heat. Stir in 1 tablespoon reserved flour mixture; cook and stir 30 seconds. Stir in wine; cook about 30 seconds or until thickened and slightly reduced. Stir in chicken broth and lemon juice; cook and stir 1 to 2 minutes until sauce is smooth and slightly thickened. Stir in capers. 3 Serve sauce over cobia; sprinkle with parsley.

Per Serving:
calories: 230 | fat: 9g | protein: 28g | carbs: 9g | sugars: 0g | fiber: 0g | sodium: 400mg

Snapper with Shallot and Tomato

Prep time: 20 minutes | Cook time: 15 minutes | Serves 2

2 snapper fillets	1 tablespoon olive oil
1 shallot, peeled and sliced	¼ teaspoon freshly ground black pepper
2 garlic cloves, halved	½ teaspoon paprika
1 bell pepper, sliced	Sea salt, to taste
1 small-sized serrano pepper, sliced	2 bay leaves
1 tomato, sliced	

1. Place two parchment sheets on a working surface. Place the fish in the center of one side of the parchment paper. 2. Top with the shallot, garlic, peppers, and tomato. Drizzle olive oil over the fish and vegetables. Season with black pepper, paprika, and salt. Add the bay leaves. 3. Fold over the other half of the parchment. Now, fold the paper around the edges tightly and create a half moon shape, sealing the fish inside. 4. Cook in the preheated air fryer at 390°F (199°C) for 15 minutes. Serve warm.

Per Serving:
calories: 325 | fat: 10g | protein: 47g | carbs: 11g | fiber: 2g | sodium: 146mg

Roasted Red Snapper and Shrimp in Parchment

Prep time: 10 minutes | Cook time: 45 minutes | Serves 8

One 3-pound whole red snapper or bass, cleaned	½ pound large shrimp, shelled and deveined
1 medium garlic clove, minced	½ pound sliced mushrooms
¼ cup extra-virgin olive oil	3 tablespoons lemon juice, divided
⅛ teaspoon freshly ground black pepper	½ cup dry white wine, divided
½ teaspoon finely chopped fresh thyme	¼ cup minced fresh parsley
1 teaspoon flour	Zest of 1 lemon

1 Preheat oven to 375 degrees. Wash the fish, inside and out, under cold running water, and pat dry with paper towels. 2 In a small bowl, combine the garlic, olive oil, pepper, thyme, and flour. Mix well. 3 Place the fish on a double thickness of parchment paper. In the cavity of the fish, place 1 tablespoon of the garlic mixture, 4 shrimp, and ½ cup sliced mushrooms. Sprinkle with 1 tablespoon of the lemon juice and 2 tablespoons of the wine. 4 Dot the top of the fish with the remaining garlic mixture, and arrange the remaining shrimp and mushrooms on top. Sprinkle with the remaining lemon juice and wine, and the parsley. 5 Bring the long sides of the parchment together over the fish, and secure with a double fold. Fold both ends of the parchment upward several times. 6 Place the fish on a baking sheet; bake for 30–35 minutes at 375 degrees. Transfer to a serving platter, garnish with lemon zest, and serve.

Per Serving:
calories: 272 | fat: 9g | protein: 40g | carbs: 3g | sugars: 1g | fiber: 1g | sodium: 273mg

Sea Bass with Ginger Sauce

Prep time: 5 minutes | Cook time: 15 minutes | Serves 2

Two 4-ounce sea bass filets	2 garlic cloves, minced
1 tablespoon extra-virgin olive oil	⅓ cup minced scallions
2 tablespoons minced fresh ginger	4 teaspoons chopped cilantro
	1 tablespoon light soy sauce

1. In a medium steamer, add water and bring to a boil. Arrange the filets on the steamer rack. Cover, and steam for 6–8 minutes. 2. Meanwhile, in a small skillet, heat the oil over medium-high heat. Add the ginger and garlic, and sauté for 2–3 minutes. 3. Transfer the steamed filets to a platter. Pour the ginger oil over the filets, and top with scallions, cilantro, and soy sauce.

Per Serving:
calories: 207 | fat: 11g | protein: 22g | carbs: 5g | sugars: 2g | fiber: 1g | sodium: 202mg

Southern-Style Catfish

Prep time: 10 minutes | Cook time: 12 minutes | Serves 4

4 (7-ounce / 198-g) catfish fillets	almond flour
⅓ cup heavy whipping cream	2 teaspoons Old Bay seasoning
1 tablespoon lemon juice	½ teaspoon salt
1 cup blanched finely ground	¼ teaspoon ground black pepper

1. Place catfish fillets into a large bowl with cream and pour in lemon juice. Stir to coat. 2. In a separate large bowl, mix flour and Old Bay seasoning. 3. Remove each fillet and gently shake off excess cream. Sprinkle with salt and pepper. Press each fillet gently into flour mixture on both sides to coat. 4. Place fillets into ungreased air fryer basket. Adjust the temperature to 400°F (204°C) and air fry for 12 minutes, turning fillets halfway through cooking. Catfish will be golden brown and have an internal temperature of at least 145°F (63°C) when done. Serve warm.

Per Serving:
calories: 438 | fat: 28g | protein: 41g | carbs: 7g | fiber: 4g | sodium: 387mg

Roasted Salmon with Honey-Mustard Sauce

Prep time: 5 minutes | Cook time: 20 minutes | Serves 4

Nonstick cooking spray	¼ teaspoon salt
2 tablespoons whole-grain mustard	¼ teaspoon freshly ground black pepper
1 tablespoon honey	1 pound salmon fillet
2 garlic cloves, minced	

1. Preheat the oven to 425°F. Spray a baking sheet with nonstick cooking spray. 2. In a small bowl, whisk together the mustard, honey, garlic, salt, and pepper. 3. Place the salmon fillet on the prepared baking sheet, skin-side down. Spoon the sauce onto the salmon and spread evenly. 4. Roast for 15 to 20 minutes, depending on the thickness of the fillet, until the flesh flakes easily.

Per Serving:
calories: 186 | fat: 7g | protein: 23g | carbs: 6g | sugars: 4g | fiber: 0g | sodium: 312mg

Baked Oysters

Prep time: 30 minutes | Cook time: 15 minutes | Serves 2

2 cups coarse salt, for holding the oysters	¼ cup finely chopped red bell pepper
1 dozen fresh oysters, scrubbed	1 garlic clove, minced
1 tablespoon butter	1 tablespoon finely chopped fresh parsley
½ cup finely chopped artichoke hearts	Zest and juice of ½ lemon
¼ cup finely chopped scallions, both white and green parts	Pinch salt
	Freshly ground black pepper

1. Pour the coarse salt into an 8-by-8-inch baking dish and spread to evenly fill the bottom of the dish. 2. Prepare a clean surface to shuck the oysters. Using a shucking knife, insert the blade at the joint of the shell, where it hinges open and shut. Firmly apply pressure to pop the blade in, and work the knife around the shell to open. Discard the empty half of the shell. Use the knife to gently loosen the oyster, and remove any shell particles. Set the oysters in their shells on the salt, being careful not to spill the juices. 3. Preheat the oven to 425°F. 4. In a large skillet, melt the butter over medium heat. Add the artichoke hearts, scallions, and bell pepper, and cook for 5 to 7 minutes. Add the garlic and cook an additional minute. Remove from the heat and mix in the parsley, lemon zest and juice, and season with salt and pepper. 5. Divide the vegetable mixture evenly among the oysters and bake for 10 to 12 minutes until the vegetables are lightly browned.

Per Serving:
calories: 134 | fat: 7g | protein: 6g | carbs: 11g | sugars: 7g | fiber: 2g | sodium: 281mg

Greek Scampi

Prep time: 10 minutes | Cook time: 5 minutes | Serves 2

2 garlic cloves, minced	6 Kalamata olives
2 tablespoons extra-virgin olive oil	Juice of ½ lemon
½ pound shrimp, peeled, deveined, and thoroughly rinsed	2 teaspoons chopped fresh dill, or ¾ teaspoon dried
1 cup diced tomatoes	Dash salt
½ cup nonfat ricotta cheese	Dash freshly ground black pepper
	Lemon wedges, for garnish

1. In a large skillet set over medium heat, sauté the garlic in the olive oil for 30 seconds. 2. Add the shrimp. Cook for 1 minute. 3. Add the tomatoes, ricotta cheese, olives, lemon juice, and dill. Reduce the heat to low. Simmer for 5 to 10 minutes, stirring so the shrimp cook on both sides. When the shrimp are pink and the tomatoes and ricotta have made a sauce, the dish is ready. 4. Sprinkle with salt and pepper. 5. Serve immediately, garnished with lemon wedges.

Per Serving:
calories: 345 | fat: 21g | protein: 31g | carbs: 11g | sugars: 3g | fiber: 2g | sodium: 406mg

Salmon en Papillote

Prep time: 15 minutes | Cook time: 15 minutes | Serves 2

For the roasted vegetables
½ pound fresh green beans, trimmed
½ onion, cut into ¼-inch-thick slices
1 tablespoon extra-virgin olive oil
1 teaspoon capers (optional)
For the salmon
2 teaspoons extra-virgin olive oil, divided
2 medium parsnips, cut into ¼-inch-thick rounds, divided
2 (4-ounce) salmon fillets
2 garlic cloves, thinly sliced, divided
1 lemon, divided (½ cut into slices, the other ½ cut into 2 wedges)
1 tablespoon chopped fresh thyme, divided
Kosher salt
Freshly ground black pepper

To make the roasted vegetables 1. Preheat the oven to 400°F. Line a baking sheet with parchment paper. 2. In a medium bowl, toss the green beans, onion, extra-virgin olive oil, and capers (if using) until well coated. 3. Spread the vegetables on half of the baking sheet and set aside until the salmon is ready to bake. To make the salmon 4. Cut two pieces of parchment paper, fold them in half, and cut each into a heart shape (about 10 to 12 inches in circumference). Lightly brush the parchment with ½ teaspoon of extra-virgin olive oil. 5. Open one of the hearts and place half the parsnips on the right half in the center, fanning them out. Place one piece of salmon on the fanned parsnips. Add half the garlic, half the lemon slices, half the thyme, ½ teaspoon of extra-virgin olive oil, and a pinch each of kosher salt and pepper. 6. Seal the packet by folding the left half of the heart over the right side. Fold along the edge of the heart and create a seal. Repeat with the other piece of parchment. 7. Place the packets on the empty side of the baking sheet and bake until the salmon is cooked through, 10 to 15 minutes. Allow the fish to rest a few minutes before serving with the roasted green beans and remaining lemon wedges. 8. Store any leftovers in an airtight container in the refrigerator for 1 to 2 days.

Per Serving:
calories: 389 | fat: 17g | protein: 28g | carbs: 35g | sugars: 11g | fiber: 10g | sodium: 261mg

Crab-Stuffed Avocado Boats

Prep time: 5 minutes | Cook time: 7 minutes | Serves 4

2 medium avocados, halved and pitted
8 ounces (227 g) cooked crab meat
¼ teaspoon Old Bay seasoning
2 tablespoons peeled and diced yellow onion
2 tablespoons mayonnaise

1. Scoop out avocado flesh in each avocado half, leaving ½ inch around edges to form a shell. Chop scooped-out avocado. 2. In a medium bowl, combine crab meat, Old Bay seasoning, onion, mayonnaise, and chopped avocado. Place ¼ mixture into each avocado shell. 3. Place avocado boats into ungreased air fryer basket. Adjust the temperature to 350°F (177°C) and air fry for 7 minutes. Avocado will be browned on the top and mixture will be bubbling when done. Serve warm.

Per Serving:
calories: 226 | fat: 17g | protein: 12g | carbs: 10g | sugars: 1g | fiber: 7g | sodium: 239mg

Lime Lobster Tails

Prep time: 10 minutes | Cook time: 6 minutes | Serves 4

4 lobster tails, peeled
2 tablespoons lime juice
½ teaspoon dried basil
½ teaspoon coconut oil, melted

1. Mix lobster tails with lime juice, dried basil, and coconut oil. 2. Put the lobster tails in the air fryer and cook at 380°F (193°C) for 6 minutes.

Per Serving:
calories: 123 | fat: 2g | protein: 25g | carbs: 1g | fiber: 0g | sodium: 635mg

Asian Cod with Brown Rice, Asparagus, and Mushrooms

Prep time: 5 minutes | Cook time: 25 minutes | Serves 2

¾ cup Minute brand brown rice
½ cup water
Two 5-ounce skinless cod fillets
1 tablespoon soy sauce or tamari
1 tablespoon fresh lemon juice
½ teaspoon peeled and grated fresh ginger
1 tablespoon extra-virgin olive oil or 1 tablespoon unsalted butter, cut into 8 pieces
2 green onions, white and green parts, thinly sliced
12 ounces asparagus, trimmed
4 ounces shiitake mushrooms, stems removed and sliced
⅛ teaspoon fine sea salt
⅛ teaspoon freshly ground black pepper
Lemon wedges for serving

1. Pour 1 cup water into the Instant Pot. Have ready two-tier stackable stainless-steel containers. 2. In one of the containers, combine the rice and ½ cup water, then gently shake the container to spread the rice into an even layer, making sure all of the grains are submerged. Place the fish fillets on top of the rice. In a small bowl, stir together the soy sauce, lemon juice, and ginger. Pour the soy sauce mixture over the fillets. Drizzle 1 teaspoon olive oil on each fillet (or top with two pieces of the butter), and sprinkle the green onions on and around the fish. 3. In the second container, arrange the asparagus in the center in as even a layer as possible. Place the mushrooms on either side of the asparagus. Drizzle with the remaining 2 teaspoons olive oil (or put the remaining six pieces butter on top of the asparagus, spacing them evenly). Sprinkle the salt and pepper evenly over the vegetables. 4. Place the container with the rice and fish on the bottom and the vegetable container on top. Cover the top container with its lid and then latch the containers together. Grasping the handle, lower the containers into the Instant Pot. 5. Secure the lid and set the Pressure Release to Sealing. Select the Pressure Cook or Manual setting and set the cooking time for 15 minutes at high pressure. (The pot will take about 10 minutes to come up to pressure before the cooking program begins.) 6. When the cooking program ends, let the pressure release naturally for 5 minutes, then move the Pressure Release to Venting to release any remaining steam. Open the pot and, wearing heat-resistant mitts, lift out the stacked containers. Unlatch, unstack, and open the containers, taking care not to get burned by the steam. 7. Transfer the vegetables, rice, and fish to plates and serve right away, with the lemon wedges on the side.

Per Serving:
calories: 344 | fat: 11g | protein: 27g | carbs: 46g | sugars: 6g | fiber: 7g | sodium: 637mg

Mediterranean Salmon with Whole-Wheat Couscous

Prep time: 5 minutes | Cook time: 30 minutes | Serves 4

Couscous	Salmon
1 cup whole-wheat couscous	1 pound skinless salmon fillet
1 cup water	2 teaspoons extra-virgin olive oil
1 tablespoon extra-virgin olive oil	1 tablespoon fresh lemon juice
1 teaspoon dried basil	1 garlic clove, minced
¼ teaspoon fine sea salt	¼ teaspoon dried oregano
1 pint cherry or grape tomatoes, halved	¼ teaspoon fine sea salt
8 ounces zucchini, halved lengthwise, then sliced crosswise ¼ inch thick	¼ teaspoon freshly ground black pepper
	1 tablespoon capers, drained
	Lemon wedges for serving

1. Pour 1 cup water into the Instant Pot. Have ready two-tier stackable stainless-steel containers. 2. To make the couscous: In one of the containers, stir together the couscous, water, oil, basil, and salt. Sprinkle the tomatoes and zucchini over the top. 3. To make the salmon: Place the salmon fillet in the second container. In a small bowl, whisk together the oil, lemon juice, garlic, oregano, salt, pepper, and capers. Spoon the oil mixture over the top of the salmon. 4. Place the container with the couscous and vegetables on the bottom and the salmon container on top. Cover the top container with its lid and then latch the containers together. Grasping the handle, lower the containers into the Instant Pot. 5. Secure the lid and set the Pressure Release to Sealing. Select the Pressure Cook or Manual setting and set the cooking time for 20 minutes at high pressure. (The pot will take about 10 minutes to come up to pressure before the cooking program begins.) 6. When the cooking program ends, let the pressure release naturally for 5 minutes, then move the Pressure Release to Venting to release any remaining steam. Open the pot and, wearing heat-resistant mitts, lift out the stacked containers. Unlatch, unstack, and open the containers, taking care not to get burned by the steam. 7. Using a fork, fluff the couscous and mix in the vegetables. Spoon the couscous onto plates, then use a spatula to cut the salmon into four pieces and place a piece on top of each couscous serving. Serve right away, with lemon wedges on the side.

Per Serving:
calories: 427 | fat: 18g | protein: 28g | carbs: 36g | sugars: 2g | fiber: 6g | sodium: 404mg

Calypso Shrimp with Black Bean Salsa

Prep time: 25 minutes | Cook time: 5 minutes | Serves 4

Shrimp	
½ teaspoon grated lime peel	1 medium mango, peeled, pitted and chopped (1 cup)
1 tablespoon lime juice	1 small red bell pepper, chopped (½ cup)
1 tablespoon canola oil	2 medium green onions, sliced (2 tablespoons)
1 teaspoon finely chopped gingerroot	1 tablespoon chopped fresh cilantro
1 clove garlic, finely chopped	½ teaspoon grated lime peel
1 lb uncooked deveined peeled large shrimp, thawed if frozen	1 to 2 tablespoons lime juice
Salsa	1 tablespoon red wine vinegar
1 can (15 oz) black beans, drained, rinsed	¼ teaspoon ground red pepper (cayenne)

1 In medium glass or plastic bowl, mix lime peel, lime juice, oil, gingerroot and garlic. Stir in shrimp; let stand 15 minutes. 2 Meanwhile, in medium bowl, mix salsa ingredients. 3 In 10-inch skillet, cook shrimp over medium-high heat about 5 minutes, turning once, until pink. Serve with salsa.

Per Serving:
calories: 300| fat: 5g | protein: 26g | carbs: 37g | sugars: 7g | fiber: 12g | sodium: 190mg

Rainbow Salmon Kebabs

Prep time: 10 minutes | Cook time: 8 minutes | Serves 2

6 ounces (170 g) boneless, skinless salmon, cut into 1-inch cubes	pieces
¼ medium red onion, peeled and cut into 1-inch pieces	½ medium zucchini, trimmed and cut into ½-inch slices
½ medium yellow bell pepper, seeded and cut into 1-inch	1 tablespoon olive oil
	½ teaspoon salt
	¼ teaspoon ground black pepper

1. Using one (6-inch) skewer, skewer 1 piece salmon, then 1 piece onion, 1 piece bell pepper, and finally 1 piece zucchini. Repeat this pattern with additional skewers to make four kebabs total. Drizzle with olive oil and sprinkle with salt and black pepper. 2. Place kebabs into ungreased air fryer basket. Adjust the temperature to 400°F (204°C) and air fry for 8 minutes, turning kebabs halfway through cooking. Salmon will easily flake and have an internal temperature of at least 145°F (63°C) when done; vegetables will be tender. Serve warm.

Per Serving:
calories: 195 | fat: 11g | protein: 19g | carbs: 6g | fiber: 2g | sodium: 651mg

Teriyaki Salmon

Prep time: 30 minutes | Cook time: 12 minutes | Serves 4

4 (6-ounce / 170-g) salmon fillets	¼ teaspoon ground ginger
½ cup soy sauce	2 teaspoons olive oil
¼ cup packed light brown sugar	½ teaspoon salt
2 teaspoons rice vinegar	¼ teaspoon freshly ground black pepper
1 teaspoon minced garlic	Oil, for spraying

1. Place the salmon in a small pan, skin-side up. 2. In a small bowl, whisk together the soy sauce, brown sugar, rice vinegar, garlic, ginger, olive oil, salt, and black pepper. 3. Pour the mixture over the salmon and marinate for about 30 minutes. 4. Line the air fryer basket with parchment and spray lightly with oil. Place the salmon in the prepared basket, skin-side down. You may need to work in batches, depending on the size of your air fryer. 5. Air fry at 400°F (204°C) for 6 minutes, brush the salmon with more marinade, and cook for another 6 minutes, or until the internal temperature reaches 145°F (63°C). Serve immediately.

Per Serving:
calories: 319 | fat: 14g | protein: 37g | carbs: 8g | sugars: 6g | fiber: 1g | sodium: 762mg

Caribbean Haddock in a Packet

Prep time: 10 minutes | Cook time: 20 minutes | Serves 2

1 tablespoon extra-virgin olive oil, divided
1 cup angel hair coleslaw, divided
1 (8-ounce) haddock fillet, halved and rinsed
1 small tomato, thinly sliced
1 small red bell pepper, thinly sliced
½ cup chopped fresh chives

2 tablespoons chopped fresh cilantro
Juice of 1 lime
4 dashes hot pepper sauce
Dash salt
Dash freshly ground black pepper

1. Preheat the oven to 450°F. 2. Fold 2 (12-by-24-inch) aluminum foil sheets in half widthwise into 2 (12-by-12-inch) squares. 3. In the center of each foil square, brush ½ teaspoon of olive oil. 4. Place ½ cup of coleslaw in each square. 5. Top each with 1 piece of haddock. 6. Add half of the tomato slices and half of the red bell pepper slices atop each fillet. 7. Sprinkle each with 1 of the remaining 2 teaspoons of olive oil, ¼ cup of chives, 1 tablespoon of cilantro, half of the lime juice, and 2 dashes of hot pepper sauce. Season with salt and pepper. 8. Fold and seal the foil into airtight packets. Place the packets in a baking dish and into the preheated oven. Bake for 20 minutes. 9. Carefully avoiding the steam that will be released, open a packet and check that the fish is cooked. It should be opaque and flake easily. To test for doneness, poke the tines of a fork into the thickest portion of the fish at a 45-degree angle. Gently twist the fork and pull up some of the fish. If the fish resists flaking, return it to the oven for another 2 minutes then test again. Fish cooks very quickly, so be careful not to overcook it. 10. Divide the fish, vegetables, and juices between 2 serving plates.

Per Serving:
calories: 310 | fat: 16g | protein: 21g | carbs: 21g | sugars: 16g | fiber: 4g | sodium: 536mg

Chapter 6   Snacks and Appetizers

Cucumber Roll-Ups

Prep time: 5 minutes | Cook time: 0 minutes | Serves 2 to 4

2 (6-inch) gluten-free wraps	long strips
2 tablespoons cream cheese	2 tablespoons fresh mint
1 medium cucumber, cut into	

1. Place the wraps on your work surface and spread them evenly with the cream cheese. Top with the cucumber and mint. 2. Roll the wraps up from one side to the other, kind of like a burrito. Slice into 1-inch bites or keep whole. 3. Serve. 4. Store any leftovers in an airtight container in the refrigerator for 1 to 2 days.

Per Serving:
calorie: 70 | fat: 1g | protein: 4g | carbs: 12g | sugars: 3g | fiber: 2g | sodium: 183mg

Zucchini Hummus Dip with Red Bell Peppers

Prep time: 10 minutes | Cook time: 0 minutes | Serves 4

2 zucchini, chopped	Juice of 1 lemon
3 garlic cloves	½ teaspoon sea salt
2 tablespoons extra-virgin olive oil	1 red bell pepper, seeded and cut into sticks
2 tablespoons tahini	

1. In a blender or food processor, combine the zucchini, garlic, olive oil, tahini, lemon juice, and salt. Blend until smooth. 2. Serve with the red bell pepper for dipping.

Per Serving:
calorie: 136 | fat: 11g | protein: 3g | carbs: 8g | sugars: 4g | fiber: 2g | sodium: 309mg

Southern Boiled Peanuts

Prep time: 5 minutes | Cook time: 1 hour 20 minutes | Makes 8 cups

1 pound raw jumbo peanuts in the shell	3 tablespoons fine sea salt

1. Remove the inner pot from the Instant Pot and add the peanuts to it. Cover the peanuts with water and use your hands to agitate them, loosening any dirt. Drain the peanuts in a colander, rinse out the pot, and return the peanuts to it. Return the inner pot to the Instant Pot housing. 2. Add the salt and 9 cups water to the pot and stir to dissolve the salt. Select a salad plate just small enough to fit inside the pot and set it on top of the peanuts to weight them down, submerging them all in the water. 3. Secure the lid and set the Pressure Release to Sealing. Select the Steam setting and set the cooking time for 1 hour at low pressure. (The pot will take about 20 minutes to come up to pressure before the cooking program begins.) 4. When the cooking program ends, let the pressure release naturally (this will take about 1 hour). Open the pot and, wearing heat-resistant mitts, remove the inner pot from the housing. Let the peanuts cool to room temperature in the brine (this will take about 1½ hours). 5. Serve at room temperature or chilled. Transfer the peanuts with their brine to an airtight container and refrigerate for up to 1 week.

Per Serving:
calories: 306 | fat: 17g | protein: 26g | carbs: 12g | sugars: 2g | fiber: 4g | sodium: 303mg

Hummus with Chickpeas and Tahini Sauce

Prep time: 10 minutes | Cook time: 55 minutes | Makes 4 cups

4 cups water	3 tablespoons fresh lemon juice
1 cup dried chickpeas	1 garlic clove
2½ teaspoons fine sea salt	¼ teaspoon ground cumin
½ cup tahini	

1. Combine the water, chickpeas, and 1 teaspoon of the salt in the Instant Pot and stir to dissolve the salt. 2. Secure the lid and set the Pressure Release to Sealing. Select the Bean/Chili, Pressure Cook, or Manual setting and set the cooking time for 40 minutes at high pressure. (The pot will take about 15 minutes to come up to pressure before the cooking program begins.) 3. When the cooking program ends, let the pressure release naturally for 15 minutes, then move the Pressure Release to Venting to release any remaining steam. 4. Place a colander over a bowl. Open the pot and, wearing heat-resistant mitts, lift out the inner pot and drain the beans in the colander. Return the chickpeas to the inner pot and place it back in the Instant Pot housing on the Keep Warm setting. Reserve the cooking liquid. 5. In a blender or food processor, combine 1 cup of the cooking liquid, the tahini, lemon juice, garlic, cumin, and 1 teaspoon salt. Blend or process on high speed, stopping to scrape down the sides of the container as needed, for about 30 seconds, until smooth and a little fluffy. Scoop out and set aside ½ cup of this sauce for the topping. 6. Set aside ½ cup of the chickpeas for the topping. Add the remaining chickpeas to the tahini sauce in the blender or food processor along with ½ cup of the cooking liquid and the remaining ½ teaspoon salt. Blend or process on high speed, stopping to scrape down the sides of the container as needed, for about 1 minute, until very smooth. 7. Transfer the hummus to a shallow serving bowl. Spoon the reserved tahini mixture over the top, then sprinkle on the reserved chickpeas. The hummus will keep in an airtight container in the refrigerator for up to 3 days. Serve at room temperature or chilled.

Per Serving:
calories: 107 | fat: 5g | protein: 4g | carbs: 10g | sugars: 3g | fiber: 4g | sodium: 753mg

Baked Parmesan Crisps

Prep time: 5 minutes | Cook time: 5 minutes | Serves 2

1 cup grated Parmesan cheese

1. Preheat the oven to 400°F. Line a rimmed baking sheet with parchment paper. 2. Spread the Parmesan on the prepared baking sheet into 4 mounds, spreading each mound out so it is flat but not touching the others. 3. Bake until brown and crisp, 3 to 5 minutes. 4. Cool for 5 minutes. Use a spatula to remove to a plate to continue cooling.

Per Serving:
calorie: 226 | fat: 15g | protein: 21g | carbs: 2g | sugars: 0g | fiber: 0g | sodium: 32mg

Spicy Cajun Onion Dip

Prep time: 15 minutes | Cook time: 0 minutes | Serves 5

Dip
¾ cup plain low-fat yogurt
½ cup reduced-fat sour cream
3 medium green onions, chopped (3 tablespoons)
1½ teaspoons Cajun seasoning
2 cloves garlic, finely chopped
Vegetables and Shrimp
1 medium red bell pepper, cut into 20 strips
½ lb fresh sugar snap pea pods, strings removed
20 cooked deveined peeled large (21 to 30 count) shrimp, thawed if frozen

1 In small bowl, mix dip ingredients with whisk until smooth. Cover; refrigerate at least 15 minutes to blend flavors. 2 Serve dip with bell pepper, pea pods and shrimp.

Per Serving:
calories: 110 | fat: 4g | protein: 9g | carbs: 9g | sugars: 6g | fiber: 2g | sodium: 430mg

Instant Popcorn

Prep time: 1 minutes | Cook time: 5 minutes | Serves 5

2 tablespoons coconut oil
½ cup popcorn kernels
¼ cup margarine spread, melted, optional
Sea salt to taste

1. Set the Instant Pot to Sauté. 2. Melt the coconut oil in the inner pot, then add the popcorn kernels and stir. 3. Press Adjust to bring the temperature up to high. 4. When the corn starts popping, secure the lid on the Instant Pot. 5. When you no longer hear popping, turn off the Instant Pot, remove the lid, and pour the popcorn into a bowl. 6. Top with the optional melted margarine and season the popcorn with sea salt to your liking.

Per Serving:
calories: 161 | fat: 12g | protein: 1g | carbs: 13g | sugars: 0g | fiber: 3g | sodium: 89mg

Low-Sugar Blueberry Muffins

Prep time: 5 minutes | Cook time: 20 to 25 minutes | Makes 12 muffins

2 large eggs
1½ cups (144 g) almond flour
1 cup (80 g) gluten-free rolled oats
½ cup (120 ml) pure maple syrup
½ cup (120 ml) avocado oil
1 tsp baking powder
1 tsp ground cinnamon
½ tsp pure vanilla extract
½ tsp pure almond extract
1 cup (150 g) fresh or frozen blueberries

1. Preheat the oven to 350°F (177°C). Line a 12-well muffin pan with paper liners or spray the wells with cooking oil spray. 2. In a blender, combine the eggs, almond flour, oats, maple syrup, oil, baking powder, cinnamon, vanilla, and almond extract. Blend the ingredients on high for 20 to 30 seconds, until the mixture is homogeneous. 3. Transfer the batter to a large bowl and gently stir in the blueberries. 4. Divide the batter evenly among the muffin wells. Bake the muffins for 20 to 25 minutes, until a toothpick inserted in the middle comes out clean. 5. Let the muffins rest for 5 minutes, then transfer them to a cooling rack.

Per Serving:
calorie: 240 | fat: 18g | protein: 5g | carbs: 19g | sugars: 10g | fiber: 3g | sodium: 19mg

Candied Pecans

Prep time: 5 minutes | Cook time: 20 minutes | Serves 10

4 cups raw pecans
1½ teaspoons liquid stevia
½ cup plus 1 tablespoon water, divided
1 teaspoon vanilla extract
1 teaspoon cinnamon
¼ teaspoon nutmeg
⅛ teaspoon ground ginger
⅛ teaspoon sea salt

1. Place the raw pecans, liquid stevia, 1 tablespoon water, vanilla, cinnamon, nutmeg, ground ginger, and sea salt into the inner pot of the Instant Pot. 2. Press the Sauté button on the Instant Pot and sauté the pecans and other ingredients until the pecans are soft. 3. Pour in the ½ cup water and secure the lid to the locked position. Set the vent to sealing. 4. Press Manual and set the Instant Pot for 15 minutes. 5. Preheat the oven to 350°F. 6. When cooking time is up, turn off the Instant Pot, then do a quick release. 7. Spread the pecans onto a greased, lined baking sheet. 8. Bake the pecans for 5 minutes or less in the oven, checking on them frequently so they do not burn.

Per Serving:
calories: 275 | fat: 28g | protein: 4g | carbs: 6g | sugars: 2g | fiber: 4g | sodium: 20mg

Creamy Cheese Dip

Prep time: 5 minutes | Cook time: 5 minutes | Serves 40

1 cup plain fat-free yogurt, strained overnight in cheesecloth over a bowl set in the refrigerator
1 cup fat-free ricotta cheese
1 cup low-fat cottage cheese

1. Combine all the ingredients in a food processor; process until smooth. Place in a covered container, and refrigerate until ready to use (this cream cheese can be refrigerated for up to 1 week).

Per Serving:
calorie: 21 | fat: 1g | protein: 2g | carbs: 1g | sugars: 1g | fiber: 0g | sodium: 81mg

Hummus

Prep time: 5 minutes | Cook time: 5 minutes | Serves 12

One 15-ounce can chickpeas, drained (reserve a little liquid)
3 cloves garlic
Juice of 1 lemon
Juice of 1 lime
1 teaspoon extra-virgin olive oil
1 teaspoon ground cumin

1. In a blender or food processor, combine all the ingredients until smooth, adding chickpea liquid or water if necessary to blend, and create a creamy texture. Refrigerate until ready to serve. Serve with crunchy vegetables, crackers, or pita bread.

Per Serving:
calorie: 56 | fat: 1g | protein: 3g | carbs: 9g | sugars: 2g | fiber: 2g | soldium: 76mg

Caprese Skewers

Prep time: 5 minutes | Cook time: 0 minutes | Serves 2

12 cherry tomatoes	cheese
12 basil leaves	¼ cup Italian Vinaigrette
8 (1-inch) pieces mozzarella	(optional, for serving)

1. On each of 4 wooden skewers, thread the following: 1 tomato, 1 basil leaf, 1 piece of cheese, 1 tomato, 1 basil leaf, 1 piece of cheese, 1 basil leaf, 1 tomato. 2. Serve with the vinaigrette, if desired, for dipping.

Per Serving:
calorie: 475 | fat: 21g | protein: 39g | carbs: 38g | sugars: 24g | fiber: 11g | sodium: 63mg

Sweet Potato Oven Fries with Spicy Sour Cream

Prep time: 10 minutes | Cook time: 35 minutes | Serves 4

1 teaspoon salt-free southwest chipotle seasoning	Olive oil cooking spray
2 large dark-orange sweet potatoes (1 lb), peeled, cut into ½-inch-thick slices	½ cup reduced-fat sour cream
	1 tablespoon sriracha sauce
	1 tablespoon chopped fresh cilantro

1 Heat oven to 425°F. Spray large cookie sheet with cooking spray. Place ¾ teaspoon of the seasoning in 1-gallon resealable food-storage plastic bag; add potatoes. Seal bag; shake until potatoes are evenly coated. Place potatoes in single layer on cookie sheet; spray lightly with cooking spray. Bake 20 minutes or until bottoms are golden brown. Turn potatoes; bake 10 to 15 minutes longer or until tender and bottoms are golden brown. 2 Meanwhile, in small bowl, stir sour cream, sriracha sauce, cilantro and remaining ¼ teaspoon seasoning; refrigerate until ready to serve. 3 Serve fries warm with spicy sour cream.

Per Serving:
calories: 120 | fat: 4g | protein: 2g | carbs: 20g | sugars: 7g | fiber: 3g | sodium: 140mg

Crab-Filled Mushrooms

Prep time: 5 minutes | Cook time: 25 minutes | Serves 10

20 large fresh mushroom caps	green onion
6 ounces canned crabmeat, rinsed, drained, and flaked	⅛ teaspoon freshly ground black pepper
½ cup crushed whole-wheat crackers	¼ cup chopped pimiento
2 tablespoons chopped fresh parsley	3 tablespoons extra-virgin olive oil
2 tablespoons finely chopped	10 tablespoons wheat germ

1. Preheat the oven to 350 degrees. Clean the mushrooms by dusting off any dirt on the cap with a mushroom brush or paper towel; remove the stems. 2. In a small mixing bowl, combine the crabmeat, crackers, parsley, onion, and pepper. 3. Place the mushroom caps in a 13-x-9-x-2-inch baking dish, crown side down. Stuff some of the crabmeat filling into each cap. Place a little pimiento on top of the filling. 4. Drizzle the olive oil over the caps and sprinkle each cap with ½ tablespoon wheat germ. Bake for 15–17 minutes. Transfer to a serving platter, and serve hot.

Per Serving:
calorie: 113 | fat: 6g | protein: 7g | carbs: 9g | sugars: 1g | fiber: 2g | sodium: 77mg

No-Added-Sugar Berries and Cream Yogurt Bowl

Prep time: 5 minutes | Cook time: 0 minutes | Serves 1

1 cup (200 g) plain nonfat Greek yogurt	½ cup (50 g) frozen mixed berries, thawed
1 tbsp (15 g) almond butter	Zest of ½ medium lemon

1. In a small bowl, combine the yogurt, almond butter, berries, and lemon zest.

Per Serving:
calorie: 270 | fat: 10g | protein: 27g | carbs: 21g | sugars: 15g | fiber: 3g | sodium: 89mg

Garlic Kale Chips

Prep time: 5 minutes | Cook time: 15 minutes | Serves 1

1 (8-ounce) bunch kale, trimmed and cut into 2-inch pieces	½ teaspoon sea salt
	¼ teaspoon garlic powder
1 tablespoon extra-virgin olive oil	Pinch cayenne (optional, to taste)

1. Preheat the oven to 350°F. Line two baking sheets with parchment paper. 2. Wash the kale and pat it completely dry. 3. In a large bowl, toss the kale with the olive oil, sea salt, garlic powder, and cayenne, if using. 4. Spread the kale in a single layer on the prepared baking sheets. 5. Bake until crisp, 12 to 15 minutes, rotating the sheets once.

Per Serving:
calorie: 78 | fat: 5g | protein: 3g | carbs: 7g | sugars: 2g | fiber: 3g | sodium: 416mg

Gruyere Apple Spread

Prep time: 5 minutes | Cook time: 5 minutes | Serves 20

4 ounces fat-free cream cheese, softened	½ cup shredded apple (unpeeled)
½ cup low-fat cottage cheese	2 tablespoons finely chopped pecans
4 ounces Gruyere cheese	2 teaspoons minced fresh chives
¼ teaspoon dry mustard	
⅛ teaspoon freshly ground black pepper	

1. Place the cheeses in a food processor, and blend until smooth. Add the mustard and pepper, and blend for 30 seconds. 2. Transfer the mixture to a serving bowl, and fold in the apple and pecans. Sprinkle the dip with chives. 3. Cover, and refrigerate the mixture for 1–2 hours. Serve chilled with crackers, or stuff into celery stalks.

Per Serving:
calorie: 46 | fat: 3g | protein: 4g | carbs: 1g | sugars: 1g | fiber: 0g | sodium: 107mg

Turkey Rollups with Veggie Cream Cheese

Prep time: 10 minutes | Cook time: 0 minutes | Serves 2

¼ cup cream cheese, at room temperature	1 tablespoon chopped fresh chives
2 tablespoons finely chopped red onion	1 teaspoon Dijon mustard
2 tablespoons finely chopped red bell pepper	1 garlic clove, minced
	¼ teaspoon sea salt
	6 slices deli turkey

1. In a small bowl, mix the cream cheese, red onion, bell pepper, chives, mustard, garlic, and salt. 2. Spread the mixture on the turkey slices and roll up.

Per Serving:
calorie: 146 | fat: 1g | protein: 24g | carbs: 8g | sugars: 6g | fiber: 1g | sodium: 572mg

7-Layer Dip

Prep time: 10 minutes | Cook time: 35 minutes | Serves 6

Cashew Sour Cream	½ teaspoon chili powder
1 cup raw whole cashews, soaked in water to cover for 1 to 2 hours and then drained	¼ teaspoon garlic powder
½ cup avocado oil	½ cup grape or cherry tomatoes, halved
½ cup water	1 avocado, diced
¼ cup fresh lemon juice	¼ cup chopped yellow onion
2 tablespoons nutritional yeast	1 jalapeño chile, sliced
1 teaspoon fine sea salt	2 tablespoons chopped cilantro
Beans	6 ounces baked corn tortilla chips
½ cup dried black beans	1 English cucumber, sliced
2 cups water	2 carrots, sliced
½ teaspoon fine sea salt	6 celery stalks, cut into sticks

1. To make the cashew sour cream: In a blender, combine the cashews, oil, water, lemon juice, nutritional yeast, and salt. Blend on high speed, stopping to scrape down the sides of the container as needed, for about 2 minutes, until very smooth. (The sour cream can be made in advance and stored in an airtight container in the refrigerator for up to 5 days.) 2. To make the beans: Pour 1 cup water into the Instant Pot. In a 1½-quart stainless-steel bowl, combine the beans, the 2 cups water, and salt and stir to dissolve the salt. Place the bowl on a long-handled silicone steam rack, then, holding the handles of the steam rack, lower it into the Instant Pot. (If you don't have the long-handled rack, use the wire metal steam rack and a homemade sling) 3. Secure the lid and set the Pressure Release to Sealing. Select the Bean/Chili, Pressure Cook, or Manual setting and set the cooking time for 25 minutes at high pressure. (The pot will take about 10 minutes to come up to pressure before the cooking program begins.) 4. When the cooking program ends, let the pressure release naturally for at least 20 minutes, then move the Pressure Release to Venting to release any remaining steam. 5. Place a colander over a bowl. Open the pot and, wearing heat-resistant mitts, lift out the inner pot and drain the beans in the colander. Transfer the liquid captured in the bowl to a measuring cup, and pour the beans into the bowl. Add ¼ cup of the cooking liquid to the beans and, using a potato masher or fork, mash the beans to your desired consistency, adding more cooking liquid as needed. Stir in the chili powder and garlic powder. 6. Using a rubber spatula, spread the black beans in an even layer in a clear-glass serving dish. Spread the cashew sour cream in an even layer on top of the beans. Add layers of the tomatoes, avocado, onion, jalapeño, and cilantro. (At this point, you can cover and refrigerate the assembled dip for up to 1 day.) Serve accompanied with the tortilla chips, cucumber, carrots, and celery on the side.

Per Serving:
calories: 259 | fat: 8g | protein: 8g | carbs: 41g | sugars: 3g | fiber: 8g | sodium: 811mg

Chicken Kabobs

Prep time: 5 minutes | Cook time: 20 minutes | Serves 6

1 pound boneless, skinless chicken breast	3 tablespoons dry vermouth
3 tablespoons light soy sauce	1 large clove garlic, finely chopped
One 1-inch cube of fresh ginger root, finely chopped	12 watercress sprigs
3 tablespoons extra-virgin olive oil	2 large lemons, cut into wedges

1. Cut the chicken into 1-inch cubes and place in a shallow bowl. 2. In a small bowl, combine the soy sauce, ginger root, oil, vermouth, and garlic and pour over the chicken. Cover the chicken, and let marinate for at least 1 hour (or overnight). 3. Thread the chicken onto 12 metal or wooden skewers (remember to soak wooden skewers in water before using). Grill or broil 6 inches from the heat source for 8 minutes, turning frequently. 4. Arrange the skewers on a platter and garnish with the watercress and lemon wedges. Serve hot with additional soy sauce, if desired.

Per Serving:
calorie: 187 | fat: 10g | protein: 18g | carbs: 4g | sugars: 2g | fiber: 1g | sodium: 158mg

Caramelized Onion–Shrimp Spread

Prep time: 30 minutes | Cook time: 20 minutes | Serves 18

1 tablespoon butter (do not use margarine)	cream cheese, softened
½ medium onion, thinly sliced (about ½ cup)	1 bag (4 oz) frozen cooked salad shrimp, thawed, well drained (about 1 cup)
1 clove garlic, finely chopped	1 teaspoon chopped fresh chives
¼ cup apple jelly	36 whole-grain crackers
1 container (8 oz) reduced-fat	

1 In 1-quart saucepan, melt butter over medium-low heat. Add onion; cook 15 minutes, stirring frequently. Add garlic; cook 1 minute, stirring occasionally, until onion and garlic are tender and browned. Stir in apple jelly. Cook, stirring constantly, until melted. Remove from heat. Let stand 5 minutes to cool. 2 Meanwhile, in small bowl, stir together cream cheese and shrimp. On 8-inch plate, spread shrimp mixture into a 5-inch round. 3 Spoon onion mixture over shrimp mixture. Sprinkle with chives. Serve with crackers.

Per Serving:
calories: 90 | fat: 4g | protein: 3g | carbs: 10g | sugars: 3g | fiber: 1g | sodium: 140mg

Cocoa Coated Almonds

Prep time: 5 minutes | Cook time: 15 minutes | Serves 4

1 cup almonds	2 packets powdered stevia
1 tablespoon cocoa powder	

1. Preheat the oven to 350°F. Line a baking sheet with parchment paper. 2. Spread the almonds in a single layer on the baking sheet. Bake for 5 minutes. 3. While the almonds bake, in a small bowl, mix the cocoa and stevia well. Add the hot almonds to the bowl. Toss to combine. 4. Return the almonds to the baking sheet and bake until fragrant, about 5 minutes more.

Per Serving:

calorie: 143 | fat: 12g | protein: 5g | carbs: 6g | sugars: 1g | fiber: 3g | sodium: 1mg

Fresh Dill Dip

Prep time: 5 minutes | Cook time: 5 minutes | Serves 6

1 cup plain fat-free yogurt	fresh chives
¼ teaspoon salt	1 tablespoon finely chopped fresh dill
¼ teaspoon freshly ground black pepper	1 tablespoon apple cider vinegar
¼ cup minced parsley	
2 tablespoons finely chopped	

1. In a small bowl, combine all the ingredients. Chill for 2–4 hours. Serve with fresh cut vegetables.

Per Serving:

calorie: 20 | fat: 0g | protein: 2g | carbs: 3g | sugars: 2g | fiber: 0g | sodium: 120mg

Baked Scallops

Prep time: 5 minutes | Cook time: 10 minutes | Serves 4

12 ounces fresh bay or dry sea scallops	
1½ teaspoons salt-free pickling spices	1 red bell pepper, cut into thin strips
½ cup cider vinegar	1 head butter lettuce, rinsed and dried
¼ cup water	
1 tablespoon finely chopped onion	⅓ cup sesame seeds, toasted

1. Preheat the oven to 350 degrees. Wash the scallops in cool water, and cut any scallops that are too big in half. 2. Spread the scallops out in a large baking dish (be careful not to overlap them). In a small bowl, combine the spices, cider vinegar, water, onion, and pepper; pour the mixture over the scallops. Season with salt, if desired. 3. Cover the baking dish and bake for 7 minutes. Remove from the oven, and allow the scallops to chill in the refrigerator (leave them in the cooking liquid/vegetable mixture). 4. Just before serving, place the lettuce leaves on individual plates or a platter, and place the scallops and vegetables over the top. Sprinkle with sesame seeds before serving.

Per Serving:

calorie: 159 | fat: 8g | protein: 14g | carbs: 7g | sugars: 2g | fiber: 3g | sodium: 344mg

Kale Chip Nachos

Prep time: 10 minutes | Cook time: 20 minutes | Serves 2 to 4

1 bunch kale, torn into bite-size pieces	½ teaspoon ground coriander
3 tablespoons extra-virgin olive oil, divided	1 teaspoon chili powder
	Optional Toppings
2 teaspoons ground cumin, divided	Avocado slices
	Salsa
1 large sweet potato, cut into ¼-inch-thick rounds	Jicama, sliced
	Red onion, sliced
	Fresh cilantro
1 (15-ounce) can black beans, rinsed and drained	Fresh chiles, minced
	Fresh tomatoes, diced

1. Preheat the oven to 225°F. Line a baking sheet with parchment paper. 2. In a large bowl, toss the kale with 1 tablespoon of oil and 1 teaspoon of cumin. Use your hands to massage the kale and evenly distribute the oil. 3. Spread the kale in a single even layer on the prepared baking sheet. (You may need two lined baking sheets for this.) Bake for 15 minutes, then flip and toss, and bake for another 5 to 10 minutes. 4. Meanwhile, heat 1 tablespoon of oil in a large skillet over medium-high heat. Arrange the sweet potato rounds in a single layer in the skillet, cover, and let them cook until they begin to brown on the bottom, about 3 minutes. Flip the potatoes over and cook for 3 to 5 minutes more. 5. Add the black beans to the skillet with the remaining 1 tablespoon of oil, remaining 1 teaspoon of cumin, the coriander, and chili powder. Cook for 3 minutes, then set aside and keep warm if the kale is not yet finished baking. 6. Serve on a platter, starting with the kale as a base, topped with sweet potatoes, black beans, and finally, any optional toppings. 7. Store any leftovers in an airtight container in the refrigerator for 3 to 4 days.

Per Serving:

calorie: 296 | fat: 14g | protein: 10g | carbs: 34g | sugars: 2g | fiber: 12g | sodium: 599mg

Creamy Spinach Dip

Prep time: 13 minutes | Cook time: 5 minutes | Serves 11

8 ounces low-fat cream cheese	¼ teaspoon black pepper
1 cup low-fat sour cream	10 ounces frozen spinach
½ cup finely chopped onion	12 ounces reduced-fat shredded Monterey Jack cheese
½ cup no-sodium vegetable broth	
5 cloves garlic, minced	12 ounces reduced-fat shredded Parmesan cheese
½ teaspoon salt	

1. Add cream cheese, sour cream, onion, vegetable broth, garlic, salt, pepper, and spinach to the inner pot of the Instant Pot. 2. Secure lid, make sure vent is set to sealing, and set to the Bean/Chili setting on high pressure for 5 minutes. 3. When done, do a manual release. 4. Add the cheeses and mix well until creamy and well combined.

Per Serving:

calorie: 274 | fat: 18g | protein: 19g | carbs: 10g | sugars: 3g | fiber: 1g | sodium: 948mg

Blood Sugar–Friendly Nutty Trail Mix

Prep time: 5 minutes | Cook time: 0 minutes | Serves 4

¼ cup (31 g) raw shelled pistachios	¼ cup (38 g) raisins
¼ cup (30 g) raw pecans	¼ cup (45 g) dairy-free dark chocolate chips
¼ cup (43 g) raw almonds	

1. In a medium bowl, combine the pistachios, pecans, almonds, raisins, and chocolate chips. 2. Divide the trail mix into four portions.

Per Serving:
calorie: 234 | fat: 17g | protein: 5g | carbs: 21g | sugars: 15g | fiber: 4g | sodium: 6mg

Green Goddess White Bean Dip

Prep time: 1 minutes | Cook time: 45 minutes | Makes 3 cups

1 cup dried navy, great Northern, or cannellini beans	plus 1 tablespoon
4 cups water	¼ cup firmly packed fresh flat-leaf parsley leaves
2 teaspoons fine sea salt	1 bunch chives, chopped
3 tablespoons fresh lemon juice	Leaves from 2 tarragon sprigs
¼ cup extra-virgin olive oil,	Freshly ground black pepper

1. Combine the beans, water, and 1 teaspoon of the salt in the Instant Pot and stir to dissolve the salt. 2. Secure the lid and set the Pressure Release to Sealing. Select the Bean/Chili, Pressure Cook, or Manual setting and set the cooking time for 30 minutes at high pressure if using navy or Great Northern beans or 40 minutes at high pressure if using cannellini beans. (The pot will take about 15 minutes to come up to pressure before the cooking program begins.) 3. When the cooking program ends, let the pressure release naturally for 15 minutes, then move the Pressure Release to Venting to release any remaining steam. Open the pot and scoop out and reserve ½ cup of the cooking liquid. Wearing heat-resistant mitts, lift out the inner pot and drain the beans in a colander. 4. In a food processor or blender, combine the beans, ½ cup cooking liquid, lemon juice, ¼ cup olive oil, ½ teaspoon parsley, chives, tarragon, remaining 1 teaspoon salt, and ½ teaspoon pepper. Process or blend on medium speed, stopping to scrape down the sides of the container as needed, for about 1 minute, until the mixture is smooth. 5. Transfer the dip to a serving bowl. Drizzle with the remaining 1 tablespoon olive oil and sprinkle with a few grinds of pepper. The dip will keep in an airtight container in the refrigerator for up to 1 week. Serve at room temperature or chilled.

Per Serving:
calorie: 70 | fat: 5g | protein: 3g | carbs: 8g | sugars: 1g | fiber: 4g | sodium: 782mg

Homemade Sun-Dried Tomato Salsa

Prep time: 5 minutes | Cook time: 0 minutes | Serves 4

½ (15-oz [425-g]) can no-salt-added diced tomatoes, drained	1 clove garlic
6 tbsp (20 g) julienned sun-dried tomatoes (see Tip)	⅛ cup (3 g) fresh basil leaves
	1 tsp balsamic vinegar
1½ cups (330 g) canned artichoke hearts, drained	2 tbsp (30 ml) olive oil
	Sea salt, as needed
	Black pepper, as needed

1. In a food processor or blender, combine the diced tomatoes, sun-dried tomatoes, artichoke hearts, garlic, basil, vinegar, oil, sea salt, and black pepper. Process or blend the ingredients to the desired consistency.

Per Serving:
calorie: 131 | fat: 7g | protein: 2g | carbs: 13g | sugars: 3g | fiber: 4g | sodium: 279mg

Almond Milk Nut Butter Mocha Smoothie

Prep time: 5 minutes | Cook time: 0 minutes | Serves 1

1 cup almond milk	1 to 2 (1-gram) packets stevia (or to taste)
2 tablespoons almond butter	
1 tablespoon cocoa powder	¼ teaspoon almond extract
1 teaspoon espresso powder (or to taste)	½ cup crushed ice

1. In a blender, combine all of the ingredients and blend on high until smooth.

Per Serving:
calorie: 249 | fat: 21g | protein: 9g | carbs: 12g | sugars: 2g | fiber: 6g | sodium: 174mg

Chapter 7 Vegetables and Sides

Potatoes with Parsley

Prep time: 10 minutes | Cook time: 5 minutes | Serves 4

3 tablespoons margarine, divided
2 pounds medium red potatoes (about 2 ounces each), halved lengthwise
1 clove garlic, minced
½ teaspoon salt
½ cup low-sodium chicken broth
2 tablespoons chopped fresh parsley

1. Place 1 tablespoon margarine in the inner pot of the Instant Pot and select Sauté. 2. After margarine is melted, add potatoes, garlic, and salt, stirring well. 3. Sauté 4 minutes, stirring frequently. 4. Add chicken broth and stir well. 5. Seal lid, make sure vent is on sealing, then select Manual for 5 minutes on high pressure. 6. When cooking time is up, manually release the pressure. 7. Strain potatoes, toss with remaining 2 tablespoons margarine and chopped parsley, and serve immediately.

Per Serving:
calories: 237 | fat: 9g | protein: 5g | carbs: 37g | sugars: 3g | fiber: 4g | sodium: 389mg

Balsamic Brussels Sprouts

Prep time: 5 minutes | Cook time: 12 minutes | Serves 4

2 cups trimmed and halved fresh Brussels sprouts
2 tablespoons olive oil
¼ teaspoon salt
¼ teaspoon ground black pepper
2 tablespoons balsamic vinegar
2 slices cooked sugar-free bacon, crumbled

1. In a large bowl, toss Brussels sprouts in olive oil, then sprinkle with salt and pepper. Place into ungreased air fryer basket. Adjust the temperature to 375°F (191°C) and set the timer for 12 minutes, shaking the basket halfway through cooking. Brussels sprouts will be tender and browned when done. 2. Place sprouts in a large serving dish and drizzle with balsamic vinegar. Sprinkle bacon over top. Serve warm.

Per Serving:
calories: 114 | fat: 9g | protein: 4g | carbs: 6g | net carbs: 4g | fiber: 2g

Cauliflower with Lime Juice

Prep time: 10 minutes | Cook time: 7 minutes | Serves 4

2 cups chopped cauliflower florets
2 tablespoons coconut oil, melted
2 teaspoons chili powder
½ teaspoon garlic powder
1 medium lime
2 tablespoons chopped cilantro

1. In a large bowl, toss cauliflower with coconut oil. Sprinkle with chili powder and garlic powder. Place seasoned cauliflower into the air fryer basket. 2. Adjust the temperature to 350°F (177°C) and set the timer for 7 minutes. 3. Cauliflower will be tender and begin to turn golden at the edges. Place into a serving bowl. 4. Cut the lime into quarters and squeeze juice over cauliflower. Garnish with cilantro.

Per Serving:
calories: 80 | fat: 7g | protein: 1g | carbs: 5g | fiber: 2g | sodium: 55mg

Italian Wild Mushrooms

Prep time: 30 minutes | Cook time: 3 minutes | Serves 10

2 tablespoons canola oil
2 large onions, chopped
4 garlic cloves, minced
3 large red bell peppers, chopped
3 large green bell peppers, chopped
12-ounce package oyster mushrooms, cleaned and chopped
3 fresh bay leaves
10 fresh basil leaves, chopped
1 teaspoon salt
1½ teaspoons pepper
28-ounce can Italian plum tomatoes, crushed or chopped

1. Press Sauté on the Instant Pot and add in the oil. Once the oil is heated, add the onions, garlic, peppers, and mushroom to the oil. Sauté just until mushrooms begin to turn brown. 2. Add remaining ingredients. Stir well. 3. Secure the lid and make sure vent is set to sealing. Press Manual and set time for 3 minutes. 4. When cook time is up, release the pressure manually. Discard bay leaves.

Per Serving:
calories: 82 | fat: 3g | protein: 3g | carbs: 13g | sugars: 8g | fiber: 4g | sodium: 356mg

Carrots Marsala

Prep time: 5 minutes | Cook time: 10 minutes | Serves 6

10 carrots (about 1 pound), peeled and diagonally sliced
¼ cup Marsala wine
¼ cup water
1 tablespoon extra-virgin olive oil
⅛ teaspoon freshly ground black pepper
1 tablespoon finely chopped fresh parsley

1. In a large saucepan, combine the carrots, wine, water, oil, and pepper. Bring to a boil, cover, reduce the heat, and simmer for 8–10 minutes, until the carrots are just tender, basting occasionally. Taste, and add salt, if desired. 2. Transfer to a serving dish, spoon any juices on top, and sprinkle with parsley.

Per Serving:
calories: 48 | fat: 2.4g | protein: 0.66g | carbs: 6.49g | sugars: 2.76g | fiber: 2.3g | sodium: 46mg

Spicy Mustard Greens

Prep time: 10 minutes | Cook time: 15 minutes | Serves 4

½ cup store-bought low-sodium vegetable broth
½ sweet onion, chopped
1 celery stalk, roughly chopped
½ large red bell pepper, thinly sliced
2 garlic cloves, minced
1 bunch mustard greens, roughly chopped

1. In a large cast iron pan, bring the broth to a simmer over medium heat. 2. Add the onion, celery, bell pepper, and garlic. Cook, uncovered, stirring occasionally, for 3 to 5 minutes, or until the onion is translucent. 3. Add the mustard greens. Cover the pan, reduce the heat to low, and cook for 10 minutes, or until the greens are wilted. 4. Serve warm.

Per Serving:
calories: 32 | fat: 0.27g | protein: 1.35g | carbs: 6.85g | sugars: 4.09g | fiber: 1.5g | sodium: 28mg

Lemon-Garlic Mushrooms

Prep time: 10 minutes | Cook time: 10 to 15 minutes | Serves 6

12 ounces (340 g) sliced mushrooms	1 teaspoon minced garlic
1 tablespoon avocado oil	1 teaspoon freshly squeezed lemon juice
Sea salt and freshly ground black pepper, to taste	½ teaspoon red pepper flakes
3 tablespoons unsalted butter	2 tablespoons chopped fresh parsley

1. Place the mushrooms in a medium bowl and toss with the oil. Season to taste with salt and pepper. 2. Place the mushrooms in a single layer in the air fryer basket. Set your air fryer to 375ºF (191ºC) and roast for 10 to 15 minutes, until the mushrooms are tender. 3. While the mushrooms cook, melt the butter in a small pot or skillet over medium-low heat. Stir in the garlic and cook for 30 seconds. Remove the pot from the heat and stir in the lemon juice and red pepper flakes. 4. Toss the mushrooms with the lemon-garlic butter and garnish with the parsley before serving.
Per Serving:
calories: 72| fat: 6g | protein: 2g | carbs: 3g | net carbs: 2g | fiber: 1g

Italian Roasted Vegetables

Prep time: 15 minutes | Cook time: 20 minutes | Serves 4

2 tablespoons extra-virgin olive oil	mushrooms
2 teaspoons chopped fresh oregano	2 cups cauliflower florets
1 teaspoon chopped fresh basil	1 zucchini, cut into 1-inch chunks
1 teaspoon minced garlic	2 cups cherry tomatoes
½ pound whole cremini	Sea salt
	Freshly ground black pepper

1. Preheat the oven to 400°F. Line a baking sheet with aluminum foil. 2. In a large bowl, stir together the oil, oregano, basil, and garlic. 3. Add the mushrooms, cauliflower, zucchini, and cherry tomatoes and toss to coat. 4. Transfer the vegetables to the baking sheet and roast until they are tender and lightly browned, about 20 minutes. 5. Season with salt and pepper and serve.
Per Serving:
calories: 297 | fat: 7.79g | protein: 8.18g | carbs: 58.58g | sugars: 12.81g | fiber: 9.9g | sodium: 182mg

Teriyaki Green Beans

Prep time: 15 minutes | Cook time: 20 minutes | Serves 4

10 oz (283 g) button mushrooms, thinly sliced	½ tsp smoked paprika
1 tbsp (15 ml) sesame oil, divided	2 cloves garlic, minced
2 tbsp (30 ml) low-sodium tamari, divided	1 lb (454 g) fresh green beans, trimmed and washed
	1 cup (165 g) finely chopped fresh pineapple

1. In a large bowl, combine the mushrooms with ½ tablespoon (8 ml) of the oil, 1½ tablespoons (23 ml) of the tamari, and the smoked paprika. Let the mushrooms rest for 10 minutes to allow them to absorb the marinade. 2. If you will be roasting the mushrooms, preheat the oven to 400°F (204°C) while the mushrooms marinate. Line a large baking sheet with parchment paper. 3. Spread out the mushrooms on the prepared baking sheet. Roast them for 20 minutes, or until they are very crispy. 4. Alternatively, if you will be stir-frying the mushrooms, heat a small skillet over medium heat. Add the mushrooms and stir-fry them for about 5 minutes, until they are tender. Note that this cooking method will yield mushrooms that are less crispy than roasting, but they will still be delicious. Meanwhile, heat the remaining ½ tablespoon (8 ml) of oil in a large skillet over medium-high heat. Add the garlic and cook it for 2 minutes, or until it is brown and fragrant. Add the green beans and pineapple. Cook the mixture for 10 minutes, until the green beans are bright green and starting to soften. Add the crispy mushrooms to the skillet. Stir to combine, then serve.
Per Serving:
calorie: 106 | fat: 3g | protein: 6g | carbs: 17g | sugars: 9g | fiber: 5g | sodium: 257mg

Sweet-and-Sour Cabbage Slaw

Prep time: 10 minutes | Cook time: 0 minutes | Serves 2

2 tablespoons apple cider vinegar	1 tart apple, cored and diced
1 tablespoon granulated stevia	½ cup shredded carrot
2 cups angel hair cabbage	2 medium scallions, sliced
	2 tablespoons sliced almonds

1. In a medium bowl, stir together the vinegar and stevia. 2. In a large bowl, mix together the cabbage, apple, carrot, and scallions. 3. Pour the sweetened vinegar over the vegetable mixture. Toss to combine. 4. Garnish with the sliced almonds and serve.
Per Serving:
calories: 125 | fat: 0.99g | protein: 2.29g | carbs: 29.51g | sugars: 20.87g | fiber: 5.4g | sodium: 47mg

Mushroom Cassoulets

Prep time: 5 minutes | Cook time: 30 minutes | Serves 6

1 pound mushrooms, sliced	Leaves from 1 celery stalk
½ cup lentils, cooked	2 tablespoons lemon juice
1 medium onion, chopped	⅛ teaspoon freshly ground black pepper
1 cup low-sodium chicken broth	½ cup wheat germ
1 sprig thyme	2 tablespoons extra-virgin olive oil
1 bay leaf	

1. Preheat the oven to 350 degrees. 2. In a saucepan, combine the mushrooms, lentils, onion, and chicken broth. Tie together the thyme, bay leaf, and celery leaves and add to the mushrooms. 3. Add the lemon juice and pepper, and bring to a boil. Boil until the liquid is reduced, about 10 minutes. Remove the bundle of herbs. 4. Divide the mushroom mixture equally into small ramekins. Mix the wheat germ and oil together, and sprinkle on top of each casserole. 5. Bake at 350 degrees for 20 minutes or until the tops are golden brown. Remove from the oven, and let cool slightly before serving. Add salt if desired.
Per Serving:
calories: 114 | fat: 6.01g | protein: 6.19g | carbs: 11.63g | sugars: 2.49g | fiber: 2.5g | sodium: 21mg

Sesame Broccoli

Prep time: 5 minutes | Cook time: 4 minutes | Serves 3

1 tablespoon tahini	ginger
1½ tablespoons coconut nectar	¼ teaspoon garlic powder
1½ tablespoons tamari	4–5 cups broccoli florets
1 teaspoon apple cider vinegar	2 teaspoons sesame seeds (raw or lightly toasted)
1 teaspoon freshly grated	

1. In a large bowl, whisk together the tahini, nectar, tamari, vinegar, ginger, and garlic powder. Set aside. Place a steamer basket in a large pot with 2" of water. Bring to a boil over high heat. Place the broccoli in the basket and steam for 3 to 4 minutes, or until it turns bright green and is just becoming tender. Drain and pat dry the broccoli. Add the broccoli to the marinade, and toss to coat thoroughly. Sprinkle with the sesame seeds and serve.

Per Serving:
calorie: 115 | fat: 4g | protein: 5g | carbs: 17g | sugars: 8g | fiber: 5g | sodium: 558mg

Roasted Garlic

Prep time: 5 minutes | Cook time: 20 minutes | Makes 12 cloves

1 medium head garlic	2 teaspoons avocado oil

1. Remove any hanging excess peel from the garlic but leave the cloves covered. Cut off ¼ of the head of garlic, exposing the tips of the cloves. 2. Drizzle with avocado oil. Place the garlic head into a small sheet of aluminum foil, completely enclosing it. Place it into the air fryer basket. 3. Adjust the temperature to 400ºF (204ºC) and air fry for 20 minutes. If your garlic head is a bit smaller, check it after 15 minutes. 4. When done, garlic should be golden brown and very soft. 5. To serve, cloves should pop out and easily be spread or sliced. Store in an airtight container in the refrigerator up to 5 days. You may also freeze individual cloves on a baking sheet, then store together in a freezer-safe storage bag once frozen.

Per Serving:
calories: 8 | fat: 1g | protein: 0g | carbs: 0g | fiber: 0g | sodium: 0mg

Sweet Potato Crisps

Prep time: 10 minutes | Cook time: 30 minutes | Serves 3

1 pound sweet potatoes	½ tablespoon pure maple syrup
½ tablespoon balsamic vinegar	Rounded ¼ teaspoon sea salt

1. Preheat the oven to 400°F. Line a large baking sheet with parchment paper. 2. Peel the sweet potatoes, then use the peeler to continue to make sweet potato peelings. (Alternatively, you can push peeled sweet potatoes through a food processor slicing blade.) Transfer the peelings to a large mixing bowl and use your hands to toss with the vinegar and syrup, coating them as evenly as possible. Spread the peelings on the prepared baking sheet, spacing well. Sprinkle with the salt. Bake for 30 minutes, tossing once or twice. The pieces around the edges of the pan can get brown quickly, so move the chips around during baking. Turn off the oven and let the chips sit in the residual heat for 20 minutes, stir again, and let sit for another 15 to 20 minutes, until they crisp up. Remove, and snack!

Per Serving:
calorie: 94 | fat: 0g | protein: 2g | carbs: 22g | sugars: 8g | fiber: 3g | sodium: 326mg

Sautéed Garlicky Mushrooms

Prep time: 10 minutes | Cook time: 12 minutes | Serves 4

1 tablespoon butter	garlic
2 teaspoons extra-virgin olive oil	1 teaspoon chopped fresh thyme
2 pounds button mushrooms, halved	Sea salt
2 teaspoons minced fresh	Freshly ground black pepper

1. Place a large skillet over medium-high heat and add the butter and olive oil. 2. Sauté the mushrooms, stirring occasionally, until they are lightly caramelized and tender, about 10 minutes. 3. Add the garlic and thyme and sauté for 2 more minutes. 4. Season the mushrooms with salt and pepper before serving.

Per Serving:
calories: 88 | fat: 4.67g | protein: 4.98g | carbs: 9.66g | sugars: 5.69g | fiber: 3.2g | sodium: 189mg

Crispy Green Beans

Prep time: 5 minutes | Cook time: 8 minutes | Serves 4

2 teaspoons olive oil	¼ teaspoon salt
½ pound (227 g) fresh green beans, ends trimmed	¼ teaspoon ground black pepper

1. In a large bowl, drizzle olive oil over green beans and sprinkle with salt and pepper. 2. Place green beans into ungreased air fryer basket. Adjust the temperature to 350ºF (177ºC) and set the timer for 8 minutes, shaking the basket two times during cooking. Green beans will be dark golden and crispy at the edges when done. Serve warm.

Per Serving:
calories: 33 | fat: 3g | protein: 1g | carbs: 3g | fiber: 1g | sodium: 147mg

Sautéed Spinach and Tomatoes

Prep time: 5 minutes | Cook time: 10 minutes | Serves 4

1 tablespoon extra-virgin olive oil	3 spinach bunches, trimmed
1 cup cherry tomatoes, halved	2 garlic cloves, minced
	¼ teaspoon salt

1. In a large skillet, heat the oil over medium heat. 2. Add the tomatoes, and cook until the skins begin to blister and split, about 2 minutes. 3. Add the spinach in batches, waiting for each batch to wilt slightly before adding the next batch. Stir continuously for 3 to 4 minutes until the spinach is tender. 4. Add the garlic to the skillet, and toss until fragrant, about 30 seconds. 5. Drain the excess liquid from the pan. Add the salt. Stir well and serve.

Per Serving:
calories: 52 | fat: 4g | protein: 2g | carbs: 4g | sugars: 1g | fiber: 2g | sodium: 183mg

Perfect Sweet Potatoes

Prep time: 5 minutes | Cook time: 15 minutes | Serves 4 to 6

4–6 medium sweet potatoes	1 cup of water

1. Scrub skin of sweet potatoes with a brush until clean. Pour water into inner pot of the Instant Pot. Place steamer basket in the bottom of the inner pot. Place sweet potatoes on top of steamer basket. 2. Secure the lid and turn valve to seal. 3. Select the Manual mode and set to pressure cook on high for 15 minutes. 4. Allow pressure to release naturally (about 10 minutes). 5. Once the pressure valve lowers, remove lid and serve immediately.

Per Serving:
calories: 112 | fat: 0g | protein: 2g | carbs: 26g | sugars: 5g | fiber: 4g | sodium: 72mg

Sun-Dried Tomato Brussels Sprouts

Prep time: 15 minutes | Cook time: 20 minutes | Serves 4

1 pound Brussels sprouts, trimmed and halved	½ cup sun-dried tomatoes, chopped
1 tablespoon extra-virgin olive oil	2 tablespoons freshly squeezed lemon juice
Sea salt	1 teaspoon lemon zest
Freshly ground black pepper	

1. Preheat the oven to 400°F. Line a large baking sheet with aluminum foil. 2. In a large bowl, toss the Brussels sprouts with oil and season with salt and pepper. 3. Spread the Brussels sprouts on the baking sheet in a single layer. 4. Roast the sprouts until they are caramelized, about 20 minutes. 5. Transfer the sprouts to a serving bowl. Mix in the sun-dried tomatoes, lemon juice, and lemon zest. 6. Stir to combine, and serve.

Per Serving:
calories: 98 | fat: 3.94g | protein: 4.83g | carbs: 14.62g | sugars: 5.26g | fiber: 5.2g | sodium: 191mg

Green Bean and Radish Potato Salad

Prep time: 10 minutes | Cook time: 20 minutes | Serves 6

Kosher salt	lemon juice
6 ounces fresh green beans, trimmed and cut into 1-inch pieces	1 tablespoon Dijon or whole-grain mustard
	1 shallot, minced
1½ pounds fingerling potatoes	8 radishes, thinly sliced
⅓ cup extra-virgin olive oil	¼ cup fresh dill, chopped
2 tablespoons freshly squeezed	Freshly ground black pepper

1. Place a small saucepan filled three-quarters full of water and a pinch of salt over high heat and bring it to a boil. Add the green beans and boil for 2 minutes, then transfer them with a slotted spoon to a colander. Run the beans under cold running water until cool and transfer to a medium bowl. 2. Place the potatoes in the same pot of boiling water, reduce the heat to low, and simmer until tender, about 12 minutes. 3. Meanwhile, combine the extra-virgin olive oil, lemon juice, mustard, and shallot in a jar. Seal with the lid and shake vigorously. If you don't have a jar with a fitted lid, you can also whisk the ingredients in a bowl. 4. Transfer the cooked potatoes to a colander and cool them under cold running water. When they're cool enough to handle, slice the potatoes into thin rounds. 5. Add the potatoes and dressing to the bowl with the green beans, along with the radishes and dill, and toss to combine. 6. Season with salt and pepper and serve. 7. Store any leftovers in an airtight container in the refrigerator for 3 to 4 days.

Per Serving:
calories: 206 | fat: 12.18g | protein: 2.86g | carbs: 22.67g | sugars: 1.3g | fiber: 3.3g | sodium: 202mg

Sautéed Spinach with Parmesan and Almonds

Prep time: 5 minutes | Cook time: 5 minutes | Serves 2

2 teaspoons extra-virgin olive oil	2 teaspoons balsamic vinegar
2 tablespoons sliced almonds	⅛ teaspoon salt
2 garlic cloves, minced	2 tablespoons soy Parmesan cheese
2 (5-ounce) bags prewashed spinach	Freshly ground black pepper, to season

1. In a large nonstick skillet or Dutch oven set over medium-high heat, heat the olive oil. 2. Add the almonds and garlic. Cook for 30 seconds, stirring, or until fragrant. 3. Add the spinach. Cook for about 2 minutes, stirring, until just wilted. Remove the pan from the heat. 4. Stir in the balsamic vinegar and salt. 5. Sprinkle with the soy Parmesan cheese. Season with pepper and serve immediately.

Per Serving:
calories: 84 | fat: 6.62g | protein: 2.55g | carbs: 4.26g | sugars: 0.96g | fiber: 0.9g | sodium: 262mg

Brussels Sprouts with Pecans and Gorgonzola

Prep time: 10 minutes | Cook time: 25 minutes | Serves 4

½ cup pecans	Salt and freshly ground black pepper, to taste
1½ pounds (680 g) fresh Brussels sprouts, trimmed and quartered	¼ cup crumbled Gorgonzola cheese
2 tablespoons olive oil	

1. Spread the pecans in a single layer of the air fryer and set the heat to 350°F (177°C). Air fry for 3 to 5 minutes until the pecans are lightly browned and fragrant. Transfer the pecans to a plate and continue preheating the air fryer, increasing the heat to 400°F (204°C). 2. In a large bowl, toss the Brussels sprouts with the olive oil and season with salt and black pepper to taste. 3. Working in batches if necessary, arrange the Brussels sprouts in a single layer in the air fryer basket. Pausing halfway through the baking time to shake the basket, air fry for 20 to 25 minutes until the sprouts are tender and starting to brown on the edges. 4. Transfer the sprouts to a serving bowl and top with the toasted pecans and Gorgonzola. Serve warm or at room temperature.

Per Serving:
calories: 253 | fat: 18g | protein: 9g | carbs: 17g | fiber: 8g | sodium: 96mg

Asparagus with Vinaigrette

Prep time: 5 minutes | Cook time: 10 minutes | Serves 6

1½ pounds fresh or frozen asparagus (thin pieces)	½ cup water
½ cup red wine vinegar	1 tablespoon extra-virgin olive oil
½ teaspoon dried or 1 teaspoon fresh tarragon	1⅓ tablespoons Dijon mustard
2 tablespoons finely chopped fresh chives	1 pound fresh spinach leaves, trimmed of stems, washed, and dried
3 tablespoons finely chopped fresh parsley	2 large tomatoes, cut into wedges

1. Place 1 inch of water in a pot, and place a steamer inside. Arrange the asparagus on top of the steamer. Steam fresh asparagus for 4 minutes or frozen asparagus for 6–8 minutes. Immediately rinse the asparagus under cold water to stop the cooking. (This helps keep asparagus bright green and crunchy.) Set aside. 2. In a small bowl or salad cruet, combine the remaining ingredients except the spinach and tomatoes. Mix, or shake well. 3. To serve, line plates with the spinach leaves, and place the asparagus on top of the spinach. Garnish with the tomato wedges, and spoon any remaining dressing on top.

Per Serving:
calories: 72 | fat: 1.82g | protein: 6.61g | carbs: 10.2g | sugars: 1.98g | fiber: 4.8g | sodium: 133mg

Roasted Lemon and Garlic Broccoli

Prep time: 10 minutes | Cook time: 25 minutes | Serves 8

2 large broccoli heads, cut into florets	¼ teaspoon salt
3 garlic cloves, minced	¼ teaspoon freshly ground black pepper
2 tablespoons extra-virgin olive oil	2 tablespoons freshly squeezed lemon juice

1. Preheat the oven to 425°F. 2. On a rimmed baking sheet, toss the broccoli, garlic, and olive oil. Season with the salt and pepper. 3. Roast, tossing occasionally, for 25 to 30 minutes until tender and browned. Season with the lemon juice and serve.

Per Serving:
calories: 30 | fat: 2g | protein: 1g | carbs: 3g | sugars: 1g | fiber: 1g | sodium: 84mg

Roasted Delicata Squash

Prep time: 10 minutes | Cook time: 20 minutes | Serves 4

1 (1- to 1½-pound) delicata squash, halved, seeded, cut into ½-inch-thick strips	½ teaspoon dried thyme
	¼ teaspoon salt
1 tablespoon extra-virgin olive oil	¼ teaspoon freshly ground black pepper

1. Preheat the oven to 400°F. Line a baking sheet with parchment paper. 2. In a large mixing bowl, toss the squash strips with the olive oil, thyme, salt, and pepper. Arrange on the prepared baking sheet in a single layer. 3. Roast for 10 minutes, flip, and continue to roast for 10 more minutes until tender and lightly browned.

Per Serving:
calories: 79 | fat: 4g | protein: 1g | carbs: 12g | sugars: 3g | fiber: 2g | sodium: 123mg

Sautéed Mixed Vegetables

Prep time: 20 minutes | Cook time: 8 minutes | Serves 4

2 teaspoons extra-virgin olive oil	1 red bell pepper, seeded and cut into long strips
2 carrots, peeled and sliced	1 cup green beans, trimmed
4 cups broccoli florets	Sea salt
4 cups cauliflower florets	Freshly ground black pepper

1. Place a large skillet over medium heat and add the olive oil. 2. Sauté the carrots, broccoli, and cauliflower until tender-crisp, about 6 minutes. 3. Add the bell pepper and green beans, and sauté 2 minutes more. 4. Season with salt and pepper, and serve.

Per Serving:
calories: 97 | fat: 3.16g | protein: 5.39g | carbs: 15.14g | sugars: 5.21g | fiber: 6g | sodium: 211mg

Spinach and Sweet Pepper Poppers

Prep time: 10 minutes | Cook time: 8 minutes | Makes 16 poppers

4 ounces (113 g) cream cheese, softened	½ teaspoon garlic powder
1 cup chopped fresh spinach leaves	8 mini sweet bell peppers, tops removed, seeded, and halved lengthwise

1. In a medium bowl, mix cream cheese, spinach, and garlic powder. Place 1 tablespoon mixture into each sweet pepper half and press down to smooth. 2. Place poppers into ungreased air fryer basket. Adjust the temperature to 400°F (204°C) and air fry for 8 minutes. Poppers will be done when cheese is browned on top and peppers are tender-crisp. Serve warm.

Per Serving:
calories: 31 | fat: 2g | protein: 1g | carbs: 3g | fiber: 0g | sodium: 34mg

Green Beans with Garlic and Onion

Prep time: 5 minutes | Cook time: 12 minutes | Serves 8

1 pound fresh green beans, trimmed and cut into 2-inch pieces	1 large garlic clove, minced
	1 tablespoon white vinegar
1 tablespoon extra-virgin olive oil	¼ cup Parmigiano-Reggiano cheese
1 small onion, chopped	⅛ teaspoon freshly ground black pepper

1. Steam the beans for 7 minutes or until just tender. Set aside. 2. In a skillet, heat the oil over low heat. Add the onion and garlic, and sauté for 4–5 minutes or until the onion is translucent. 3. Transfer the beans to a serving bowl, and add the onion mixture and vinegar, tossing well. Sprinkle with cheese and pepper, and serve.

Per Serving:
calories: 43 | fat: 2.87g | protein: 1.45g | carbs: 3.55g | sugars: 0.91g | fiber: 1.2g | sodium: 30mg

Wilted Kale and Chard

Prep time: 10 minutes | Cook time: 10 minutes | Serves 4

2 tablespoons extra-virgin olive oil	chopped
1 pound kale, coarse stems removed and leaves chopped	1 tablespoon freshly squeezed lemon juice
1 pound Swiss chard, coarse stems removed and leaves	½ teaspoon ground cardamom
	Sea salt
	Freshly ground black pepper

1. Place a large skillet over medium-high heat and add the olive oil. 2. Add the kale, chard, lemon juice, and cardamom to the skillet. Use tongs to toss the greens continuously until they are wilted, about 10 minutes or less. 3. Season the greens with salt and pepper. 4. Serve immediately.

Per Serving:
calories: 139 | fat: 8.06g | protein: 6.95g | carbs: 14.69g | sugars: 3.91g | fiber: 6g | sodium: 430mg

Parmesan Cauliflower Mash

Prep time: 7 minutes | Cook time: 5 minutes | Serves 4

1 head cauliflower, cored and cut into large florets	¾ cup freshly grated Parmesan cheese
½ teaspoon kosher salt	1 tablespoon unsalted butter or ghee (optional)
½ teaspoon garlic pepper	Chopped fresh chives
2 tablespoons plain Greek yogurt	

1. Pour 1 cup of water into the electric pressure cooker and insert a steamer basket or wire rack. 2. Place the cauliflower in the basket. 3. Close and lock the lid of the pressure cooker. Set the valve to sealing. 4. Cook on high pressure for 5 minutes. 5. When the cooking is complete, hit Cancel and quick release the pressure. 6. Once the pin drops, unlock and remove the lid. 7. Remove the cauliflower from the pot and pour out the water. Return the cauliflower to the pot and add the salt, garlic pepper, yogurt, and cheese. Use an immersion blender or potato masher to purée or mash the cauliflower in the pot. 8. Spoon into a serving bowl, and garnish with butter (if using) and chives.

Per Serving:
calories: 141 | fat: 6g | protein: 12g | carbs: 12g | sugars: 9g | fiber: 4g | sodium: 592mg

Bacon-Wrapped Asparagus

Prep time: 10 minutes | Cook time: 10 minutes | Serves 4

8 slices reduced-sodium bacon, cut in half	g) asparagus spears, trimmed of woody ends
16 thick (about 1 pound / 454	

1. Preheat the air fryer to 350°F (177°C). 2. Wrap a half piece of bacon around the center of each stalk of asparagus. 3. Working in batches, if necessary, arrange seam-side down in a single layer in the air fryer basket. Air fry for 10 minutes until the bacon is crisp and the stalks are tender.

Per Serving:
calories: 214| fat: 20g | protein: 7g | carbs: 1g | net carbs: 1g | fiber: 0g

Zucchini on the Half Shell

Prep time: 15 minutes | Cook time: 30 minutes | Serves 4 to 8

4 zucchini, cut lengthwise, seeded, pulp removed	1 cup coarsely chopped tomatoes
1 (13.4-ounce) box borlotti beans, rinsed	2 teaspoons Creole seasoning
½ onion, finely chopped	½ cup grated reduced-fat Cheddar cheese
1 garlic clove, minced	

1. Preheat the oven to 350°F. 2. Arrange the zucchini on a rimmed baking sheet in a single layer, cavity-side up. 3. Transfer the baking sheet to the oven, and bake for 10 minutes, or until the exterior of the zucchini is soft. 4. Meanwhile, in a small pan, combine the beans, onion, garlic, tomatoes, and Creole seasoning. Cook over medium heat, stirring often, for 3 to 5 minutes, or until the onion and garlic are translucent. Remove from the heat. 5. Remove the zucchini from the oven, and spoon the tomato and bean mixture into the cavities. 6. Sprinkle 1 tablespoon of cheese on top of each stuffed zucchini. 7. Return the baking sheet to the oven and cook for 10 to 15 minutes, or until the cheese is melted and golden brown. Serve warm and enjoy.

Per Serving:
calories: 63 | fat: 1.45g | protein: 5.13g | carbs: 8.66g | sugars: 4.81g | fiber: 2.7g | sodium: 177mg

Broccoli Cauliflower Bake

Prep time: 15 minutes | Cook time: 40 minutes | Serves 6

½ cup ground almonds	1 head cauliflower, cut into small florets
¼ cup grated Parmesan cheese	1 sweet onion, chopped
1 tablespoon butter, melted, plus 2 tablespoons butter	1 teaspoon minced garlic
Pinch freshly ground black pepper	2 tablespoons all-purpose flour
1 head broccoli, cut into small florets	1 cup skim milk
	2 ounces goat cheese
	¼ teaspoon ground nutmeg

1. Preheat the oven to 350°F. 2. In a small bowl, mix together the almonds, Parmesan cheese, melted butter, and pepper. Set it aside. 3. Place a large pot full of water over high heat and bring to a boil. 4. Blanch the broccoli and cauliflower for 1 minute, drain, and set them aside. 5. Place a large skillet over medium-high heat and melt the 2 tablespoons of butter. 6. Sauté the onion and garlic until tender, about 3 minutes. Whisk in the flour and cook, stirring constantly, for 1 minute. Whisk in the milk and cook, stirring constantly, until the sauce has thickened, about 4 minutes. 7. Remove the skillet from the heat and whisk in the goat cheese and nutmeg. 8. Add the broccoli and cauliflower, then spoon the mixture into a 1½-quart casserole dish. 9. Sprinkle the almond mixture over the top and bake until the casserole is heated through, about 30 minutes.

Per Serving:
calories: 212 | fat: 8g | protein: 13g | carbs: 27g | sugars: 10g | fiber: 7g | sodium: 241mg

Snow Peas with Sesame Seeds

Prep time: 5 minutes | **Cook time:** 5 minutes | **Serves 6**

2 cups water	¼ teaspoon salt
1 pound trimmed fresh snow peas	⅛ teaspoon freshly ground black pepper
3 tablespoons sesame seeds	1 teaspoon ground ginger
1 tablespoon chopped shallots	

1. In a saucepan over high heat, boil the water. Add the snow peas, and then turn off the heat. After 1 minute, rinse the snow peas under cold running water to stop the cooking process; drain. (This method of blanching helps the snow peas to retain their bright green color and crispness.) 2. In a skillet, toast the sesame seeds for 1 minute over medium heat. Add the snow peas, shallots, salt, pepper, and ginger. Continue sautéing for 1–2 minutes until the snow peas are coated with sesame seeds. Serve.

Per Serving:
calories: 59 | fat: 2.62g | protein: 3.01g | carbs: 6.71g | sugars: 3.18g | fiber: 2.5g | sodium: 104mg

Best Brown Rice

Prep time: 5 minutes | **Cook time:** 22 minutes | **Serves 6 to 12**

2 cups brown rice	2½ cups water

1. Rinse brown rice in a fine-mesh strainer. 2. Add rice and water to the inner pot of the Instant Pot. 3. Secure the lid and make sure vent is on sealing. 4. Use Manual setting and select 22 minutes cooking time on high pressure. 5. When cooking time is done, let the pressure release naturally for 10 minutes, then press Cancel and manually release any remaining pressure.

Per Serving:
calorie: 114 | fat: 1g | protein: 2g | carbs: 23g | sugars: 0g | fiber: 1g | sodium: 3mg

Horseradish Mashed Cauliflower

Prep time: 5 minutes | **Cook time:** 10 minutes | **Serves 4**

1 large head cauliflower (about 3 pounds), cut into small florets	horseradish
½ cup skim milk	¼ teaspoon sea salt
2 tablespoons prepared	2 teaspoons chopped fresh chives

1. Place a large pot of water on high heat and bring it to a boil. 2. Blanch the cauliflower until it is tender, about 5 minutes. 3. Drain the cauliflower completely and transfer it to a food processor. 4. Add the milk and horseradish to the cauliflower and purée until it is smooth and thick, about 2 minutes. Or mash it by hand with a potato masher. 5. Transfer the mashed cauliflower to a bowl and season with salt. 6. Serve immediately, topped with the chopped chives.

Per Serving:
calories: 102 | fat: 1g | protein: 8g | carbs: 19g | sugars: 9g | fiber: 7g | sodium: 292mg

Callaloo Redux

Prep time: 15 minutes | **Cook time:** 25 minutes | **Serves 6**

3 cups store-bought low-sodium vegetable broth	chunks
1 (13.5-ounce) can light coconut milk	1 small onion, chopped
¼ cup coconut cream	½ butternut squash, peeled, seeded, and cut into 4-inch chunks
1 tablespoon unsalted non-hydrogenated plant-based butter	1 bunch collard greens, stemmed and chopped
12 ounces okra, cut into 1-inch	1 hot pepper (Scotch bonnet or habanero)

1. In an electric pressure cooker, combine the vegetable broth, coconut milk, coconut cream, and butter. 2. Layer the okra, onion, squash, collard greens, and whole hot pepper on top. 3. Close and lock the lid, and set the pressure valve to sealing. 4. Select the Manual/Pressure Cook setting, and cook for 20 minutes. 5. Once cooking is complete, quick-release the pressure. Carefully remove the lid. 6. Remove and discard the hot pepper. Carefully transfer the callaloo to a blender, and blend until smooth. Serve spooned over grits.

Per Serving:
calories: 258 | fat: 21.43g | protein: 4.81g | carbs: 16.98g | sugars: 7.82g | fiber: 4.9g | sodium: 88mg

Radish Chips

Prep time: 10 minutes | **Cook time:** 5 minutes | **Serves 4**

2 cups water	½ teaspoon garlic powder
1 pound (454 g) radishes	2 tablespoons coconut oil, melted
¼ teaspoon onion powder	
¼ teaspoon paprika	

1. Place water in a medium saucepan and bring to a boil on stovetop. 2. Remove the top and bottom from each radish, then use a mandoline to slice each radish thin and uniformly. You may also use the slicing blade in the food processor for this step. 3. Place the radish slices into the boiling water for 5 minutes or until translucent. Remove them from the water and place them into a clean kitchen towel to absorb excess moisture. 4. Toss the radish chips in a large bowl with remaining ingredients until fully coated in oil and seasoning. Place radish chips into the air fryer basket. 5. Adjust the temperature to 320ºF (160ºC) and air fry for 5 minutes. 6. Shake the basket two or three times during the cooking time. Serve warm.

Per Serving:
calories: 81 | fat: 7g | protein: 1g | carbs: 5g | fiber: 2g | sodium: 27mg

Chapter 8   Vegetarian Mains

Italian Zucchini Boats

Prep time: 5 minutes | Cook time: 15 minutes | Serves 4

1 cup canned low-sodium chickpeas, drained and rinsed	2 zucchini
1 cup no-sugar-added spaghetti sauce	¼ cup shredded Parmesan cheese

1. Preheat the oven to 425°F. 2. In a medium bowl, mix the chickpeas and spaghetti sauce together. 3. Cut the zucchini in half lengthwise, and scrape a spoon gently down the length of each half to remove the seeds. 4. Fill each zucchini half with the chickpea sauce, and top with one-quarter of the Parmesan cheese. 5. Place the zucchini halves on a baking sheet and roast in the oven for 15 minutes.

Per Serving:
calories: 120 | fat: 4.48g | protein: 6.69g | carbs: 13.56g | sugars: 4.79g | fiber: 3.8g | sodium: 441mg

Chickpea-Spinach Curry

Prep time: 5 minutes | Cook time: 10 minutes | Serves 2

1 cup frozen chopped spinach, thawed	chopped tomatoes, undrained
1 cup canned chickpeas, drained and rinsed	1 tablespoon curry powder
½ cup frozen green beans	1 tablespoon granulated garlic
½ cup frozen broccoli florets	Salt, to season
½ cup no-salt-added canned	Freshly ground black pepper, to season
	½ cup chopped fresh parsley

1. In a medium saucepan set over high heat, stir together the spinach, chickpeas, green beans, broccoli, tomatoes and their juice, curry powder, and garlic. Season with salt and pepper. Bring to a fast boil. Reduce the heat to low. Cover and simmer for 10 minutes, or until heated through. 2. Top with the parsley, serve, and enjoy!

Per Serving:
calories: 203 | fat: 3.42g | protein: 12.63g | carbs: 34.72g | sugars: 6.94g | fiber: 13g | sodium: 375mg

Stuffed Peppers

Prep time: 20 minutes | Cook time: 50 minutes | Serves 2

½ cup water	Salt, to season
¼ cup uncooked quinoa, thoroughly rinsed	Freshly ground black pepper, to season
1 tablespoon extra-virgin olive oil	1 red bell pepper, halved and seeded
1 garlic clove, minced	1 orange bell pepper, halved and seeded
6 ounces extra-firm tofu, drained and sliced	½ cup nonfat shredded mozzarella cheese, divided
½ cup marinara sauce, divided	4 tomato slices, divided
¼ cup finely chopped walnuts	
1 teaspoon dried basil	

1. Preheat the oven to 350°F. 2. In a small pot set over high heat, bring the water to a boil. 3. Add the quinoa. Reduce the heat to low. Cover and simmer for about 15 minutes, or until tender and all the water is absorbed. Let cool. Fluff with a fork. Set aside. 4. In a skillet set over medium heat, stir together the olive oil, garlic, and tofu. Cook for about 5 minutes, or until the tofu is evenly brown. 5. Mix in ¼ cup of marinara, the walnuts, and basil. Season with salt and pepper. Cook for 5 minutes more, stirring. 6. Using a wooden spoon or spatula, press one-quarter of the cooked quinoa into each pepper half. 7. Top each with about 1 tablespoon of the remaining ¼ cup of marinara. 8. Sprinkle each with about 1 tablespoon of mozzarella cheese. 9. Place 1 tomato slice on each filled pepper. 10. Finish with about 1 tablespoon of the remaining ¼ cup of mozzarella cheese. 11. Transfer the stuffed peppers to a baking dish. Place the dish in the preheated oven. Bake for 25 minutes, or until the cheese melts. 12. Serve 1 stuffed red bell pepper half and 1 stuffed orange bell pepper half to each person and enjoy!

Per Serving:
calories: 399 | fat: 20.88g | protein: 24.71g | carbs: 33.3g | sugars: 6.65g | fiber: 6.2g | sodium: 535mg

Italian Tofu with Mushrooms and Peppers

Prep time: 5 minutes | Cook time: 10 minutes | Serves 2

1 teaspoon extra-virgin olive oil	mushrooms
¼ cup chopped bell pepper, any color	1 portobello mushroom cap, chopped
¼ cup chopped onions	1 tablespoon balsamic vinegar
1 garlic clove, minced	1 teaspoon dried basil
8 ounces firm tofu, drained and rinsed	Salt, to season
½ cup sliced fresh button	Freshly ground black pepper, to season

1. In a medium skillet set over medium heat, heat the olive oil. 2. Add the bell pepper, onions, and garlic. Sauté for 5 minutes, or until soft. 3. Add the tofu, button mushrooms, and portobello mushrooms, tossing and stirring. Reduce the heat to low. 4. Stir in the balsamic vinegar and basil. Season with salt and pepper. Simmer for 2 minutes. 5. Enjoy!

Per Serving:
calories: 142 | fat: 7.81g | protein: 12.76g | carbs: 8.58g | sugars: 3.77g | fiber: 1.8g | sodium: 326mg

Black-Eyed Pea Sauté with Garlic and Olives

Prep time: 5 minutes | Cook time: 5 minutes | Serves 2

2 teaspoons extra-virgin olive oil	¼ cup water
1 garlic clove, minced	¼ teaspoon salt
½ red onion, chopped	¼ teaspoon freshly ground black pepper
1 cup cooked black-eyed peas; if canned, drain and rinse	6 Kalamata olives, pitted and halved
½ teaspoon dried thyme	

1. In a medium saucepan set over medium heat, stir together the olive oil, garlic, and red onion. Cook for 2 minutes, continuing to stir. 2. Add the black-eyed peas and thyme. Cook for 1 minute. 3. Stir in the water, salt, pepper, and olives. Cook for 2 minutes more, or until heated through.

Per Serving:
calories: 140 | fat: 6.13g | protein: 4.65g | carbs: 18.02g | sugars: 7.75g | fiber: 4.6g | sodium: 426mg

Caprese Eggplant Stacks

Prep time: 5 minutes | Cook time: 12 minutes | Serves 4

1 medium eggplant, cut into ¼-inch slices	Mozzarella, cut into ½-ounce / 14-g slices
2 large tomatoes, cut into ¼-inch slices	2 tablespoons olive oil
4 ounces (113 g) fresh	¼ cup fresh basil, sliced

1. In a baking dish, place four slices of eggplant on the bottom. Place a slice of tomato on top of each eggplant round, then Mozzarella, then eggplant. Repeat as necessary. 2. Drizzle with olive oil. Cover dish with foil and place dish into the air fryer basket. 3. Adjust the temperature to 350ºF (177ºC) and bake for 12 minutes. 4. When done, eggplant will be tender. Garnish with fresh basil to serve.

Per Serving:
calories: 97 | fat: 7g | protein: 2g | carbs: 8g | fiber: 4g | sodium: 11mg

No-Bake Spaghetti Squash Casserole

Prep time: 10 minutes | Cook time: 45 minutes | Serves 6

Marinara	soaked in water to cover for 1 to 2 hours and then drained
3 tablespoons extra-virgin olive oil	3 tablespoons nutritional yeast
3 garlic cloves, minced	2 tablespoons extra-virgin olive oil
One 28-ounce can whole San Marzano tomatoes and their liquid	1 teaspoon finely grated lemon zest, plus 2 tablespoons fresh lemon juice
2 teaspoons Italian seasoning	½ cup firmly packed fresh flat-leaf parsley leaves
1 teaspoon fine sea salt	
½ teaspoon red pepper flakes (optional)	1½ teaspoons Italian seasoning
Vegan Parmesan	1 teaspoon garlic powder
½ cup raw whole cashews	1 teaspoon fine sea salt
2 tablespoons nutritional yeast	½ teaspoon freshly ground black pepper
½ teaspoon garlic powder	
½ teaspoon fine sea salt	One 3½-pound steamed spaghetti squash
Vegan Ricotta	
One 14-ounce package firm tofu, drained	2 tablespoons chopped fresh flat-leaf parsley
½ cup raw whole cashews,	

1. To make the marinara: Select the Sauté setting on the Instant Pot and heat the oil and garlic for about 2 minutes, until the garlic is bubbling but not browned. Add the tomatoes and their liquid and use a wooden spoon or spatula to crush the tomatoes against the side of the pot. Stir in the Italian seasoning, salt, and pepper flakes (if using) and cook, stirring occasionally, for about 10 minutes, until the sauce has thickened a bit. Press the Cancel button to turn off the pot and let the sauce cook from the residual heat for about 5 minutes more, until it is no longer simmering. Wearing heat-resistant mitts, lift the pot out of the housing, pour the sauce into a medium heatproof bowl, and set aside. (You can make the sauce up to 4 days in advance, then let it cool, transfer it to an airtight container, and refrigerate.) 2. To make the vegan Parmesan: In a food processor, combine the cashews, nutritional yeast, garlic powder, and salt. Using 1-second pulses, pulse about ten times, until the mixture resembles grated Parmesan cheese. Transfer to a small bowl and set aside. Do not wash the food processor bowl and blade. 3. To make the vegan ricotta: Cut the tofu crosswise into eight ½-inch-thick slices. Sandwich the slices between double layers of paper towels or a folded kitchen towel and press gently to remove excess moisture. Add the tofu to the food processor along with the cashews, nutritional yeast, oil, lemon zest, lemon juice, parsley, Italian seasoning, garlic powder, salt, and pepper. Process for about 1 minute, until the mixture is mostly smooth with flecks of parsley throughout. Set aside. 4. Return the marinara to the pot. Select the Sauté setting and heat the marinara sauce for about 3 minutes, until it starts to simmer. Add the spaghetti squash and vegan ricotta to the pot and stir to combine. Continue to heat, stirring often, for 8 to 10 minutes, until piping hot. Press the Cancel button to turn off the pot. 5. Spoon the spaghetti squash into bowls, top with the vegan Parmesan and parsley, and serve right away.

Per Serving:
calorie: 307 | fat: 17g | protein: 16g | carbs: 25g | sugars: 2g | fiber: 5g | sodium: 985mg

No-Tuna Lettuce Wraps

Prep time: 10 minutes | Cook time: 0 minutes | Serves 4

1 (15-ounce) can low-sodium chickpeas, drained and rinsed	red onion
1 celery stalk, thinly sliced	2 tablespoons unsalted tahini
3 tablespoons honey mustard	1 tablespoon capers, undrained
2 tablespoons finely chopped	12 butter lettuce leaves

1. In a large bowl, mash the chickpeas. 2. Add the celery, honey mustard, onion, tahini, and capers, and mix well. 3. For each serving, place three lettuce leaves on a plate so they overlap, top with one-fourth of the chickpea filling, and roll up into a wrap. Repeat with the remaining lettuce leaves and filling.

Per Serving:
calories: 163 | fat: 8.42g | protein: 6.47g | carbs: 17.06g | sugars: 3.51g | fiber: 5.9g | sodium: 333mg

Greek Stuffed Eggplant

Prep time: 15 minutes | Cook time: 20 minutes | Serves 2

1 large eggplant	1 cup fresh spinach
2 tablespoons unsalted butter	2 tablespoons diced red bell pepper
¼ medium yellow onion, diced	
¼ cup chopped artichoke hearts	½ cup crumbled feta

1. Slice eggplant in half lengthwise and scoop out flesh, leaving enough inside for shell to remain intact. Take eggplant that was scooped out, chop it, and set aside. 2. In a medium skillet over medium heat, add butter and onion. Sauté until onions begin to soften, about 3 to 5 minutes. Add chopped eggplant, artichokes, spinach, and bell pepper. Continue cooking 5 minutes until peppers soften and spinach wilts. Remove from the heat and gently fold in the feta. 3. Place filling into each eggplant shell and place into the air fryer basket. 4. Adjust the temperature to 320ºF (160ºC) and air fry for 20 minutes. 5. Eggplant will be tender when done. Serve warm.

Per Serving:
calories: 259 | fat: 16.32g | protein: 9.81g | carbs: 22.16g | sugars: 12.44g | fiber: 10.1g | sodium: 386mg

Palak Tofu

Prep time: 5 minutes | Cook time: 40 minutes | Serves 4

One 14-ounce package extra-firm tofu, drained	One 16-ounce bag frozen chopped spinach
5 tablespoons cold-pressed avocado oil	⅓ cup water
1 yellow onion, diced	One 14½-ounce can fire-roasted diced tomatoes and their liquid
1-inch piece fresh ginger, peeled and minced	¼ cup coconut milk
3 garlic cloves, minced	2 teaspoons garam masala
1 teaspoon fine sea salt	Cooked brown rice or cauliflower "rice" or whole-grain flatbread for serving
½ teaspoon freshly ground black pepper	
¼ teaspoon cayenne pepper	

1. Cut the tofu crosswise into eight ½-inch-thick slices. Sandwich the slices between double layers of paper towels or a folded kitchen towel and press firmly to wick away as much moisture as possible. Cut the slices into ½-inch cubes. 2. Select the Sauté setting on the Instant Pot and and heat 4 tablespoons of the oil for 2 minutes. Add the onion and sauté for about 10 minutes, until it begins to brown. 3. While the onion is cooking in the Instant Pot, in a large nonstick skillet over medium-high heat, warm the remaining 1 tablespoon oil. Add the tofu in a single layer and cook without stirring for about 3 minutes, until lightly browned. 4. Using a spatula, turn the cubes over and cook for about 3 minutes more, until browned on the other side. Remove from the heat and set aside. 5. Add the ginger and garlic to the onion in the Instant Pot and sauté for about 2 minutes, until the garlic is bubbling but not browned. Add the sautéed tofu, salt, black pepper, and cayenne and stir gently to combine, taking care not to break up the tofu. Add the spinach and stir gently. Pour in the water and then pour the tomatoes and their liquid over the top in an even layer. Do not stir them in. 6. Secure the lid and set the Pressure Release to Sealing. Press the Cancel button to reset the cooking program, then select the Manual or Pressure Cook setting and set the cooking time for 10 minutes at low pressure. (The pot will take about 15 minutes to come up to pressure before the cooking program begins.) 7. When the cooking program ends, let the pressure release naturally for 10 minutes, then move the Pressure Release to Venting to release any remaining steam. Open the pot, add the coconut milk and garam masala, and stir to combine. 8. Ladle the tofu onto plates or into bowls. Serve piping hot, with the "rice" alongside.

Per Serving:
calories: 345 | fat: 24g | protein: 14g | carbs: 18g | sugars: 5g | fiber: 6g | sodium: 777mg

Parmesan Artichokes

Prep time: 10 minutes | Cook time: 10 minutes | Serves 4

2 medium artichokes, trimmed and quartered, center removed	Parmesan cheese
2 tablespoons coconut oil	¼ cup blanched finely ground almond flour
1 large egg, beaten	½ teaspoon crushed red pepper flakes
½ cup grated vegetarian	

1. In a large bowl, toss artichokes in coconut oil and then dip each piece into the egg. 2. Mix the Parmesan and almond flour in a large bowl. Add artichoke pieces and toss to cover as completely as possible, sprinkle with pepper flakes. Place into the air fryer basket. 3. Adjust the temperature to 400ºF (204ºC) and air fry for 10 minutes. 4. Toss the basket two times during cooking. Serve warm.

Per Serving:
calories: 207 | fat: 13g | protein: 10g | carbs: 15g | fiber: 5g | sodium: 211mg

Seitan Curry

Prep time: 10 minutes | Cook time: 15 minutes | Serves 2

1 tablespoon extra-virgin olive oil	1 cup diced tomatoes
½ cup chopped onion	⅓ cup unsweetened light canned coconut milk
2 garlic cloves, chopped	¼ cup water
1 cup cauliflower florets	Salt, to season
½ cup diced carrots	Freshly ground black pepper, to season
6 ounces seitan (wheat gluten), finely chopped	2 tablespoons chopped cashews, for garnish
2 teaspoons garam masala	

1. In a large wok or skillet set over high heat, heat the olive oil. 2. Add the onion and garlic. Sauté for 3 minutes. 3. Add the cauliflower, carrots, seitan, and garam masala. Mix well. Reduce the heat to medium-high. 4. Stir in the tomatoes, coconut milk, and water. Cover and bring to a simmer. Cook for about 10 minutes, covered, or until the cauliflower and carrots are tender. 5. Season with salt and pepper. Garnish with the cashews. 6. Serve and enjoy!

Per Serving:
calories: 617 | fat: 28.29g | protein: 5.32 g | carbs: 43g | sugars: 8.31g | fiber: 5.7g | sodium: 434.3mg

Veggie Fajitas

Prep time: 10 minutes | Cook time: 15 minutes | Serves 4

For The Guacamole	1 green bell pepper
2 small avocados pitted and peeled	1 small white onion
1 teaspoon freshly squeezed lime juice	Avocado oil cooking spray
	1 cup canned low-sodium black beans, drained and rinsed
¼ teaspoon salt	½ teaspoon ground cumin
9 cherry tomatoes, halved	¼ teaspoon chili powder
For The Fajitas	¼ teaspoon garlic powder
1 red bell pepper	4 (6-inch) yellow corn tortillas

To Make The Guacamole 1. In a medium bowl, use a fork to mash the avocados with the lime juice and salt. 2. Gently stir in the cherry tomatoes. To Make The Fajitas 1. Cut the red bell pepper, green bell pepper, and onion into ½-inch slices. 2. Heat a large skillet over medium heat. When hot, coat the cooking surface with cooking spray. Put the peppers, onion, and beans into the skillet. 3. Add the cumin, chili powder, and garlic powder, and stir. 4. Cover and cook for 15 minutes, stirring halfway through. 5. Divide the fajita mixture equally between the tortillas, and top with guacamole and any preferred garnishes.

Per Serving:
calories: 269 | fat: 15g | protein: 8g | carbs: 30g | sugars: 5g | fiber: 11g | sodium: 175mg

Vegan Dal Makhani

Prep time: 0 minutes | Cook time: 55 minutes | Serves 6

1 cup dried kidney beans	diced
⅓ cup urad dal or beluga or Puy lentils	1 tablespoon garam masala
	1 teaspoon ground turmeric
4 cups water	¼ teaspoon cayenne pepper (optional)
1 teaspoon fine sea salt	
1 tablespoon cold-pressed avocado oil	One 15-ounce can fire-roasted diced tomatoes and liquid
1 tablespoon cumin seeds	2 tablespoons vegan buttery spread
1-inch piece fresh ginger, peeled and minced	
	Cooked cauliflower "rice" for serving
4 garlic cloves, minced	
1 large yellow onion, diced	2 tablespoons chopped fresh cilantro
2 jalapeño chiles, seeded and diced	
	6 tablespoons plain coconut yogurt
1 green bell pepper, seeded and	

1. In a medium bowl, combine the kidney beans, urad dal, water, and salt and stir to dissolve the salt. Let soak for 12 hours. 2. Select the Sauté setting on the Instant Pot and heat the oil and cumin seeds for 3 minutes, until the seeds are bubbling, lightly toasted, and aromatic. Add the ginger and garlic and sauté for 1 minute, until bubbling and fragrant. Add the onion, jalapeños, and bell pepper and sauté for 5 minutes, until the onion begins to soften. 3. Add the garam masala, turmeric, cayenne (if using), and the soaked beans and their liquid and stir to mix. Pour the tomatoes and their liquid on top. Do not stir them in. 4. Secure the lid and set the Pressure Release to Sealing. Press the Cancel button to reset the cooking program, then select the Pressure Cook or Manual setting and set the cooking time for 30 minutes at high pressure. (The pot will take about 15 minutes to come up to pressure before the cooking program begins.) 5. When the cooking program ends, let the pressure release naturally for 30 minutes, then move the Pressure Release to Venting to release any remaining steam. Open the pot and stir to combine, then stir in the buttery spread. If you prefer a smoother texture, ladle 1½ cups of the dal into a blender and blend until smooth, about 30 seconds, then stir the blended mixture into the rest of the dal in the pot. 6. Spoon the cauliflower "rice" into bowls and ladle the dal on top. Sprinkle with the cilantro, top with a dollop of coconut yogurt, and serve.

Per Serving:
calorie: 245 | fat: 7g | protein: 11g | carbs: 37g | sugars: 4g | fiber: 10g | sodium: 518mg

Roasted Veggie Bowl

Prep time: 10 minutes | Cook time: 15 minutes | Serves 2

1 cup broccoli florets	½ medium green bell pepper, seeded and sliced ¼ inch thick
1 cup quartered Brussels sprouts	
	1 tablespoon coconut oil
½ cup cauliflower florets	2 teaspoons chili powder
¼ medium white onion, peeled and sliced ¼ inch thick	½ teaspoon garlic powder
	½ teaspoon cumin

1. Toss all ingredients together in a large bowl until vegetables are fully coated with oil and seasoning. 2. Pour vegetables into the air fryer basket. 3. Adjust the temperature to 360°F (182°C) and roast for 15 minutes. 4. Shake two or three times during cooking. Serve warm.

Per Serving:
calories: 112 | fat: 7.68g | protein: 3.64g | carbs: 10.67

Asparagus, Sun-Dried Tomato, and Green Pea Sauté

Prep time: 10 minutes | Cook time: 10 minutes | Serves 2

6 packaged sun-dried tomatoes (not packed in oil)	mushrooms
	¼ cup reduced-sodium vegetable broth
½ cup boiling water	
1 tablespoon extra-virgin olive oil	2 tablespoons sliced almonds
	1 large tomato, diced (about 1 cup)
2 garlic cloves, minced	
¾ pound fresh asparagus, trimmed and cut into 2-inch pieces	1½ teaspoons dried tarragon
	½ cup frozen peas
	Freshly ground black pepper, to season
¼ cup chopped red bell pepper	
½ cup sliced fresh button	

1. In a small heatproof bowl, place the sun-dried tomatoes. Cover with the boiling water. Set aside. 2. In a large skillet or wok set over high heat, heat the olive oil. 3. Add the garlic. Swirl in the oil for a few seconds. 4. Toss in the asparagus, red bell pepper, and mushrooms. Stir-fry for 30 seconds. 5. Add the vegetable broth and almonds. Cover and steam for about 2 minutes. Uncover the skillet. 6. Add the tomato and tarragon. Cook for 2 to 3 minutes to reduce the liquid. 7. Drain and chop the sun-dried tomatoes. Add them and the peas to the skillet. Stir-fry for 3 to 4 minutes, or until the vegetables are crisp-tender and the liquid is reduced to a sauce. 8. Season with pepper and serve immediately.

Per Serving:
calories: 165 | fat: 8.22g | protein: 7.51g | carbs: 20g | sugars: 9.15g | fiber: 7.3g | sodium: 46mg

Orange Tofu

Prep time: 10 minutes | Cook time: 20 minutes | Serves 4

⅓ cup freshly squeezed orange juice (zest orange first; see orange zest ingredient below)	ginger
	1 large clove garlic, grated
	½–1 teaspoon orange zest
1 tablespoon tamari	¼ teaspoon sea salt
1 tablespoon tahini	Few pinches of crushed red-pepper flakes (optional)
½ tablespoon coconut nectar or pure maple syrup	
	1 package (12 ounces) extra-firm tofu, sliced into ¼"–½" thick squares and patted to remove excess moisture
2 tablespoons apple cider vinegar	
½ tablespoon freshly grated	

1. Preheat the oven to 400°F. 2. In a small bowl, combine the orange juice, tamari, tahini, nectar or syrup, vinegar, ginger, garlic, orange zest, salt, and red-pepper flakes (if using). Whisk until well combined. Pour the sauce into an 8" x 12" baking dish. Add the tofu and turn to coat both sides. Bake for 20 minutes. Add salt to taste.

Per Serving:
calorie: 122 | fat: 7g | protein: 10g | carbs: 7g | sugars: 4g | fiber: 1g | sodium: 410mg

Cashew-Kale and Chickpeas

Prep time: 15 minutes | Cook time: 15 minutes | Serves 2

For the cashew sauce	1 cup canned chickpeas, drained and rinsed
½ cup unsalted cashews soaked in ½ cup hot water for at least 20 minutes	1 bunch kale, thoroughly washed, central stems removed, leaves thinly sliced (about 2½ cups)
1 cup reduced-sodium vegetable broth	2 to 3 tablespoons water
1 garlic clove, minced	1 teaspoon red pepper flakes
For the kale	½ teaspoon salt
1 medium red bell pepper, diced	Freshly ground black pepper, to season
1 medium carrot, julienned	¼ cup minced fresh cilantro
½ cup sliced fresh mushrooms	

To make the cashew sauce 1. Drain the cashews. 2. In a blender or food processor, blend together the cashews, vegetable broth, and garlic until completely smooth. Set aside. To make the kale 1. In a large nonstick skillet or Dutch oven set over medium-low heat, stir together the red bell pepper, carrot, and mushrooms. Cook for 5 to 7 minutes, or until softened. 2. Stir in the chickpeas. Increase the heat to high. 3. Add the kale and the water. Stir to combine. Cover and cook for 5 minutes, or until the kale is tender. 4. Stir in the cashew sauce, red pepper flakes, and salt. Season with pepper. Cook for 2 to 3 minutes more, uncovered, or until the sauce thickens. 5. Garnish with the cilantro before serving. 6. Enjoy!

Per Serving:

calories: 480 | fat: 19.73g | protein: 20.16g | carbs: 62.12g | sugars: 17g | fiber: 15.3g | sodium: 843mg

Instant Pot Hoppin' John with Skillet Cauli "Rice"

Prep time: 0 minutes | Cook time: 30 minutes | Serves 6

Hoppin' John	diced
1 pound dried black-eyed peas (about 2¼ cups)	½ teaspoon smoked paprika
8⅔ cups water	½ teaspoon dried thyme
1½ teaspoons fine sea salt	½ teaspoon dried sage
2 tablespoons extra-virgin olive oil	¼ teaspoon cayenne pepper
2 garlic cloves, minced	2 cups low-sodium vegetable broth
8 ounces shiitake mushrooms, stemmed and chopped, or cremini mushrooms, chopped	Cauli "Rice"
	1 tablespoon vegan buttery spread or unsalted butter
1 small yellow onion, diced	1 pound riced cauliflower
1 green bell pepper, seeded and diced	½ teaspoon fine sea salt
2 celery stalks, diced	2 green onions, white and green parts, sliced
2 jalapeño chiles, seeded and	Hot sauce (such as Tabasco or Crystal) for serving

1. To make the Hoppin' John: In a large bowl, combine the black-eyed peas, 8 cups of the water, and 1 teaspoon of the salt and stir to dissolve the salt. Let soak for at least 8 hours or up to overnight. 2. Select the Sauté setting on the Instant Pot and heat the oil and garlic for 3 minutes, until the garlic is bubbling but not browned. Add the mushrooms and the remaining ½ teaspoon salt and sauté for 5 minutes, until the mushrooms have wilted and begun to give up their liquid. Add the onion, bell pepper, celery, and jalapeños and sauté for 4 minutes, until the onion is softened. Add the paprika, thyme, sage, and cayenne and sauté for 1 minute. 3. Drain the black-eyed peas and add them to the pot along with the broth and remaining ⅔ cup water. The liquid should just barely cover the beans. (Add an additional splash of water if needed.) 4. Secure the lid and set the Pressure Release to Sealing. Press the Cancel button to reset the cooking program, then select the Bean/Chili, Pressure Cook, or Manual setting and set the cooking time for 5 minutes at high pressure. (The pot will take about 10 minutes to come up to pressure before the cooking program begins.) 5. When the cooking program ends, let the pressure release naturally for 10 minutes, then move the Pressure Release to Venting to release any remaining steam. 6. To make the cauli "rice": While the pressure is releasing, in a large skillet over medium heat, melt the buttery spread. Add the cauliflower and salt and sauté for 3 to 5 minutes, until cooked through and piping hot. (If using frozen riced cauliflower, this may take another 2 minutes or so.) 7. Spoon the cauli "rice" onto individual plates. Open the pot and spoon the black-eyed peas on top of the cauli "rice". Sprinkle with the green onions and serve right away, with the hot sauce on the side.

Per Serving:

calories: 287 | fat: 7g | protein: 23g | carbs: 56g | sugars: 8g | fiber: 24g | sodium: 894mg

Grilled Vegetables on White Bean Mash

Prep time: 15 minutes | Cook time: 30 minutes | Serves 2

2 medium zucchini, sliced	½ cup low-sodium vegetable broth
1 red bell pepper, seeded and quartered	4 cups baby spinach, divided
2 portobello mushroom caps, quartered	Salt, to season
	Freshly ground black pepper, to season
3 teaspoons extra-virgin olive oil, divided	1 tablespoon chopped fresh parsley
1 (8-ounce) can cannellini beans, drained and rinsed	2 lemon wedges, divided, for garnish
1 garlic clove, minced	

1. Preheat the grill. Use a stove-top grill pan or broiler if a grill is not available. 2. Lightly brush the zucchini, red bell pepper, and mushrooms with 1½ teaspoons of olive oil. Arrange them in a barbecue grill pan. Place the pan on the preheated grill. Cook the vegetables for 5 to 8 minutes, or until lightly browned. Turn the vegetables. Brush with the remaining 1½ teaspoons of olive oil. Cook for 5 to 8 minutes more, or until tender. 3. To a small pan set over high heat, add the cannellini beans, garlic, and vegetable broth. Bring to a boil. Reduce the heat to low. Simmer for 10 minutes, uncovered. Using a potato masher, roughly mash the beans, adding a little more broth if they seem too dry. 4. Place 2 cups of spinach on each serving plate. 5. Top each with half of the bean mash and half of the grilled vegetables. Season with salt and pepper. Garnish with parsley. 6. Place 1 lemon wedge on each plate and serve.

Per Serving:

calories: 289.5 | fat: 8.55g | protein: 11.3g | carbs:28.91 g | sugars: 7.88g | fiber: 4.4g | sodium: 398mg

Stuffed Portobellos

Prep time: 10 minutes | Cook time: 8 minutes | Serves 4

3 ounces (85 g) cream cheese, softened	leaves
½ medium zucchini, trimmed and chopped	4 large portobello mushrooms, stems removed
¼ cup seeded and chopped red bell pepper	2 tablespoons coconut oil, melted
1½ cups chopped fresh spinach	½ teaspoon salt

1. In a medium bowl, mix cream cheese, zucchini, pepper, and spinach. 2. Drizzle mushrooms with coconut oil and sprinkle with salt. Scoop ¼ zucchini mixture into each mushroom. 3. Place mushrooms into ungreased air fryer basket. Adjust the temperature to 400ºF (204ºC) and air fry for 8 minutes. Portobellos will be tender and tops will be browned when done. Serve warm.

Per Serving:
calories: 151 | fat: 13g | protein: 4g | carbs: 6g | fiber: 2g | sodium: 427mg

Pra Ram Vegetables and Peanut Sauce with Seared Tofu

Prep time: 5 minutes | Cook time: 20 minutes | Serves 4

Peanut Sauce	8 ounces zucchini, julienned ¼ inch thick
2 tablespoons cold-pressed avocado oil	1 pound broccoli florets
2 garlic cloves, minced	½ small head green cabbage, cut into 1-inch-thick wedges (with core intact so wedges hold together)
½ cup creamy natural peanut butter	
½ cup coconut milk	Tofu
2 tablespoons brown rice syrup	One 14-ounce package extra-firm tofu, drained
1 tablespoon plus 1 teaspoon soy sauce, tamari, or coconut aminos	¼ teaspoon fine sea salt
¼ cup water	¼ teaspoon freshly ground black pepper
Vegetables	1 tablespoon cornstarch
2 carrots, sliced on the diagonal ¼ inch thick	2 tablespoons coconut oil

1. To make the peanut sauce: In a small saucepan over medium heat, warm the oil and garlic for about 2 minutes, until the garlic is bubbling but not browned. Add the peanut butter, coconut milk, brown rice syrup, soy sauce, and water; stir to combine; and bring to a simmer (this will take about 3 minutes). As soon as the mixture is fully combined and at a simmer, remove from the heat and keep warm. The peanut sauce will keep in an airtight container in the refrigerator for up to 5 days. 2. To make the vegetables: Pour 1 cup water into the Instant Pot and place a steamer basket into the pot. In order, layer the carrots, zucchini, broccoli, and cabbage in the steamer basket, finishing with the cabbage. 3. Secure the lid and set the Pressure Release to Sealing. Select the Steam setting and set the cooking time for 0 (zero) minutes at low pressure. (The pot will take about 15 minutes to come up to pressure before the cooking program begins.) 4. To prepare the tofu: While the vegetables are steaming, cut the tofu crosswise into eight ½-inch-thick slices. Cut each of the slices in half crosswise, creating squares. Sandwich the squares between double layers of paper towels or a folded kitchen towel and press firmly to wick away as much moisture as possible. Sprinkle the tofu squares on both sides with the salt and pepper, then sprinkle them on both sides with the cornstarch. Using your fingers, spread the cornstarch on the top and bottom of each square to coat evenly. 5. In a large nonstick skillet over medium-high heat, warm the oil for about 3 minutes, until shimmering. Add the tofu and sear, turning once, for about 6 minutes per side, until crispy and golden. Divide the tofu evenly among four plates. 6. When the cooking program ends, perform a quick pressure release by moving the Pressure Release to Venting. Open the pot and, wearing heat-resistant mitts, grasp the handles of the steamer basket and lift it out of the pot. 7. Divide the vegetables among the plates, arranging them around the tofu. Spoon the peanut sauce over the tofu and serve.

Per Serving:
calories: 380 | fat: 22g | protein: 18g | carbs: 30g | sugars: 9g | fiber: 10g | sodium: 381mg

Gingered Tofu and Greens

Prep time: 15 minutes | Cook time: 20 minutes | Serves 2

For the marinade	oil, divided
2 tablespoons low-sodium soy sauce	1 tablespoon grated fresh ginger
¼ cup rice vinegar	2 cups coarsely shredded bok choy
⅓ cup water	
1 tablespoon grated fresh ginger	2 cups coarsely shredded kale, thoroughly washed
1 tablespoon coconut flour	½ cup fresh, or frozen, chopped green beans
1 teaspoon granulated stevia	
1 garlic clove, minced	1 tablespoon freshly squeezed lime juice
For the tofu and greens	
8 ounces extra-firm tofu, drained, cut into 1-inch cubes	1 tablespoon chopped fresh cilantro
3 teaspoons extra-virgin olive	2 tablespoons hemp hearts

To make the marinade 1. In a small bowl, whisk together the soy sauce, rice vinegar, water, ginger, coconut flour, stevia, and garlic until well combined. 2. Place a small saucepan set over high heat. Add the marinade. Bring to a boil. Cook for 1 minute. Remove from the heat. To make the tofu and greens 1. In a medium ovenproof pan, place the tofu in a single layer. Pour the marinade over. Drizzle with 1½ teaspoons of olive oil. Let sit for 5 minutes. 2. Preheat the broiler to high. 3. Place the pan under the broiler. Broil the tofu for 7 to 8 minutes, or until lightly browned. Using a spatula, turn the tofu over. Continue to broil for 7 to 8 minutes more, or until browned on this side. 4. In a large wok or skillet set over high heat, heat the remaining 1½ teaspoons of olive oil. 5. Stir in the ginger. 6. Add the bok choy, kale, and green beans. Cook for 2 to 3 minutes, stirring constantly, until the greens wilt. 7. Add the lime juice and cilantro. Remove from the heat. 8. Add the browned tofu with any remaining marinade in the pan to the bok choy, kale, and green beans. Toss gently to combine. 9. Top with the hemp hearts and serve immediately.

Per Serving:
calories: 252 | fat: 13.79g | protein: 15.05g | carbs: 19.62g | sugars: 3.87g | fiber: 2.7g | sodium: 679mg
g | sugars: 3.08g | fiber: 4.6g | sodium: 106mg

Edamame Falafel with Roasted Vegetables

Prep time: 10 minutes | Cook time: 55 minutes | Serves 2

For the roasted vegetables	1 small onion, chopped
1 cup broccoli florets	1 garlic clove, chopped
1 medium zucchini, sliced	1 tablespoon freshly squeezed lemon juice
½ cup cherry tomatoes, halved	
1½ teaspoons extra-virgin olive oil	2 tablespoons hemp hearts
	1 teaspoon ground cumin
Salt, to season	2 tablespoons oat flour
Freshly ground black pepper, to season	¼ teaspoon salt
	Pinch freshly ground black pepper
Extra-virgin olive oil cooking spray	2 tablespoons extra-virgin olive oil, divided
For the falafel	
1 cup frozen shelled edamame, thawed	Prepared hummus, for serving (optional)

To make the roasted vegetables 1. Preheat the oven to 425°F. 2. In a large bowl, toss together the broccoli, zucchini, tomatoes, and olive oil to coat. Season with salt and pepper. 3. Spray a baking sheet with cooking spray. 4. Spread the vegetables evenly atop the sheet. Place the sheet in the preheated oven. Roast for 35 to 40 minutes, stirring every 15 minutes, or until the vegetables are soft and cooked through. 5. Remove from the oven. Set aside. To make the falafel 1. In a food processor, pulse the edamame until coarsely ground. 2. Add the onion, garlic, lemon juice, and hemp hearts. Process until finely ground. Transfer the mixture to a medium bowl. 3. By hand, mix in the cumin, oat flour, salt, and pepper. 4. Roll the dough into 1-inch balls. Flatten slightly. You should have about 12 silver dollar–size patties. 5. In a large skillet set over medium heat, heat 1 tablespoon of olive oil. 6. Add 4 falafel patties to the pan at a time (or as many as will fit without crowding), and cook for about 3 minutes on each side, or until lightly browned. Remove from the pan. Repeat with the remaining 1 tablespoon of olive oil and falafel patties. 7. Serve immediately with the roasted vegetables and hummus (if using) and enjoy!

Per Serving:
calories: 316 | fat: 22.48g | protein: 11.78g | carbs: 20.68g | sugars: 3.73g | fiber: 5.8g | sodium: 649mg

Chickpea and Tofu Bolognese

Prep time: 5 minutes | Cook time: 25 minutes | Serves 4

1 (3- to 4-pound) spaghetti squash	sauce
½ teaspoon ground cumin	1 (15-ounce) can low-sodium chickpeas, drained and rinsed
1 cup no-sugar-added spaghetti	6 ounces extra-firm tofu

1. Preheat the oven to 400°F. 2. Cut the squash in half lengthwise. Scoop out the seeds and discard. 3. Season both halves of the squash with the cumin, and place them on a baking sheet cut-side down. Roast for 25 minutes. 4. Meanwhile, heat a medium saucepan over low heat, and pour in the spaghetti sauce and chickpeas. 5. Press the tofu between two layers of paper towels, and gently squeeze out any excess water. 6. Crumble the tofu into the sauce and cook for 15 minutes. 7. Remove the squash from the oven, and comb through the flesh of each half with a fork to make thin strands. 8. Divide the "spaghetti" into four portions, and top each portion with one-quarter of the sauce.

Per Serving:
calories: 221 | fat: 6.39g | protein: 12.46g | carbs: 31.8g | sugars: 6.36g | fiber: 7.8g | sodium: 405mg

Easy Cheesy Vegetable Frittata

Prep time: 10 minutes | Cook time: 15 minutes | Serves 2

Extra-virgin olive oil cooking spray	basil
	Pinch freshly ground black pepper
½ cup sliced onion	
½ cup sliced green bell pepper	½ cup liquid egg substitute
½ cup sliced eggplant	½ cup nonfat cottage cheese
½ cup frozen spinach	¼ cup fat-free evaporated milk
½ cup sliced fresh mushrooms	¼ cup nonfat shredded Cheddar cheese
1 tablespoon chopped fresh	

1. Coat an ovenproof 10-inch skillet with cooking spray. Place it over medium-low heat until hot. 2. Add the onion, green bell pepper, eggplant, spinach, and mushrooms. Sauté for 2 to 3 minutes, or until lightly browned. 3. Add the basil. Season with pepper. Stir to combine. Cook for 2 to 3 minutes more, or until the flavors blend. Remove from the heat. 4. Preheat the broiler. 5. In a blender, combine the egg substitute, cottage cheese, Cheddar cheese, and evaporated milk. Process until smooth. Pour the egg mixture over the vegetables in the skillet. 6. Return the skillet to medium-low heat. Cover and cook for about 5 minutes, or until the bottom sets and the top is still slightly wet. 7. Transfer the ovenproof skillet to the broiler. Broil for 2 to 3 minutes, or until the top is set. 8. Serve one-half of the frittata per person and enjoy!

Per Serving:
calories: 177 | fat: 7.23g | protein: 17.07g | carbs: 12.4g | sugars: 6.22g | fiber: 2.6g | sodium: 408mg

Vegetable Burgers

Prep time: 10 minutes | Cook time: 12 minutes | Serves 4

8 ounces (227 g) cremini mushrooms	yellow onion
2 large egg yolks	1 clove garlic, peeled and finely minced
½ medium zucchini, trimmed and chopped	½ teaspoon salt
¼ cup peeled and chopped	¼ teaspoon ground black pepper

1. Place all ingredients into a food processor and pulse twenty times until finely chopped and combined. 2. Separate mixture into four equal sections and press each into a burger shape. Place burgers into ungreased air fryer basket. Adjust the temperature to 375°F (191°C) and air fry for 12 minutes, turning burgers halfway through cooking. Burgers will be browned and firm when done. 3. Place burgers on a large plate and let cool 5 minutes before serving.

Per Serving:
calories: 50 | fat: 3g | protein: 3g | carbs: 4g | fiber: 1g | sodium: 299mg

Chile Relleno Casserole with Salsa Salad

Prep time: 10 minutes | Cook time: 55 minutes | Serves 4

Casserole
- ½ cup gluten-free flour (such as King Arthur or Cup4Cup brand)
- 1 teaspoon baking powder
- 6 large eggs
- ½ cup nondairy milk or whole milk
- Three 4-ounce cans fire-roasted diced green chiles, drained
- 1 cup nondairy cheese shreds or shredded mozzarella cheese

Salad
- 1 head green leaf lettuce, shredded
- 2 Roma tomatoes, seeded and diced
- 1 green bell pepper, seeded and diced
- ½ small yellow onion, diced
- 1 jalapeño chile, seeded and diced (optional)
- 2 tablespoons chopped fresh cilantro
- 4 teaspoons extra-virgin olive oil
- 4 teaspoons fresh lime juice
- ⅛ teaspoon fine sea salt

1. To make the casserole: Pour 1 cup water into the Instant Pot. Butter a 7-cup round heatproof glass dish or coat with nonstick cooking spray and place the dish on a long-handled silicone steam rack. (If you don't have the long-handled rack, use the wire metal steam rack and a homemade sling) 2. In a medium bowl, whisk together the flour and baking powder. Add the eggs and milk and whisk until well blended, forming a batter. Stir in the chiles and ¾ cup of the cheese. 3. Pour the batter into the prepared dish and cover tightly with aluminum foil. Holding the handles of the steam rack, lower the dish into the Instant Pot. 4. Secure the lid and set the Pressure Release to Sealing. Select the Pressure Cook or Manual setting and set the cooking time for 40 minutes at high pressure. (The pot will take about 10 minutes to come up to pressure before the cooking program begins.) 5. When the cooking program ends, let the pressure release naturally for at least 10 minutes, then move the Pressure Release to Venting to release any remaining steam. Open the pot and, wearing heat-resistant mitts, grasp the handles of the steam rack and lift it out of the pot. Uncover the dish, taking care not to get burned by the steam or to drip condensation onto the casserole. While the casserole is still piping hot, sprinkle the remaining ¼ cup cheese evenly on top. Let the cheese melt for 5 minutes. 6. To make the salad: While the cheese is melting, in a large bowl, combine the lettuce, tomatoes, bell pepper, onion, jalapeño (if using), cilantro, oil, lime juice, and salt. Toss until evenly combined. 7. Cut the casserole into wedges. Serve warm, with the salad on the side.

Per Serving:
calorie: 361 | fat: 22g | protein: 21g | carbs: 23g | sugars: 8g | fiber: 3g | sodium: 421mg

Stuffed Portobello Mushrooms

Prep time: 5 minutes | Cook time: 20 minutes | Serves 4

- 8 large portobello mushrooms
- 3 teaspoons extra-virgin olive oil, divided
- 4 cups fresh spinach
- 1 medium red bell pepper, diced
- ¼ cup crumbled feta

1. Preheat the oven to 450ºF. 2. Remove the stems from the mushrooms, and gently scoop out the gills and discard. Coat the mushrooms with 2 teaspoons of olive oil. 3. On a baking sheet, place the mushrooms cap-side down, and roast for 20 minutes. 4. Meanwhile, heat the remaining 1 teaspoon of olive oil in a medium skillet over medium heat. When hot, sauté the spinach and red bell pepper for 8 to 10 minutes, stirring occasionally. 5. Remove the mushrooms from the oven. Drain, if necessary. Spoon the spinach and pepper mix into the mushrooms, and top with feta.

Per Serving:
calories: 91 | fat: 4.24g | protein: 6.04g | carbs: 9.77g | sugars: 5.96g | fiber: 3.5g | sodium: 155mg

Southwest Tofu

Prep time: 10 minutes | Cook time: 20 minutes | Serves 4

- 3½ tablespoons freshly squeezed lime juice
- 2 teaspoons pure maple syrup
- 1½ teaspoons ground cumin
- 1 teaspoon dried oregano leaves
- 1 teaspoon chili powder
- ½ teaspoon paprika
- ½ teaspoon sea salt
- ⅛ teaspoon allspice
- 1 package (12 ounces) extra-firm tofu, sliced into ¼"–½" thick squares and patted to remove excess moisture

1. In a 9" x 12" baking dish, combine the lime juice, syrup, cumin, oregano, chili powder, paprika, salt, and allspice. Add the tofu and turn to coat both sides. Bake uncovered for 20 minutes, or until the marinade is absorbed, turning once.

Per Serving:
calorie: 78 | fat: 4g | protein: 7g | carbs: 6g | sugars: 3g | fiber: 1g | sodium: 324mg

Chapter 9   Stews and Soups

Potlikker Soup

Prep time: 15 minutes | Cook time: 20 minutes | Serves 6

3 cups store-bought low-sodium chicken broth, divided	1 fresh ham bone
1 medium onion, chopped	5 carrots, peeled and cut into 1-inch rounds
3 garlic cloves, minced	2 fresh thyme sprigs
1 bunch collard greens or mustard greens including stems, roughly chopped	3 bay leaves
	Freshly ground black pepper

1. Select the Sauté setting on an electric pressure cooker, and combine ½ cup of chicken broth, the onion, and garlic and cook for 3 to 5 minutes, or until the onion and garlic are translucent. 2. Add the collard greens, ham bone, carrots, remaining 2½ cups of broth, the thyme, and bay leaves. 3. Close and lock the lid and set the pressure valve to sealing. 4. Change to the Manual/Pressure Cook setting, and cook for 15 minutes. 5. Once cooking is complete, quick-release the pressure. Carefully remove the lid. Discard the bay leaves. 6. Serve.

Per Serving:
calories: 107 | fat: 2.61g | protein: 11.74g | carbs: 11.83g | sugars: 2.62g | fiber: 4.7g | sodium: 556mg

Coconut, Miso, and Sweet Potato White Bean Chili

Prep time: 10 minutes | Cook time: 35 minutes | Serves 4

2 tsp (10 ml) sesame oil, divided	1 (15-oz [425-g]) can navy beans, drained and rinsed
1 medium white onion, coarsely chopped	8 oz (227 g) tempeh, crumbled (see Tips)
2 tsp (6 g) minced fresh garlic	2 green onions, finely chopped
2 tsp (4 g) grated fresh ginger	2 tbsp (30 ml) low-sodium tamari
1 tbsp (17 g) miso of choice dissolved in 3 tbsp (45 ml) warm water (see Tips)	3 cups (200 g) coarsely chopped kale
1 (14-oz [397-ml]) can light coconut milk	Pinch of cayenne pepper (optional)
2 cups (480 ml) water	Sea salt, as needed
2 medium sweet potatoes, cubed	Black pepper, as needed

1. Heat 1 teaspoon of the oil in a large pot over medium heat. Add the onion, garlic, and ginger and sauté the mixture for about 5 minutes, or until the edges of the onion start to caramelize. 2. Add the miso-water mixture, coconut milk, water, sweet potatoes, and beans to the pot. Cover the pot and simmer the chili for about 30 minutes, or until the sweet potatoes are fork-tender. 3. Meanwhile, heat the remaining 1 teaspoon of oil in a medium skillet over medium heat. Add the tempeh, green onions, and tamari. Cook the mixture for 7 to 10 minutes, or until the tempeh is crispy. 4. Stir the tempeh mixture, kale, cayenne pepper (if using), sea salt, and black pepper into the chili, then serve.

Per Serving:
calorie: 407 | fat: 16g | protein: 22g | carbs: 45g | sugars: 5g | fiber: 12g | sodium: 1134mg

Easy Southern Brunswick Stew

Prep time: 20 minutes | Cook time: 8 minutes | Serves 12

2 pounds pork butt, visible fat removed	10-ounce package frozen peas
17-ounce can white corn	2 10¾-ounce cans reduced-sodium tomato soup
1¼ cups ketchup	Hot sauce to taste, optional
2 cups diced, cooked potatoes	

1. Place pork in the Instant Pot and secure the lid. 2. Press the Slow Cook setting and cook on low 6–8 hours. 3. When cook time is over, remove the meat from the bone and shred, removing and discarding all visible fat. 4. Combine all the meat and remaining ingredients (except the hot sauce) in the inner pot of the Instant Pot. 5. Secure the lid once more and cook in Slow Cook mode on low for 30 minutes more. Add hot sauce if you wish.

Per Serving:
calories: 213 | fat: 7g | protein: 13g | carbs: 27g | sugars: 9g | fiber: 3g | sodium: 584mg

Black Bean Soup with Sweet Potatoes

Prep time: 10 minutes | Cook time: 30 minutes | Serves 4

1 tablespoon balsamic vinegar	minced or grated
1½–1¾ cups chopped onion	2 tablespoons tomato paste
1½ cups combination of chopped red and green bell peppers	2 tablespoons freshly squeezed lime juice
1 teaspoon sea salt	½–1 teaspoon pure maple syrup
Freshly ground black pepper to taste	4½ cups (about 3 cans, 15 ounces each) black beans, drained and rinsed
2 teaspoons cumin seeds	1 bay leaf
2 teaspoons dried oregano leaves	1½ cups ½" cubes yellow sweet potato (can substitute white potato)
Rounded ¼ teaspoon allspice	
¼ teaspoon red-pepper flakes, or to taste	
1–4 tablespoons + 3 cups water	Chopped cilantro (optional)
4 medium-large cloves garlic,	Extra lime wedges (optional)

1. In a large pot over medium-high heat, combine the vinegar, onion, bell peppers, salt, black pepper, cumin seeds, oregano, allspice, and red-pepper flakes. Cook for 5 to 7 minutes, or until the onions and red peppers start to soften. Add 1 to 2 tablespoons of water if needed to keep the vegetables from sticking. Add the garlic and stir. Cover, reduce the heat to medium, and cook for another few minutes, until the garlic is softened. If anything is sticking or burning, add another 1 to 2 tablespoons of water. When the garlic is soft, add the tomato paste, lime juice, ½ teaspoon of the syrup, 3½ cups of the beans, and the remaining 3 cups water. Use an immersion blender to puree the soup until it's fairly smooth. Add the bay leaf and sweet potato, increase the heat to high to bring to a boil, then reduce the heat to low and simmer for 20 to 30 minutes. Add the remaining 1 cup black beans. Taste, and add the remaining ½ teaspoon syrup, if desired. Stir, simmer for another few minutes, then serve, seasoning to taste and topping with the cilantro (if using) and lime wedges (if using).

Per Serving:
calorie: 368 | fat: 2g | protein: 19g | carbs: 73g | sugars: 10g | fiber: 24g | sodium: 1049mg

Cauliflower Leek Soup

Prep time: 10 minutes | Cook time: 20 minutes | Serves 2

Avocado oil cooking spray	broth
2½ cups chopped leeks (2 to 3 leeks)	½ cup half-and-half
2½ cups cauliflower florets	¼ teaspoon salt
1 garlic clove, peeled	¼ teaspoon freshly ground black pepper
⅓ cup low-sodium vegetable	

1. Heat a large stockpot over medium-low heat. When hot, coat the cooking surface with cooking spray. Put the leeks and cauliflower into the pot. 2. Increase the heat to medium and cover the pan. Cook for 10 minutes, stirring halfway through. 3. Add the garlic and cook for 5 minutes. 4. Add the broth and deglaze the pan, stirring to scrape up the browned bits from the bottom. 5. Transfer the broth and vegetables to a food processor or blender and add the half-and-half, salt, and pepper. Blend well.

Per Serving:
calories: 208 | fat: 8.67g | protein: 6.26g | carbs: 29.93g | sugars: 10.99g | fiber: 5g | sodium: 434mg

Lentil Soup

Prep time: 10 minutes | Cook time: 55 minutes | Serves 8

1 large onion, diced	or beef broth
1 large carrot, peeled and diced	2 medium russet or white potatoes, peeled and diced
2 stalks celery, diced	1 tablespoon finely chopped fresh oregano
2 tablespoons extra-virgin olive oil	1 teaspoon finely chopped fresh thyme
1 pound lentils	
1½ quarts low-sodium chicken	

1. In a stockpot or Dutch oven, sauté the onion, carrot, and celery in the olive oil for 10 minutes. Add the lentils, broth, and potatoes. 2. Continue to cook for 30–45 minutes, adding the oregano and thyme 15 minutes before serving. Soup will keep for 3 days in the refrigerator or can be frozen for 3 months.

Per Serving:
calories: 174 | fat: 1.63g | protein: 7.71g | carbs: 36.34g | sugars: 1.88g | fiber: 3g | sodium: 81mg

Slow Cooker Chicken and Vegetable Soup

Prep time: 10 minutes | Cook time: 4 hours | Serves 4

1 medium potato, peeled and chopped into 1-inch pieces	2 cups low-sodium chicken broth
3 celery stalks, chopped into 1-inch pieces	2 tablespoons tomato paste
2 cups chopped baby carrots	2 tablespoons Italian seasoning
1 cup chopped white onion	1 pound boneless, skinless chicken breasts, chopped
2 cups chopped green beans	Freshly ground black pepper

1. Put the potato, celery, carrots, onion, green beans, broth, tomato paste, Italian seasoning, and chicken into a slow cooker and cook on high for 4 hours. 2. Season with freshly ground black pepper.

Per Serving:
calories: 256 | fat: 1.84g | protein: 25.68g | carbs: 36.11g | sugars: 7.14g | fiber: 6.8g | sodium: 980mg

Four-Bean Field Stew

Prep time: 10 minutes | Cook time: 40 minutes | Serves 8 to 10

6 cups store-bought low-sodium vegetable broth	1 zucchini, chopped
1 cup dried lima beans	½ cup chopped white onion
1 cup dried black beans	1 celery stalk, roughly chopped
1 cup dried pinto beans	2 garlic cloves, minced
1 cup dried kidney beans	1 teaspoon dried oregano
1 cup roughly chopped tomato	1 teaspoon dried thyme
2 carrots, peeled and roughly chopped	¼ teaspoon freshly ground black pepper

1. In an electric pressure cooker, combine the broth, lima beans, black beans, pinto beans, kidney beans, tomato, carrots, zucchini, onion, celery, garlic, oregano, thyme, and pepper. 2. Close and lock the lid, and set the pressure valve to sealing. 3. Select the Manual/Pressure Cook setting, and cook for 40 minutes. 4. Once cooking is complete, quick-release the pressure. Carefully remove the lid. 5. Serve.

Per Serving:
calories: 262 | fat: 2.98g | protein: 14.57g | carbs: 46.7g | sugars: 7.74g | fiber: 10.4g | sodium: 143mg

Robust Crimson Bean Stew

Prep time: 10 minutes | Cook time: 20 minutes | Serves 4

1 cup chopped red onion	rice (can substitute quinoa)
2 teaspoons dried oregano	3 cloves minced or grated garlic
1 teaspoon dried rosemary	1 can (28 ounces) crushed tomatoes
1 teaspoon Dijon mustard	
Freshly ground black pepper to taste	1 can (15 ounces) adzuki, black, or kidney beans, rinsed and drained
2 tablespoons + 2½ cups water	
2 cups cubed yellow or red potatoes	1–1½ cups chopped red peppers
½ cup dry black beluga or French lentils (can substitute green or brown lentils)	2 tablespoons vegan Worcestershire sauce
½ cup uncooked brown or red	¼ teaspoon sea salt

1. In an instant pot set on the sauté function, combine the onion, oregano, rosemary, mustard, black pepper, and 2 tablespoons of the water. Cook for 3 to 4 minutes. Turn off the sauté function and stir in the potatoes, lentils, rice, garlic, tomatoes, beans, and remaining 2½ cups water. Cook on high pressure for 15 minutes, and either release the pressure manually or let it naturally release. Add the red peppers, Worcestershire sauce, and salt to the instant pot. Stir, replace the cover, and let sit for 5 to 8 minutes. Taste, season as desired, and serve.

Per Serving:
calorie: 596 | fat: 2g | protein: 29g | carbs: 120g | sugars: 11g | fiber: 28g | sodium: 523mg

Mexican Tortilla Soup

Prep time: 10 minutes | Cook time: 40 minutes | Serves 8

2 tablespoons extra-virgin olive oil	whole tomatoes, drained and coarsely chopped
1 onion, chopped	1 medium zucchini, sliced
2 cloves garlic, minced	1 medium yellow squash, sliced
¼ cup freshly chopped cilantro	1 cup yellow corn
1 tablespoon cumin	Six 6-inch corn tortillas
1 teaspoon cayenne pepper	½ cup reduced-fat shredded cheddar cheese
1 quart low-sodium chicken broth	
One 15-ounce can low-sodium	

1. Preheat the oven to 350 degrees. 2. In a large saucepan, heat the oil, and sauté the onion and garlic for 5 minutes. 3. Add the cilantro, cumin, and cayenne pepper; sauté for 3 more minutes. Add the remaining ingredients except the tortillas and cheese. Bring to a boil; cover and let simmer for 30 minutes. 4. Cut each tortilla into about 10 strips (use a pizza cutter to do this easily). Place the strips on a cookie sheet and bake for 5–6 minutes at 350 degrees until slightly browned and toasted. Remove from the oven. 5. To serve the soup, place strips of tortilla into each bowl. Ladle the soup on top of the tortilla strips. Top with cheese.

Per Serving:
calories: 193 | fat: 4.48g | protein: 9.22g | carbs: 31.23g | sugars: 3.25g | fiber: 3.4g | sodium: 172mg

Comforting Chicken and Mushroom Soup

Prep time: 5 minutes | Cook time: 20 minutes | Serves 6

1 quart low-sodium chicken broth	1 tablespoon finely chopped scallions
1 tablespoon light soy sauce	1 tablespoon dry sherry
1 cup sliced mushrooms, stems removed	½ pound boneless, skinless chicken breast, cubed

1. In a stockpot, simmer all ingredients except the chicken for 10 minutes. 2. Add the chicken cubes, and simmer for 6–8 minutes more. Serve with additional soy sauce if desired (but be aware that this will raise the sodium level of the soup).

Per Serving:
calories: 88 | fat: 4.44g | protein: 9.64g | carbs: 2.27g | sugars: 1.17g | fiber: 0.2g | sodium: 88mg

Spanish Black Bean Soup

Prep time: 5 minutes | Cook time: 1 hour 10 minutes | Serves 6

1 ½ cups plus 2 teaspoons low-sodium chicken broth, divided	1 teaspoon cumin
1 teaspoon extra-virgin olive oil	1 teaspoon chili powder or ½ teaspoon cayenne pepper
3 garlic cloves, minced	1 red bell pepper, chopped
1 yellow onion, minced	1 carrot, coarsely chopped
1 teaspoon minced fresh oregano	3 cups cooked black beans
	½ cup dry red wine

1. In a large pot, heat 2 teaspoons of the chicken broth and the olive oil. Add the garlic and onion, and sauté for 3 minutes. Add the oregano, cumin, and chili powder; stir for another minute. Add the red pepper and carrot. 2. Puree 1½ cups of the black beans in a blender or food processor. Add the pureed beans, the remaining 1½ cups of whole black beans, the remaining 1½ cups of chicken broth, and the red wine to the stockpot. Simmer 1 hour. 3. Taste before serving; add additional spices if you like.

Per Serving:
calories: 160 | fat: 2.91g | protein: 9.4g | carbs: 24.58g | sugars: 1.44g | fiber: 8.4g | sodium: 48mg

Manhattan Clam Chowder

Prep time: 10 minutes | Cook time: 1 hour 30 minutes | Serves 8

3 medium carrots, peeled and coarsely chopped	2½ cups minced clams, drained
3 large white or russet potatoes, peeled and coarsely chopped	2 cups canned tomatoes, slightly crushed
4 celery stalks, coarsely chopped	½ teaspoon dried thyme or 1 teaspoon minced fresh thyme
	Freshly ground black pepper

1. Add all the ingredients to a large stockpot. Cover and let simmer for 1½ hours. Taste and add a dash of salt if needed. Serve hot.

Per Serving:
calories: 164 | fat: 0.42g | protein: 4.05g | carbs: 37.36g | sugars: 5.54g | fiber: 3.4g | sodium: 305mg

Quick Moroccan-Inspired Chicken Stew

Prep time: 5 minutes | Cook time: 15 minutes | Serves 4 to 6

2 teaspoons ground cumin	5 garlic cloves, smashed and coarsely chopped
1 teaspoon ground cinnamon	2 onions, thinly sliced
½ teaspoon turmeric	1 tablespoon fresh lemon zest
½ teaspoon paprika	½ cup coarsely chopped olives
1½ pounds boneless, skinless chicken, cut into strips	2 cups low-sodium chicken broth
2 tablespoons extra-virgin olive oil	Cilantro, for garnish (optional)

1. In a medium bowl, mix together the cumin, cinnamon, turmeric, and paprika until well blended. Add the chicken, tossing to coat, and set aside. 2. Heat the extra-virgin olive oil in a large skillet or medium Dutch oven over medium-high heat. Add the chicken and garlic in one layer and cook, browning on all sides, about 2 minutes. 3. Add the onions, lemon zest, olives, and broth and bring the soup to a boil. Reduce the heat to medium low, cover, and simmer for 8 minutes. 4. Uncover the soup and let it simmer for another 2 to 3 minutes for the sauce to thicken slightly. Adjust the seasonings as desired and serve garnished with cilantro (if using). 5. Store the cooled soup in an airtight container in the refrigerator for up to 5 days.

Per Serving:
calories: 252 | fat: 10.35g | protein: 12.62g | carbs: 27.57g | sugars: 6.45g | fiber: 2.6g | sodium: 451mg

Cauli-Curry Bean Soup

Prep time: 10 minutes | Cook time: 25 minutes | Serves 8

2 cups chopped onion	4–5 tablespoons + 4 cups water
1½ cups chopped carrot or sweet potato	3–4 cups cauliflower florets
1½ tablespoons curry powder (or to taste; use more if you really love curry)	1 can (15 ounces) chickpeas, rinsed and drained
	1 can (15 ounces) adzuki or black beans, rinsed and drained
1¼ teaspoons sea salt	1 cup dried red lentils
Freshly ground black pepper to taste	1 can (28 ounces) crushed tomatoes
1 teaspoon mustard seeds	1 tablespoon grated fresh ginger
1 teaspoon ground cumin	
1 teaspoon ground turmeric	1–2 teaspoons pure maple syrup (optional)
¼ teaspoon ground cardamom	
⅛ teaspoon ground cinnamon	

1. In a large pot over medium-high heat, combine the onion, carrot or sweet potato, curry powder, salt, pepper, mustard seeds, cumin, turmeric, cardamom, cinnamon, and 3 tablespoons of the water. Stir, cover, and cook for 4 to 5 minutes, stirring occasionally. (Add another 1 to 2 tablespoons of water if needed to keep the vegetables and spices from sticking.) Add the cauliflower, chickpeas, beans, lentils, tomatoes, and remaining 4 cups water. Stir and increase the heat to high to bring to a boil. Reduce the heat to low, cover, and simmer for 15 to 20 minutes. Stir in the ginger and syrup (if using). Season to taste, and serve.

Per Serving:
calorie: 226 | fat: 2g | protein: 14g | carbs: 42g | sugars: 7g | fiber: 13g | sodium: 577mg

Sweet Potato Bisque with White Beans

Prep time: 10 minutes | Cook time: 40 minutes | Serves 4

1½ tablespoons balsamic vinegar	substitute smoked paprika, for extra flavor)
2 cups chopped onions	Freshly ground black pepper to taste
1 cup chopped red pepper (roasted or raw)	3–3½ cups peeled, cubed yellow sweet potatoes
1¼ teaspoons sea salt + more to taste	1½–2 teaspoons Dijon mustard
1 teaspoon dried rosemary or 2 teaspoons fresh, roughly chopped	4 cups water
	2 cans (15 ounces each) white beans, drained and rinsed
1 teaspoon paprika (can	

1. In a soup pot over medium-high heat, combine the vinegar, onions, red pepper, salt, rosemary, paprika, and black pepper. Cover, reduce the heat to medium or medium-low, and cook for 8 to 9 minutes, or until the onions are softened and starting to caramelize. Add the sweet potatoes and mustard, and stir with 1 to 2 tablespoons of the water. Cover and cook for a few minutes. Add the remaining water and increase the heat to high to bring to a boil. Reduce the heat to low, cover, and simmer for 15 to 20 minutes, or until the sweet potatoes are cooked through. Turn off the heat and add 1 cup of the white beans. Use an immersion blender to puree until the bisque is smooth and silky. Add the remaining beans, cover, and simmer for 5 to 10 minutes. Serve.

Per Serving:
calorie: 327 | fat: 1g | protein: 17g | carbs: 65g | sugars: 12g | fiber: 13g | sodium: 1044mg

Hearty Hamburger and Lentil Stew

Prep time: 0 minutes | Cook time: 55 minutes | Serves 8

2 tablespoons cold-pressed avocado oil	broth
	1 tablespoon Italian seasoning
2 garlic cloves, chopped	1 tablespoon paprika
1 large yellow onion, diced	1½ teaspoons fine sea salt
2 carrots, diced	1 extra-large russet potato, diced
2 celery stalks, diced	1 cup frozen green peas
2 pounds 95 percent lean ground beef	1 cup frozen corn
½ cup small green lentils	One 14½-ounce can no-salt petite diced tomatoes and their liquid
2 cups low-sodium roasted beef bone broth or vegetable	¼ cup tomato paste

1. Select the Sauté setting on the Instant Pot and heat the oil and garlic for 3 minutes, until the garlic is bubbling but not browned. Add the onion, carrots, and celery and sauté for 5 minutes, until the onion begins to soften. Add the beef and sauté, using a wooden spoon or spatula to break up the meat as it cooks, for 6 minutes, until cooked through and no streaks of pink remain. 2. Stir in the lentils, broth, Italian seasoning, paprika, and salt. Add the potato, peas, corn, and tomatoes and their liquid in layers on top of the lentils and beef, then add the tomato paste in a dollop on top. Do not stir in the vegetables and tomato paste. 3. Secure the lid and set the Pressure Release to Sealing. Press the Cancel button to reset the cooking program, then select the Pressure Cook or Manual setting and set the cooking time for 20 minutes at high pressure. (The pot will take about 20 minutes to come up to pressure before the cooking program begins.) 4. When the cooking program ends, let the pressure release naturally for at least 15 minutes, then move the Pressure Release to Venting to release any remaining steam. Open the pot and stir the stew to mix all of the ingredients. 5. Ladle the stew into bowls and serve hot.

Per Serving:
calories: 334 | fat: 8g | protein: 34g | carbs: 30g | sugars: 6g | fiber: 7g | sodium: 902mg

Nancy's Vegetable Beef Soup

Prep time: 25 minutes | Cook time: 8 hours | Serves 8

2-pound roast, cubed, or 2 pounds stewing meat	stewed tomatoes
	5 teaspoons salt-free beef bouillon powder
15-ounce can corn	
15-ounce can green beans	Tabasco, to taste
1-pound bag frozen peas	½ teaspoons salt
40-ounce can no-added-salt	

1. Combine all ingredients in the Instant Pot. Do not drain vegetables. 2. Add water to fill inner pot only to the fill line. 3. Secure the lid, or use the glass lid and set the Instant Pot on Slow Cook mode, Low for 8 hours, or until meat is tender and vegetables are soft.

Per Serving:
calories: 229 | fat: 5g | protein: 23g | carbs: 24g | sugars: 10g | fiber: 6g | sodium: 545mg

Pork Chili

Prep time: 15 minutes | Cook time: 4 hour to 8 minutes | Serves 5

1 pound boneless pork ribs	chiles, drained
2 14½-ounce cans fire-roasted diced tomatoes	½ cup chopped onion
	1 clove garlic, minced
4¼-ounce cans diced green	1 tablespoon chili powder

1. Layer the ingredients into the Instant Pot inner pot in the order given. 2. Secure the lid. Cook on the high Slow Cook function for 4 hours or on low 6–8 hours, or until pork is tender but not dry. 3. Cut up or shred meat. Stir into the chili and serve.

Per Serving:
calories: 180 | fat: 7g | protein: 18g | carbs: 12g | sugars: 6g | fiber: 3g | sodium: 495mg

Kickin' Chili

Prep time: 10 minutes | Cook time: 45 minutes | Serves 2

1 tablespoon extra-virgin olive oil	1 (15-ounce) can pinto beans, drained and rinsed
½ cup chopped onions	2 cups water
1 garlic clove, minced	2 teaspoons ground cumin
1 celery stalk, chopped	2 teaspoons chili powder
½ cup chopped bell peppers, any color	½ teaspoon cayenne pepper
	Salt, to season
1 cup diced tomatoes, undrained	Freshly ground black pepper, to season
1 cup frozen broccoli florets	

1. In a large pot set over medium heat, heat the olive oil. 2. Add the onions. Cook for about 5 minutes, or until tender. 3. Add the garlic. Cook for 2 to 3 minutes, or until lightly browned. 4. Add the celery and bell peppers. Cook for 5 minutes, or until the vegetables are soft. 5. Stir in the tomatoes, broccoli, pinto beans, and water. 6. Add the cumin, chili powder, and cayenne pepper. Season with salt and pepper. Stir to combine. Simmer for 30 minutes, stirring frequently. 7. Serve hot and enjoy!

Per Serving:
calories: 249 | fat: 4.9g | protein: 14.08g | carbs: 42.04g | sugars: 5.97g | fiber: 13.1g | sodium: 739mg

Favorite Chili

Prep time: 10 minutes | Cook time: 35 minutes | Serves 5

1 pound extra-lean ground beef	2 tablespoons chili powder
1 teaspoon salt	½ teaspoons cumin
½ teaspoons black pepper	1 cup water
1 tablespoon olive oil	16-ounce can chili beans
1 small onion, chopped	15-ounce can low-sodium crushed tomatoes
2 cloves garlic, minced	
1 green pepper, chopped	

1. Press Sauté button and adjust once to Sauté More function. Wait until indicator says "hot." 2. Season the ground beef with salt and black pepper. 3. Add the olive oil into the inner pot. Coat the whole bottom of the pot with the oil. 4. Add ground beef into the inner pot. The ground beef will start to release moisture. Allow the ground beef to brown and crisp slightly, stirring occasionally to break it up. Taste and adjust the seasoning with more salt and ground black pepper. 5. Add diced onion, minced garlic, chopped pepper, chili powder, and cumin. Sauté for about 5 minutes, until the spices start to release their fragrance. Stir frequently. 6. Add water and 1 can of chili beans, not drained. Mix well. Pour in 1 can of crushed tomatoes. 7. Close and secure lid, making sure vent is set to sealing, and pressure cook on Manual at high pressure for 10 minutes. 8. Let the pressure release naturally when cooking time is up. Open the lid carefully.

Per Serving:
calories: 213 | fat: 10g | protein: 18g | carbs: 11g | sugars: 4g | fiber: 4g | sodium: 385mg

Pumpkin Soup

Prep time: 15 minutes | Cook time: 30 minutes | Serves 6

2 cups store-bought low-sodium seafood broth, divided	winter squash, peeled and cut into 1-inch cubes
1 bunch collard greens, stemmed and cut into ribbons	1 teaspoon paprika
	1 teaspoon dried dill
1 tomato, chopped	2 (5-ounce) cans boneless, skinless salmon in water, rinsed
1 garlic clove, minced	
1 butternut squash or other	

1. In a heavy-bottomed large stockpot, bring ½ cup of broth to a simmer over medium heat. 2. Add the collard greens, tomato, and garlic and cook for 5 minutes, or until the greens are wilted and the garlic is softened. 3. Add the squash, paprika, dill, and remaining 1½ cups of broth. Cover and cook for 20 minutes, or until the squash is tender. 4. Add the salmon and cook for 3 minutes, or just enough for the flavors to come together.

Per Serving:
calories: 161 | fat: 5.5g | protein: 23.92g | carbs: 4.51g | sugars: 1.18g | fiber: 1g | sodium: 579mg

Green Chile Corn Chowder

Prep time: 20 minutes | Cook time: 7 to 8 hours | Serves 8

16-ounce can cream-style corn	½ cup chopped cooked ham
3 potatoes, peeled and diced	2 10½-ounce cans 100% fat-free lower-sodium chicken broth
2 tablespoons chopped fresh chives	
4-ounce can diced green chilies, drained	Pepper to taste
	Tabasco sauce to taste
2-ounce jar chopped pimentos, drained	1 cup fat-free milk

1. Combine all ingredients, except milk, in the inner pot of the Instant Pot. 2. Secure the lid and cook using the Slow Cook function on low 7–8 hours or until potatoes are tender. 3. When cook time is up, remove the lid and stir in the milk. Cover and let simmer another 20 minutes.

Per Serving:
calories: 124 | fat: 2g | protein: 6g | carbs: 21g | sugars: 7g | fiber: 2g | sodium: 563mg

Lentil Stew

Prep time: 10 minutes | Cook time: 30 minutes | Serves 2

½ cup dry lentils, picked through, debris removed, rinsed and drained
2½ cups water
1 bay leaf
2 teaspoons dried tarragon
2 teaspoons dried thyme
2 garlic cloves, minced
2 medium carrots, chopped
2 medium tomatoes, diced
1 celery stalk, chopped
1 tablespoon extra-virgin olive oil
1 medium onion, diced
1 cup frozen spinach
Salt, to season
Freshly ground black pepper, to season

1. In a soup pot set over high heat, stir together the lentils, water, bay leaf, tarragon, thyme, and garlic. 2. Add the carrots, tomatoes, and celery. Cover. Bring to a boil. Reduce the heat to low and stir the soup. Simmer for 15 to 20 minutes, covered, or until the lentils are tender. 3. While the vegetables simmer, place a skillet over medium heat. Add the olive oil and onion. Sauté for about 10 minutes, or until browned. Remove the skillet from the heat. 4. When the lentils are tender, remove and discard the bay leaf. Add the cooked onion and the spinach to the soup. Heat for 5 to 10 minutes more, or until the spinach is cooked. 5. Season with salt and pepper. 6. Enjoy immediately.

Per Serving:
calories: 214 | fat: 7.4g | protein: 9.84g | carbs: 31.38g | sugars: 9.94g | fiber: 10.9g | sodium: 871mg

Green Ginger Soup

Prep time: 10 minutes | Cook time: 30 minutes | Serves 2

½ cup chopped onion
½ cup peeled, chopped fennel
1 small zucchini, chopped
½ cup frozen lima beans
¼ cup uncooked brown rice
1 bay leaf
1 teaspoon dried basil
⅛ teaspoon freshly ground black pepper
2 cups water
1 cup frozen green beans
¼ cup fresh parsley, chopped
1 (3-inch) piece fresh ginger, peeled, grated, and pressed through a strainer to extract the juice (about 2 to 3 tablespoons)
Salt, to season
2 tablespoons chopped fresh chives

1. In a large pot set over medium-high heat, stir together the onion, fennel, zucchini, lima beans, rice, bay leaf, basil, pepper, and water. Bring to a boil. Reduce the heat to low. Simmer for 15 minutes. 2. Add the green beans. Simmer for about 5 minutes, uncovered, until tender. 3. Stir in the parsley. 4. Remove and discard the bay leaf. 5. In a blender or food processor, purée the soup in batches until smooth, adding water if necessary to thin. 6. Blend in the ginger juice. 7. Season with salt. Garnish with the chives. 8. Serve hot and enjoy immediately!

Per Serving:
calories: 189 | fat: 1.52g | protein: 7.14g | carbs: 38.58g | sugars: 3.1g | fiber: 6.8g | sodium: 338mg

Thai Corn and Sweet Potato Stew

Prep time: 10 minutes | Cook time: 20 minutes | Serves 4

1 small can (5.5 ounces) light coconut milk
1 cup chopped onion
½ cup chopped celery
2 cups cubed sweet potato (can use frozen)
¾–1 teaspoon sea salt
2 cups water
1½ tablespoons Thai yellow or red curry paste
1½ cups frozen corn kernels
1½ cups chopped red bell pepper
1 package (12–14 ounces) tofu, cut into cubes, or 1 can (14 ounces) black beans, rinsed and drained
2½ tablespoons freshly squeezed lime juice
4–5 cups baby spinach leaves
⅓–½ cup fresh cilantro or Thai basil, chopped
Lime wedges (optional)

1. In a soup pot over high heat, warm 2 tablespoons of the coconut milk. Add the onion, celery, sweet potato, and ¾ teaspoon of the salt, and sauté for 4 to 5 minutes. Add the water, Thai paste, and remaining coconut milk. Increase the heat to high to bring to a boil. Cover and reduce the heat to medium-low, and let the mixture simmer for 8 to 10 minutes, or until the sweet potato has softened. Turn off the heat, and use an immersion blender to puree the soup base. Add the corn, bell pepper, and tofu or beans, and turn the heat to medium-low. Cover and cook for 3 to 4 minutes to heat through. Add the lime juice, spinach, and cilantro or basil, and stir until the spinach has just wilted. Taste, and season with the remaining ¼ teaspoon salt, if desired. Serve with the lime wedges (if using).

Per Serving:
calorie: 223 | fat: 7g | protein: 10g | carbs: 36g | sugars: 11g | fiber: 6g | sodium: 723mg

Golden Lentil–Pea Soup

Prep time: 10 minutes | Cook time: 50 minutes | Serves 6

1 cup diced onion
1 cup chopped celery
1 tablespoon smoked paprika
1 teaspoon dried rosemary
1 teaspoon ground cumin
¼ teaspoon allspice
¼ teaspoon sea salt
2–3 tablespoons + 4 cups water
4 cups chopped yellow sweet potato (or 2 cups chopped sweet potato and 2 cups chopped carrot)
1½ cups dried red lentils
1 cup dried yellow split peas
2 cups vegetable broth
1½ tablespoons apple cider vinegar

1. In a large soup pot over medium-high heat, combine the onion, celery, paprika, rosemary, cumin, allspice, salt, and 2 to 3 tablespoons of the water, and stir. Cook for 8 to 9 minutes, then add the potato, lentils, split peas, broth, and the remaining 4 cups of water. Stir to combine. Increase the heat to high to bring to a boil. Reduce the heat to low, cover, and simmer for 40 to 45 minutes, or until the peas are completely softened. Stir in the apple cider vinegar, season with additional salt and pepper if desired, and serve.

Per Serving:
calorie: 340 | fat: 1g | protein: 21g | carbs: 64g | sugars: 8g | fiber: 20g | sodium: 363mg

Ham and Potato Chowder

Prep time: 25 minutes | Cook time: 8 hour s | Serves 5

5-ounce package scalloped potatoes	1 cup chopped celery
Sauce mix from potato package	⅓ cup chopped onions
1 cup extra-lean, reduced-sodium, cooked ham, cut into narrow strips	Pepper to taste
4 teaspoons sodium-free bouillon powder	2 cups fat-free half-and-half
4 cups water	⅓ cup flour

1. Combine potatoes, sauce mix, ham, bouillon powder, water, celery, onions, and pepper in the inner pot of the Instant Pot. 2. Secure the lid and cook using the Slow Cook function on low for 7 hours. 3. Combine half-and-half and flour. Remove the lid and gradually add to the inner pot, blending well. 4. Secure the lid once more and cook on the low Slow Cook function for up to 1 hour more, stirring occasionally until thickened.

Per Serving:
calories: 241 | fat: 3g | protein: 11g | carbs: 41g | sugars: 8g | fiber: 3g | sodium: 836mg

French Market Soup

Prep time: 20 minutes | Cook time: 1 hour | Serves 8

2 cups mixed dry beans, washed with stones removed	16-ounce can low-sodium tomatoes
7 cups water	1 large onion, chopped
1 ham hock, all visible fat removed	1 garlic clove, minced
1 teaspoon salt	1 chile, chopped, or 1 teaspoon chili powder
¼ teaspoon pepper	¼ cup lemon juice

1. Combine all ingredients in the inner pot of the Instant Pot. 2. Secure the lid and make sure vent is set to sealing. Using Manual, set the Instant Pot to cook for 60 minutes. 3. When cooking time is over, let the pressure release naturally. When the Instant Pot is ready, unlock the lid, then remove the bone and any hard or fatty pieces. Pull the meat off the bone and chop into small pieces. Add the ham back into the Instant Pot.

Per Serving:
calories: 191 | fat: 4g | protein: 12g | carbs: 29g | sugars: 5g | fiber: 7g | sodium: 488mg

Hearty Beef and Veggie Stew

Prep time: 15 minutes | Cook time: 45 minutes | Serves 4

2 tbsp (30 ml) avocado oil	3 cups (720 ml) low-sodium beef broth
1 lb (454 g) extra lean beef stew meat	½ tsp salt
1 medium yellow onion, cut into large chunks	½ tsp black pepper
4 large carrots, cut into 2-inch (5-cm) chunks	¼ to ⅓ cup (16 to 21 g) finely chopped fresh herbs of choice (see Tip)
5 to 6 small red potatoes, quartered	

1. Heat the oil in a large Dutch oven or pot over medium-high heat. 2. Add the stew meat and cook it for 2 to 3 minutes on each side, until it is brown on all sides but still pink in the center. Remove the stew meat from the Dutch oven and set it aside. 3. Add the onion and carrots to the Dutch oven and cook them for 5 to 10 minutes, until they start to soften. 4. Add the potatoes, broth, salt, black pepper, and herbs. Bring the mixture to a boil. Reduce the heat to low and simmer the stew for 30 minutes, until the vegetables are fork-tender. 5. Add the stew meat to the stew and cook it for 5 to 10 minutes to warm the meat through. Serve the stew immediately.

Per Serving:
calorie: 400 | fat: 11g | protein: 32g | carbs: 45g | sugars: 8g | fiber: 6g | sodium: 742mg

Chapter 10 Desserts

Orange Praline with Yogurt

Prep time: 10 minutes | Cook time: 10 minutes | Serves 6

3 tablespoons sugar	⅛ teaspoon ground cloves
4 teaspoons water	1 tablespoon orange zest (optional)
⅓ cup slivered almonds, toasted	Pinch kosher salt
½ teaspoon ground cinnamon	3 cups plain Greek yogurt

1. Preheat the oven to 375°F. Line a baking sheet with parchment paper. 2. In a small saucepan, stir together the sugar and water and cook over high heat until light golden-brown in color, 3 to 4 minutes. Do not stir, but instead gently swirl to help the sugar dissolve. Add the almonds and cook for 1 minute. The goal is to coat the almonds with the heated sugar (think caramel here) without burning. Pour the mixture onto the prepared baking sheet and set aside to cool for about 5 minutes. 3. Meanwhile, in a medium bowl, stir together the cinnamon, cloves, orange zest (if using), and salt. 4. Break the praline into smaller pieces and toss them in the spices. 5. Evenly divide the yogurt among six bowls and serve topped with the spiced praline. Store the praline in a sealed container at room temperature for up to 2 weeks.

Per Serving:
calories: 126 | fat: 3g | protein: 8g | carbs: 16g | sugars: 15g | fiber: 1g | sodium: 250mg

Banana Pineapple Freeze

Prep time: 30 minutes | Cook time: 0 minutes | Serves 12

2 cups mashed ripe bananas	1 cup unsweetened crushed pineapple, undrained
2 cups unsweetened orange juice	½ teaspoon ground cinnamon
2 tablespoon fresh lemon juice	

1. In a food processor, combine all ingredients, and process until smooth and creamy. 2. Pour the mixture into a 9-x-9-x-2-inch baking dish, and freeze overnight or until firm. Serve chilled.

Per Serving:
calories: 60 | fat: 0g | protein: 1g | carbs: 15g | sugars: 9g | fiber: 1g | sodium: 1mg

Baked Berry Cups with Crispy Cinnamon Wedges

Prep time: 25 minutes | Cook time: 30 minutes | Serves 4

2 teaspoons sugar	1 teaspoon grated orange peel, if desired
¾ teaspoon ground cinnamon	1½ cups fresh blueberries
Butter-flavor cooking spray	1½ cups fresh raspberries
1 balanced carb whole wheat tortilla (6 inch)	About 1 cup fat-free whipped cream topping (from aerosol can)
¼ cup sugar	
2 tablespoons white whole wheat flour	

1 Heat oven to 375°F. In sandwich-size resealable food-storage plastic bag, combine 2 teaspoons sugar and ½ teaspoon of the cinnamon. Using cooking spray, spray both sides of tortilla, about 3 seconds per side; cut tortilla into 8 wedges. In bag with cinnamon-sugar, add wedges; seal bag. Shake to coat wedges evenly. 2 On ungreased cookie sheet, spread out wedges. Bake 7 to 9 minutes, turning once, until just beginning to crisp (wedges will continue to crisp while cooling). Cool about 15 minutes. 3 Meanwhile, spray 4 (6-oz) custard cups or ramekins with cooking spray; place cups on another cookie sheet. In small bowl, stir ¼ cup sugar, the flour, orange peel and remaining ¼ teaspoon cinnamon until blended. In medium bowl, gently toss berries with sugar mixture; divide evenly among custard cups. 4 Bake 15 minutes; stir gently. Bake 5 to 7 minutes longer or until liquid is bubbling around edges. Cool at least 15 minutes. 5 To serve, top each cup with about ¼ cup whipped cream topping; serve tortilla wedges with berry cups. Serve warm.

Per Serving:
calorie: 180 | fat: 2g | protein: 3g | carbs: 37g | sugars: 25g | fiber: 7g | sodium: 60mg

Oatmeal Cookies

Prep time: 5 minutes | Cook time: 15 minutes | Serves 16

¾ cup almond flour	¼ teaspoon salt
¾ cup old-fashioned oats	¼ cup unsweetened applesauce
¼ cup shredded unsweetened coconut	1 large egg
1 teaspoon baking powder	1 tablespoon pure maple syrup
1 teaspoon ground cinnamon	2 tablespoons coconut oil, melted

1. Preheat the oven to 350°F. 2. In a medium mixing bowl, combine the almond flour, oats, coconut, baking powder, cinnamon, and salt, and mix well. 3. In another medium bowl, combine the applesauce, egg, maple syrup, and coconut oil, and mix. Stir the wet mixture into the dry mixture. 4. Form the dough into balls a little bigger than a tablespoon and place on a baking sheet, leaving at least 1 inch between them. Bake for 12 minutes until the cookies are just browned. Remove from the oven and let cool for 5 minutes. 5. Using a spatula, remove the cookies and cool on a rack.

Per Serving:
calorie: 76 | fat: 6g | protein: 2g | carbs: 5g | sugars: 1g | fiber: 1g | sodium: 57mg

Raspberry Nice Cream

Prep time: 5 minutes | Cook time: 0 minutes | Serves 3

2 cups frozen, sliced, overripe bananas	Pinch of sea salt
2 cups frozen or fresh raspberries	1–2 tablespoons coconut nectar or 1–1½ tablespoons pure maple syrup

1. In a food processor or high-speed blender, combine the bananas, raspberries, salt, and 1 tablespoon of the nectar or syrup. Puree until smooth. Taste, and add the remaining nectar or syrup, if desired. Serve immediately, if you like a soft-serve consistency, or transfer to an airtight container and freeze for an hour or more, if you like a firmer texture.

Per Serving:
calorie: 193| fat: 1g | protein: 3g | carbs: 47g | sugars: 24g | fiber: 13g | sodium: 101mg

Creamy Orange Cheesecake

Prep time: 35 minutes | Cook time: 35 minutes | Serves 10

Sauce:	⅔ cup sugar
¾ cup graham cracker crumbs	2 eggs
2 tablespoons sugar	1 egg yolk
3 tablespoons melted, light, soft tub margarine	¼ cup frozen orange juice concentrate
Sauce:	1 teaspoon orange zest
2 (8-ounce) packages fat-free cream cheese, at room temperature	1 tablespoon flour
	½ teaspoon vanilla
	1½ cups water

1. Combine crust ingredients. Pat into 7" springform pan. 2. Cream together cream cheese and sugar. Add eggs and yolk. Beat for 3 minutes. 3. Beat in juice, zest, flour, and vanilla. Beat 2 minutes. 4. Pour batter into crust. Cover with foil. 5. Place the trivet into your Instant Pot and pour in 1½ cups water. Place a foil sling on top of the trivet, then place the springform pan on top. 6. Secure the lid and make sure lid is set to sealing. Press Manual and set for 35 minutes. 7. When cook time is up, press Cancel and allow the pressure to release naturally for 7 minutes, then release the remaining pressure manually. 8. Carefully remove the springform pan by using hot pads to lift the pan up by the foil sling. Uncover and place on a cooling rack until cool, then refrigerate for 8 hours.

Per Serving:
calories: 159 | fat: 3g | protein: 9g | carbs: 25g | sugars: 19g | fiber: 0g | sodium: 300mg

Chocolate Tahini Bombs

Prep time: 20 minutes | Cook time: 8 minutes | Makes 15 each

15 whole dates, pits removed (date intact, not split in half completely)	4 ounces dark chocolate, chopped
2½ tablespoons tahini, divided	1 tablespoon toasted sesame seeds
½ cup canned coconut milk	

1. Line a baking sheet with parchment paper. 2. Fill each date with a small amount of the tahini, roughly ¼ teaspoon, and place them on the prepared baking sheet. Put the filled dates in the freezer for 10 to 15 minutes. 3. Meanwhile, heat the coconut milk in a small saucepan over medium-low until simmering. 4. Place the chocolate in a medium heatproof bowl, and when the milk is simmering, pour it into the bowl and let stand for 3 minutes to soften the chocolate. 5. Stir the mixture until it is smooth and the chocolate is completely melted. 6. Remove the dates from the freezer and dip one date at a time into the chocolate. Coat evenly using a fork and place them back on the baking sheet. Sprinkle the dates with the sesame seeds and repeat until all dates are coated in chocolate. 7. Allow to cool completely for the chocolate to harden, or eat immediately.

Per Serving:
calories: 98 | fat: 6g | protein: 1g | carbs: 9g | sugars: 6g | fiber: 2g | sodium: 6mg

Cherry Delight

Prep time: 20 minutes | Cook time: 50 minutes | Serves 12

20-ounce can cherry pie filling, light	melted
½ package yellow cake mix	⅓ cup walnuts, optional
¼ cup light, soft tub margarine,	1 cup water

1. Grease a 7" springform pan then pour the pie filing inside. 2. Combine dry cake mix and margarine (mixture will be crumbly) in a bowl. Sprinkle over filling. Sprinkle with walnuts. 3. Cover the pan with foil. 4. Place the trivet into your Instant Pot and pour in 1 cup of water. Place a foil sling on top of the trivet, then place the springform pan on top. 5. Secure the lid and make sure lid is set to sealing. Press Steam and set for 50 minutes. 6. When cook time is up, release the pressure manually, then carefully remove the springform pan by using hot pads to lift the pan up by the foil sling. Place on a cooling rack for 1–2 hours.

Per Serving:
calories: 137| fat: 4g | protein: 1g | carbs: 26g | sugars: 19g | fiber: 1g | sodium: 174mg

Creamy Pineapple-Pecan Dessert Squares

Prep time: 25 minutes | Cook time: 0 minutes | Serves 18

¾ cup boiling water	¼ cup chopped pecans
1 package (4-serving size) lemon sugar-free gelatin	3 tablespoons butter or margarine, melted
1 cup unsweetened pineapple juice	1 package (8 oz) fat-free cream cheese
1½ cups graham cracker crumbs	1 container (8 oz) fat-free sour cream
½ cup sugar	1 can (8 oz) crushed pineapple, undrained
¼ cup shredded coconut	

1 In large bowl, pour boiling water over gelatin; stir about 2 minutes or until gelatin is completely dissolved. Stir in pineapple juice. Refrigerate about 30 minutes or until mixture is syrupy and just beginning to thicken. 2 Meanwhile, in 13x9-inch (3-quart) glass baking dish, toss cracker crumbs, ¼ cup of the sugar, the coconut, pecans and melted butter until well mixed. Reserve ½ cup crumb mixture for topping. Press remaining mixture in bottom of dish. 3 In medium bowl, beat cream cheese, sour cream and remaining ¼ cup sugar with electric mixer on medium speed until smooth; set aside. 4 Beat gelatin mixture with electric mixer on low speed until foamy; beat on high speed until light and fluffy (mixture will look like beaten egg whites). Beat in cream cheese mixture just until mixed. Gently stir in pineapple (with liquid). Pour into crust-lined dish; smooth top. Sprinkle reserved ½ cup crumb mixture over top. Refrigerate about 4 hours or until set. For servings, cut into 6 rows by 3 rows.

Per Serving:
calorie: 120 | fat: 4.5g | protein: 3g | carbs: 18g | sugars: 11g | fiber: 0g | sodium: 180mg

Spiced Rice Pudding

Prep time: 5 minutes | Cook time: 35 minutes | Serves 6

2 cups short-grain brown rice	¼ teaspoon orange extract
6 cups fat-free milk	Juice of 2 oranges (about ¾ cup)
1 teaspoon ground nutmeg, plus more for serving	½ cup erythritol or other brown sugar replacement
1 teaspoon ground cinnamon, plus more for serving	

1. In an electric pressure cooker, stir the rice, milk, nutmeg, cinnamon, orange extract, orange juice, and erythritol together. 2. Close and lock the lid, and set the pressure valve to sealing. 3. Select the Manual/Pressure Cook setting, and cook for 35 minutes. 4. Once cooking is complete, quick-release the pressure. Carefully remove the lid. 5. Stir well and spoon into serving dishes. Enjoy with an additional sprinkle of nutmeg and cinnamon.

Per Serving:
calories: 339 | fat: 2g | protein: 13g | carbs: 62g | sugars: 14g | fiber: 3g | sodium: 142mg

Apple Crunch

Prep time: 13 minutes | Cook time: 2 minutes | Serves 4

3 apples, peeled, cored, and sliced (about 1½ pounds)	ground cinnamon
1 teaspoon pure maple syrup	¼ cup unsweetened apple juice, apple cider, or water
1 teaspoon apple pie spice or	¼ cup low-sugar granola

1. In the electric pressure cooker, combine the apples, maple syrup, apple pie spice, and apple juice. 2. Close and lock the lid of the pressure cooker. Set the valve to sealing. 3. Cook on high pressure for 2 minutes. 4. When the cooking is complete, hit Cancel and quick release the pressure. 5. Once the pin drops, unlock and remove the lid. 6. Spoon the apples into 4 serving bowls and sprinkle each with 1 tablespoon of granola.

Per Serving:
calories: 103 | fat: 1g | protein: 1g | carbs: 26g | sugars: 18g | fiber: 4g | sodium: 13mg

Berry Bubble

Prep time: 10 minutes | Cook time: 45 minutes | Serves 4

Batter Topping	1 teaspoon lemon zest
1 cup spelt flour	Berry Base
2 tablespoons coconut sugar	4–4½ cups fresh or frozen berries
1 teaspoon baking powder	2 tablespoons coconut sugar
½ teaspoon cinnamon	2 teaspoons tapioca starch
⅛ teaspoon sea salt	1 teaspoon pure vanilla extract
½ cup plain low-fat nondairy milk	Pinch of sea salt
¼ cup unsweetened applesauce	¼ cup water
2 teaspoons lemon juice	

1. Preheat the oven to 350°F. 2. To prepare the batter topping: In a large bowl, combine the flour, sugar, baking powder, cinnamon, and salt. In a small bowl, combine the milk, applesauce, lemon juice, and lemon zest. Add the wet mixture to the dry and stir until just well combined. The batter should be fairly thick. 3. To make the fruit base: In an 8" x 8" glass baking dish, combine the berries, sugar, tapioca starch, vanilla, and salt, and toss thoroughly. Add the water and toss again. Roughly distribute the batter over the top of the berry base. (It doesn't need to fully cover the berries.) Bake for about 45 minutes, or until the topping is fully baked through.

Per Serving:
calorie: 225 | fat: 1g | protein: 6g | carbs: 51g | sugars: 24g | fiber: 7g | sodium: 285mg

Apple Cinnamon Bread Pudding

Prep time: 5 minutes | Cook time: 1 hour | Serves 10

9 slices whole-wheat bread, cubed (about 5–6 cups)	1 cup egg substitute
2 cups cubed apples (Granny Smith apples work well)	2 teaspoon vanilla
	2 teaspoon cinnamon
4 cups fat-free milk	¼ cup agave nectar
	½ cup raisins

1 Preheat the oven to 350 degrees. 2 In a large baking dish, combine the bread and apples. 3 In a bowl, whisk together the milk, egg substitute, vanilla, cinnamon, and agave nectar. Add the raisins. Pour the milk mixture over the bread, and let stand for 15 minutes so the bread can absorb some of the liquid. 4 Bake at 350 degrees for 40–45 minutes, until the bread pudding is set and firm. Cut into squares, and serve warm with whipped topping or low-fat ice cream.

Per Serving:
calories: 175 | fat: 1g | protein: 10g | carbs: 28g | sugars: 15g | fiber: 3g | sodium: 232mg

Double-Ginger Cookies

Prep time: 45 minutes | Cook time: 8 to 10 minutes | Makes 5 dozen cookies

¾ cup sugar	½ teaspoon ground cinnamon
¼ cup butter or margarine, softened	½ teaspoon ground ginger
	¼ teaspoon ground cloves
1 egg or ¼ cup fat-free egg product	¼ teaspoon salt
	¼ cup sugar
¼ cup molasses	¼ cup orange marmalade
1¾ cups all-purpose flour	2 tablespoons finely chopped crystallized ginger
1 teaspoon baking soda	

1 In medium bowl, beat ¾ cup sugar, the butter, egg and molasses with electric mixer on medium speed, or mix with spoon. Stir in flour, baking soda, cinnamon, ground ginger, cloves and salt. Cover and refrigerate at least 2 hours, until firm. 2 Heat oven to 350°F. Lightly spray cookie sheets with cooking spray. Place ¼ cup sugar in small bowl. Shape dough into ¾-inch balls; roll in sugar. Place balls about 2 inches apart on cookie sheet. Make indentation in center of each ball, using finger. Fill each indentation with slightly less than ¼ teaspoon of the marmalade. Sprinkle with crystallized ginger. 3 Bake 8 to 10 minutes or until set. Immediately transfer from cookie sheets to cooling racks. Cool completely, about 30 minutes.

Per Serving:
1 Cookie: calorie: 45 | fat: 1g | protein: 0g | carbs: 9g | sugars: 5g | fiber: 0g | sodium: 40mg

Goat Cheese–Stuffed Pears

Prep time: 6 minutes | Cook time: 2 minutes | Serves 4

2 ounces goat cheese, at room temperature	lengthwise and cored
2 teaspoons pure maple syrup	2 tablespoons chopped pistachios, toasted
2 ripe, firm pears, halved	

1. Pour 1 cup of water into the electric pressure cooker and insert a wire rack or trivet. 2. In a small bowl, combine the goat cheese and maple syrup. 3. Spoon the goat cheese mixture into the cored pear halves. Place the pears on the rack inside the pot, cut-side up. 4. Close and lock the lid of the pressure cooker. Set the valve to sealing. 5. Cook on high pressure for 2 minutes. 6. When the cooking is complete, hit Cancel and quick release the pressure. 7. Once the pin drops, unlock and remove the lid. 8. Using tongs, carefully transfer the pears to serving plates. 9. Sprinkle with pistachios and serve immediately.

Per Serving:
(½ pear): calories: 120 | fat: 5g | protein: 4g | carbs: 17g | sugars: 11g | fiber: 3g | sodium: 54mg

Grilled Watermelon with Avocado Mousse

Prep time: 10 minutes | Cook time: 10 minutes | Serves 8

1 small, seedless watermelon, halved and cut into 1-inch rounds	peeled
	½ cup fat-free plain yogurt
2 ripe avocados, pitted and	¼ teaspoon cayenne pepper

1. On a hot grill, grill the watermelon slices for 2 to 3 minutes on each side, or until you can see the grill marks. 2. To make the avocado mousse, in a blender, combine the avocados, yogurt, and cayenne and process until smooth. 3. To serve, cut each watermelon round in half. Top each with a generous dollop of avocado mousse.

Per Serving:
calories: 162 | fat: 8g | protein: 3g | carbs: 22g | sugars: 14g | fiber: 5g | sodium: 13mg

Oatmeal Chippers

Prep time: 10 minutes | Cook time: 11 minutes | Makes 20 chippers

3–3½ tablespoons almond butter (or tigernut butter, for nut-free)	1 cup + 2 tablespoons rolled oats
¼ cup pure maple syrup	1½ teaspoons baking powder
¼ cup brown rice syrup	½ teaspoon cinnamon
2 teaspoons pure vanilla extract	¼ teaspoon sea salt
1⅓ cups oat flour	2–3 tablespoons sugar-free nondairy chocolate chips

1. Preheat the oven to 350°F. Line a baking sheet with parchment paper. 2. In the bowl of a mixer, combine the almond butter, maple syrup, brown rice syrup, and vanilla. Using the paddle attachment, mix on low speed for a couple of minutes, until creamy. Turn off the mixer and add the flour, oats, baking powder, cinnamon, salt, and chocolate chips. Mix on low speed until incorporated. Place 1½-tablespoon mounds on the prepared baking sheet, spacing them 1" to 2" apart, and flatten slightly. Bake for 11 minutes, or until just set to the touch. Remove from the oven, let cool on the pan for just a minute, and then transfer the cookies to a cooling rack.

Per Serving:
calorie: 90 | fat: 2g | protein: 2g | carbs: 16g | sugars: 4g | fiber: 2g | sodium: 75mg

Cream Cheese Swirl Brownies

Prep time: 10 minutes | Cook time: 20 minutes | Serves 12

2 eggs	powder
¼ cup unsweetened applesauce	¼ cup coconut flour
¼ cup coconut oil, melted	¼ teaspoon salt
3 tablespoons pure maple syrup, divided	1 teaspoon baking powder
	2 tablespoons low-fat cream cheese
¼ cup unsweetened cocoa	

1. Preheat the oven to 350°F. Grease an 8-by-8-inch baking dish. 2. In a large mixing bowl, beat the eggs with the applesauce, coconut oil, and 2 tablespoons of maple syrup. 3. Stir in the cocoa powder and coconut flour, and mix well. Sprinkle the salt and baking powder evenly over the surface and mix well to incorporate. Transfer the mixture to the prepared baking dish. 4. In a small, microwave-safe bowl, microwave the cream cheese for 10 to 20 seconds until softened. Add the remaining 1 tablespoon of maple syrup and mix to combine. 5. Drop the cream cheese onto the batter, and use a toothpick or chopstick to swirl it on the surface. Bake for 20 minutes, until a toothpick inserted in the center comes out clean. Cool and cut into 12 squares. 6. Store refrigerated in a covered container for up to 5 days.

Per Serving:
calories: 84 | fat: 6g | protein: 2g | carbs: 6g | sugars: 4g | fiber: 2g | sodium: 93mg

Dump Cake

Prep time: 20 minutes | Cook time: 50 minutes | Serves 15

20-ounce can crushed pineapple	cake mix
	Cinnamon
21-ounce can light blueberry or cherry pie filling	⅓ cup light, soft tub margarine
	⅓ cup chopped walnuts
18½-ounce package yellow	1 cup water

1. Grease bottom and sides of a 7" springform pan. 2. Spread layers of pineapple, blueberry pie filling, and dry cake mix. Be careful not to mix the layers. 3. Sprinkle with cinnamon. 4. Top with thin layers of margarine chunks and nuts. 5. Cover the pan with foil. 6. Place the trivet into your Instant Pot and pour in 1 cup of water. Place a foil sling on top of the trivet, then place the springform pan on top. 7. Secure the lid and make sure lid is set to sealing. Press Steam and set for 50 minutes. 8. When cook time is up, release the pressure manually, then carefully remove the springform pan by using hot pads to lift the pan up by the foil sling. Place on a cooling rack until cool.

Per Serving:
calories: 219 | fat: 6g | protein: 2g | carbs: 41g | sugars: 28g | fiber: 1g | sodium: 250mg

Chai Pear-Fig Compote

Prep time: 20 minutes | Cook time: 3 minutes | Serves 4

1 vanilla chai tea bag	1½ pounds pears, peeled and chopped (about 3 cups)
1 (3-inch) cinnamon stick	½ cup chopped dried figs
1 strip lemon peel (about 2-by-½ inches)	2 tablespoons raisins

1. Pour 1 cup of water into the electric pressure cooker and hit Sauté/More. When the water comes to a boil, add the tea bag and cinnamon stick. Hit Cancel. Let the tea steep for 5 minutes, then remove and discard the tea bag. 2. Add the lemon peel, pears, figs, and raisins to the pot. 3. Close and lock the lid of the pressure cooker. Set the valve to sealing. 4. Cook on high pressure for 3 minutes. 5. When the cooking is complete, hit Cancel and quick release the pressure. 6. Once the pin drops, unlock and remove the lid. 7. Remove the lemon peel and cinnamon stick. Serve warm or cool to room temperature and refrigerate.

Per Serving:
calories: 167 | fat: 1g | protein: 2g | carbs: 44g | sugars: 29g | fiber: 9g | sodium: 4mg

Crustless Peanut Butter Cheesecake

Prep time: 10 minutes | Cook time: 10 minutes | Serves 2

4 ounces (113 g) cream cheese, softened	1 tablespoon all-natural, no-sugar-added peanut butter
2 tablespoons confectioners' erythritol	½ teaspoon vanilla extract
	1 large egg, whisked

1. In a medium bowl, mix cream cheese and erythritol until smooth. Add peanut butter and vanilla, mixing until smooth. Add egg and stir just until combined. 2. Spoon mixture into an ungreased springform pan and place into air fryer basket. Adjust the temperature to 300°F (149°C) and bake for 10 minutes. Edges will be firm, but center will be mostly set with only a small amount of jiggle when done. 3. Let pan cool at room temperature 30 minutes, cover with plastic wrap, then place into refrigerator at least 2 hours. Serve chilled.

Per Serving:
calories: 281 | fat: 26g | protein: 8g | carbs: 4g | net carbs: 4g | fiber: 0g

Mango Nice Cream

Prep time: 10 minutes | Cook time: 0 minutes | Serves 4

2 cups frozen mango chunks	½ teaspoon pure vanilla extract
1 cup frozen, sliced, overripe banana (can use room temperature, but must be overripe)	¼ cup + 1–2 tablespoons low-fat nondairy milk
	2–3 tablespoons coconut nectar or pure maple syrup (optional)
Pinch of sea salt	

1. In a food processor or high-speed blender, combine the mango, banana, salt, vanilla, and ¼ cup of the milk. Pulse to get things moving, and then puree, adding the remaining 1 to 2 tablespoons milk if needed. Taste, and add the nectar or syrup, if desired. Serve, or transfer to an airtight container and freeze for an hour or more to set more firmly before serving.

Per Serving:
calorie: 116 | fat: 0.5g | protein: 1g | carbs: 29g | sugars: 22g | fiber: 2g | sodium: 81mg

Instant Pot Tapioca

Prep time: 10 minutes | Cook time: 7 minutes | Serves 6

2 cups water	Sugar substitute to equal ¼ cup sugar
1 cup small pearl tapioca	1 teaspoon vanilla
½ cup sugar	Fruit of choice, optional
4 eggs	
½ cup evaporated skim milk	

1. Combine water and tapioca in Instant Pot. 2. Secure lid and make sure vent is set to sealing. Press Manual and set for 5 minutes. 3. Perform a quick release. Press Cancel, remove lid, and press Sauté. 4. Whisk together eggs and evaporated milk. SLOWLY add to the Instant Pot, stirring constantly so the eggs don't scramble. 5. Stir in the sugar substitute until it's dissolved, press Cancel, then stir in the vanilla. 6. Allow to cool thoroughly, then refrigerate at least 4 hours.

Per Serving:
calorie: 262 | fat: 3g | protein: 6g | carbs: 50g | sugars: 28g | fiber: 0g | sodium: 75mg

Crumb Pie Shell

Prep time: 10 minutes | Cook time: 10 minutes | Serves 10

1¼ cups finely crumbled high-fiber bran crisp breads (such as Fiber Rich+ Bran Crisp Breads)	2 tablespoons canola oil
	1 tablespoon water
	⅛ teaspoon cinnamon

1. Preheat the oven to 325 degrees. In a medium mixing bowl, combine all the ingredients, mixing thoroughly. 2. Spread the mixture evenly into a 10-inch pie pan. Press the mixture firmly onto the sides and bottom of the pan. 3. Bake the pie shell for 8–10 minutes. You can refrigerate it after baking until ready to use.

Per Serving:
calories: 78 | fat: 4g | protein: 2g | carbs: 10g | sugars: 1g | fiber: 1g | sodium: 99mg

Frozen Mocha Milkshake

Prep time: 5 minutes | Cook time: 0 minutes | Serves 1

1 cup (240 ml) unsweetened vanilla almond milk	1½ cups (210 g) crushed ice
3 tbsp (18 g) unsweetened cocoa powder	½ medium avocado, peeled and pitted
2 tsp (4 g) instant espresso powder	1 tbsp (15 ml) pure maple syrup
	1 tsp pure vanilla extract

1. In a blender, combine the almond milk, cocoa powder, espresso powder, ice, avocado, maple syrup, and vanilla. Blend the ingredients on high speed for 60 seconds, until the milkshake is smooth.

Per Serving:
calorie: 307 | fat: 20g | protein: 6g | carbs: 33g | sugars: 13g | fiber: 13g | sodium: 173mg

Blueberry Chocolate Clusters

Prep time: 5 minutes | Cook time: 5 minutes | Serves 10

1½ cups dark chocolate chips	½ cups chopped, toasted pecans
1 tablespoon coconut oil, melted	2 cups blueberries

1. Line a baking sheet with parchment paper. 2. Melt the chocolate in a microwave-safe bowl in 20- to 30-second intervals. 3. In a medium bowl, combine the melted chocolate with the coconut oil and pecans. 4. Spoon a small amount of chocolate mixture (about 1 teaspoon) on the prepared baking sheet. 5. Place a cluster of about 5 blueberries on top of the chocolate. You should get about 20 clusters in total. 6. Drizzle a small amount of chocolate over the berries. 7. Freeze until set, about 15 minutes. 8. Store in an airtight container in the refrigerator for up to 5 days or in the freezer for up to 1 month.

Per Serving:
calories: 224 | fat: 17g | protein: 3g | carbs: 17g | sugars: 9g | fiber: 4g | sodium: 6mg

Spiced Pear Applesauce

Prep time: 15 minutes | Cook time: 5 minutes | Makes: 3½ cups

1 pound pears, peeled, cored, and sliced	cinnamon
2 teaspoons apple pie spice or	Pinch kosher salt
	Juice of ½ small lemon

1. In the electric pressure cooker, combine the apples, pears, apple pie spice, salt, lemon juice, and ¼ cup of water. 2. Close and lock the lid of the pressure cooker. Set the valve to sealing. 3. Cook on high pressure for 5 minutes. 4. When the cooking is complete, hit Cancel and let the pressure release naturally. 5. Once the pin drops, unlock and remove the lid. 6. Mash the apples and pears with a potato masher to the consistency you like. 7. Serve warm, or cool to room temperature and refrigerate.

Per Serving:
(½ cup): calories: 108 | fat: 1g | protein: 1g | carbs: 29g | sugars: 20g | fiber: 6g | sodium: 15mg

Banana Bread Nice Cream

Prep time: 5 minutes | Cook time: 0 minutes | Serves 3

½ cup (packed) pitted dates	¼ teaspoon ground nutmeg
¼–⅓ cup plain or vanilla low-fat nondairy milk	A couple pinches of sea salt
1 tablespoon raw cashew or raw almond butter	2 cups frozen, sliced, overripe bananas

1. In a blender, combine the dates with ¼ cup of the milk. (If you're using a high-speed blender, that should be enough milk, but if you're using a regular blender you may need to use ⅓ cup of the milk.) Blend until smooth. Add the nut butter, nutmeg, and salt, and blend. Add about half of the bananas and puree until the mixture is smooth, then add the remaining bananas and puree again until smooth. Transfer to a container and freeze for 1 to 2 hours (for soft serve) or 4 to 5 hours or overnight for a firmer-set ice cream.

Per Serving:
calorie: 198 | fat: 3g | protein: 3g | carbs: 44g | sugars: 29g | fiber: 5g | sodium: 205mg

Cream Cheese Shortbread Cookies

Prep time: 30 minutes | Cook time: 20 minutes | Makes 12 cookies

¼ cup coconut oil, melted	1 large egg, whisked
2 ounces (57 g) cream cheese, softened	2 cups blanched finely ground almond flour
½ cup granular erythritol	1 teaspoon almond extract

1. Combine all ingredients in a large bowl to form a firm ball. 2. Place dough on a sheet of plastic wrap and roll into a 12-inch-long log shape. Roll log in plastic wrap and place in refrigerator 30 minutes to chill. 3. Remove log from plastic and slice into twelve equal cookies. Cut two sheets of parchment paper to fit air fryer basket. Place six cookies on each ungreased sheet. Place one sheet with cookies into air fryer basket. Adjust the temperature to 320°F (160°C) and bake for 10 minutes, turning cookies halfway through cooking. They will be lightly golden when done. Repeat with remaining cookies. 4. Let cool 15 minutes before serving to avoid crumbling.

Per Serving:
1 cookie: calories: 154 | fat: 14g | protein: 4g | carbs: 4g | net carbs: 2g | fiber: 2g

5-Ingredient Chunky Cherry and Peanut Butter Cookies

Prep time: 5 minutes | Cook time: 10 to 12 minutes | Makes 12 cookies

1 cup (240 g) all-natural peanut butter	1 large egg, beaten
¼ cup (60 ml) pure maple syrup	1 cup (80 g) gluten-free rolled or quick oats
	½ cup (80 g) dried cherries

1. Preheat the oven to 350°F (177°C). Line a large baking sheet with parchment paper. 2. In a large bowl, whisk together the peanut butter, maple syrup, and egg. Add the oats and cherries, and mix until the ingredients are combined. 3. Chill the dough for 10 to 15 minutes. 4. Use a cookie scoop to scoop balls of the dough onto the prepared baking sheet. 5. Using a fork, gently flatten the dough balls into your desired shape (the cookies will not change shape much during baking). Bake the cookies for 10 to 12 minutes, until they are lightly golden on top. 6. Remove the cookies from the oven and let them cool for 5 minutes before transferring them to a wire rack.

Per Serving:
calorie: 198 | fat: 12g | protein: 7g | carbs: 19g | sugars: 11g | fiber: 3g | sodium: 13mg

Chapter 11 Salads

Herbed Spring Peas

Prep time: 10 minutes | Cook time: 15 minutes | Serves 6

1 tablespoon unsalted non-hydrogenated plant-based butter	vegetable broth
½ Vidalia onion, thinly sliced	3 cups fresh shelled peas
1 cup store-bought low-sodium	1 tablespoon minced fresh tarragon

1. In a skillet, melt the butter over medium heat. 2. Add the onion and sauté for 2 to 3 minutes, or until the onion is translucent. 3. Add the broth, and reduce the heat to low. 4. Add the peas and tarragon, cover, and cook for 7 to 10 minutes, or until the peas soften. 5. Serve.

Per Serving:
calorie: 43 | fat: 2g | protein: 2g | carbs: 6g | sugars: 3g | fiber: 2g | sodium: 159mg

Celery and Apple Salad with Cider Vinaigrette

Prep time: 20 minutes | Cook time: 0 minutes | Serves 4

Dressing	2 cups chopped romaine lettuce
2 tablespoons apple cider or apple juice	2 cups diagonally sliced celery
1 tablespoon cider vinegar	½ medium apple, unpeeled, sliced very thin (about 1 cup)
2 teaspoons canola oil	⅓ cup sweetened dried cranberries
2 teaspoons finely chopped shallots	2 tablespoons chopped walnuts
½ teaspoon Dijon mustard	2 tablespoons crumbled blue cheese
½ teaspoon honey	
½ teaspoon salt	
Salad	

1 In small bowl, beat all dressing ingredients with whisk until blended; set aside. 2 In medium bowl, place lettuce, celery, apple and cranberries; toss with dressing. To serve, arrange salad on 4 plates. Sprinkle with walnuts and blue cheese. Serve immediately.

Per Serving:
calorie: 130 | fat: 6g | protein: 2g | carbs: 17g | sugars: 13g | fiber: 3g | sodium: 410mg

Chicken, Cantaloupe, Kale, and Almond Salad

Prep time: 10 minutes | Cook time: 0 minutes | Serves 3

For The Salad	For The Dressing
4 cups chopped kale, packed	2 teaspoons honey
1½ cups diced cantaloupe	2 tablespoons extra-virgin olive oil
1½ cups shredded rotisserie chicken	2 teaspoons apple cider vinegar or freshly squeezed lemon juice
½ cup sliced almonds	
¼ cup crumbled feta	

To Make The Salad 1. Divide the kale into three portions. Layer ⅓ of the cantaloupe, chicken, almonds, and feta on each portion. 2. Drizzle some of the dressing over each portion of salad. Serve immediately. To Make The Dressing 3. In a small bowl, whisk together the honey, olive oil, and vinegar.

Per Serving:
calorie: 376 | fat: 23g | protein: 30g | carbs: 16g | sugars: 12g | fiber: 3g | sodium: 415mg

Edamame and Walnut Salad

Prep time: 10 minutes | Cook time: 0 minutes | Serves 2

For the vinaigrette	to season
2 tablespoons balsamic vinegar	For the salad
1 tablespoon extra-virgin olive oil	1 cup shelled edamame
1 teaspoon grated fresh ginger	½ cup shredded carrots
½ teaspoon Dijon mustard	½ cup shredded red cabbage
Pinch salt	½ cup walnut halves
Freshly ground black pepper,	6 cups prewashed baby spinach, divided

To make the vinaigrette In a small bowl, whisk together the balsamic vinegar, olive oil, ginger, Dijon mustard, and salt. Season with pepper. Set aside. To make the salad 1. In a medium bowl, mix together the edamame, carrots, red cabbage, and walnuts. 2. Add the vinaigrette. Toss to coat. 3. Place 3 cups of spinach on each of 2 serving plates. 4. Top each serving with half of the dressed vegetables. 5. Enjoy immediately!

Per Serving:
calorie: 341 | fat: 26g | protein: 13g | carbs: 19g | sugars: 7g | fiber: 8g | sodium: 117mg

Sesame Chicken-Almond Slaw

Prep time: 20 minutes | Cook time: 40 minutes | Serves 2

For the dressing	pepper
1 tablespoon rice vinegar	For the salad
1 teaspoon granulated stevia	8 ounces chicken breast, rinsed and drained
2 teaspoons extra-virgin olive oil	4 cups angel hair cabbage
1 teaspoon water	1 cup shredded romaine lettuce
½ teaspoon sesame oil	2 tablespoons sliced scallions
¼ teaspoon reduced-sodium soy sauce	2 tablespoons toasted slivered almonds
Pinch salt	2 teaspoons toasted sesame seeds
Pinch freshly ground black	

To make the dressing In a jar with a tight-fitting lid, add the rice vinegar, stevia, olive oil, water, sesame oil, soy sauce, salt, and pepper. Shake well to combine. Set aside. To make the salad 1. Preheat the oven to 400°F. 2. To a medium baking dish, add the chicken. Place the dish in the preheated oven. Bake for 30 to 40 minutes, or until completely opaque and the temperature registers 165°F on an instant-read thermometer. 3. Remove from the oven. Slice into strips. Set aside. 4. In a large bowl, toss together the cabbage, romaine, scallions, almonds, sesame seeds, and chicken strips. Add the dressing. Toss again to coat the ingredients evenly. 5. Serve immediately.

Per Serving:
calorie: 318 | fat: 15g | protein: 31g | carbs: 17g | sugars: 8g | fiber: 6g | sodium: 125mg

Sweet Beet Grain Bowl

Prep time: 10 minutes | Cook time: 20 minutes | Serves 2

3 cups water	pepper
1 cup farro, rinsed	4 small cooked beets, sliced
2 tablespoons extra-virgin olive oil	1 pear, cored and diced
1 tablespoon honey	6 cups mixed greens
3 tablespoons cider vinegar	⅓ cup pumpkin seeds, roasted
Pinch freshly ground black	¼ cup ricotta cheese

1. In a medium saucepan, stir together the water and farro over high heat and bring to a boil. Reduce the heat to medium and simmer until the farro is tender, 15 to 20 minutes. Drain and rinse the farro under cold running water until cool. Set aside. 2. Meanwhile, in a small bowl, whisk together the extra-virgin olive oil, honey, and vinegar. Season with black pepper. 3. Evenly divide the farro between two bowls. Top each with the beets, pear, greens, pumpkin seeds, and ricotta. Drizzle the bowls with the dressing before serving and adjust the seasonings as desired.

Per Serving:
calorie: 750 | fat: 28g | protein: 21g | carbs: 104g | sugars: 18g | fiber: 12g | sodium: 174mg

Rainbow Quinoa Salad

Prep time: 10 minutes | Cook time: 0 minutes | Serves 3

Dressing	½ cup corn kernels
3½ tablespoons orange juice	½ cup diced apple tossed in ½ teaspoon lemon juice
1 tablespoon apple cider vinegar	¼ cup diced red pepper
1 tablespoon pure maple syrup	¼ cup sliced green onions or chives
1½ teaspoons yellow mustard	
Couple pinches of cloves	1 can (15 ounces) black beans, rinsed and drained
Rounded ½ teaspoon sea salt	
Freshly ground black pepper to taste	Sea salt to taste
Salad	Freshly ground black pepper to taste
2 cups cooked quinoa, cooled	

1. To make the dressing: In a large bowl, whisk together the orange juice, vinegar, syrup, mustard, cloves, salt, and pepper. 2. To make the salad: Add the quinoa, corn, apple, red pepper, green onion or chives, and black beans, and stir to combine well. Season with the salt and black pepper to taste. Serve, or store in an airtight container in the fridge.

Per Serving:
calorie: 355 | fat: 4g | protein: 15g | carbs: 68g | sugars: 12g | fiber: 15g | sodium: 955mg

Mandarin Orange Chicken Salad

Prep time: 10 minutes | Cook time: 0 minutes | Serves 4

1 (8-ounce) container plain Greek yogurt	peas in the pod, thawed
½ teaspoon ground ginger	1 (8-ounce) can water chestnuts, drained and chopped
1½ cups cooked cubed chicken	1 (11-ounce) can mandarin orange segments, drained
1 (8-ounce) package frozen	
½ cup unsalted peanuts	romaine lettuce, divided
1 (10-ounce) bag chopped	

1. In a large bowl, mix the Greek yogurt with the ground ginger. Add the chicken and mix to coat. 2. Add the pea pods, water chestnuts, mandarin oranges, and peanuts. Stir all the ingredients together until well mixed. 3. Divide ¼ of the bag of romaine into 4 bowls and top with the chicken salad.

Per Serving:
calorie: 338 | fat: 18g | protein: 28g | carbs: 19g | sugars: 10g | fiber: 5g | sodium: 85mg

Romaine Lettuce Salad with Cranberry, Feta, and Beans

Prep time: 10 minutes | Cook time: 0 minutes | Serves 2

1 cup chopped fresh green beans	½ cup cranberries, fresh or frozen
6 cups washed and chopped romaine lettuce	¼ cup crumbled fat-free feta cheese
1 cup sliced radishes	1 tablespoon extra-virgin olive oil
2 scallions, sliced	
¼ cup chopped fresh oregano	Salt, to season
1 cup canned kidney beans, drained and rinsed	Freshly ground black pepper, to season

1. In a microwave-safe dish, add the green beans and a small amount of water. Microwave on high for about 2 minutes, or until tender. 2. In a large bowl, toss together the romaine lettuce, radishes, scallions, and oregano. 3. Add the green beans, kidney beans, cranberries, feta cheese, and olive oil. Season with salt and pepper. Toss to coat. 4. Evenly divide between 2 plates and enjoy immediately.

Per Serving:
calorie: 271 | fat: 9g | protein: 16g | carbs: 36g | sugars: 10g | fiber: 13g | sodium: 573mg

Three Bean and Basil Salad

Prep time: 10 minutes | Cook time: 0 minutes | Serves 8

1 (15-ounce) can low-sodium chickpeas, drained and rinsed	white and green parts
	¼ cup finely chopped fresh basil
1 (15-ounce) can low-sodium kidney beans, drained and rinsed	3 garlic cloves, minced
	2 tablespoons extra-virgin olive oil
1 (15-ounce) can low-sodium white beans, drained and rinsed	1 tablespoon red wine vinegar
	1 teaspoon Dijon mustard
1 red bell pepper, seeded and finely chopped	¼ teaspoon freshly ground black pepper
¼ cup chopped scallions, both	

1. In a large mixing bowl, combine the chickpeas, kidney beans, white beans, bell pepper, scallions, basil, and garlic. Toss gently to combine. 2. In a small bowl, combine the olive oil, vinegar, mustard, and pepper. Toss with the salad. 3. Cover and refrigerate for an hour before serving, to allow the flavors to mix.

Per Serving:
Calorie: 193 | fat: 5g | protein: 10g | carbs: 29g | sugars: 3g | fiber: 8g | sodium: 246mg

BLT Potato Salad

Prep time: 20 minutes | Cook time: 10 to 15 minutes | Serves 6

4 small new red potatoes (about 12 oz), cut into ½-inch cubes	¼ teaspoon salt
¼ cup reduced-fat mayonnaise or salad dressing	⅛ teaspoon pepper
1 teaspoon Dijon mustard	½ cup grape tomatoes or halved cherry tomatoes
2 teaspoons chopped fresh or ½ teaspoon dried dill weed	1½ cups bite-size pieces romaine lettuce
	2 slices turkey bacon, cooked, crumbled

1 In 2-quart saucepan, place potatoes. Add enough water to cover. Heat to boiling; reduce heat to low. Cover; cook 10 to 15 minutes or until potatoes are tender. Drain; cool about 10 minutes. 2 Meanwhile, in medium bowl, mix mayonnaise, mustard, dill weed, salt and pepper. Stir in potatoes, tomatoes and lettuce until coated. Sprinkle with bacon.

Per Serving:
calorie: 100 | fat: 5g | protein: 3g | carbs: 12g | sugars: 2g | fiber: 1g | sodium: 300mg

Broccoli "Tabouli"

Prep time: 15 minutes | Cook time: 0 minutes | Serves 2

1 broccoli head, trimmed into florets (about 2 cups)	¼ cup chopped red onion
1 large jicama, peeled	¼ cup freshly squeezed lemon juice
1 cup chickpeas, drained and rinsed	2 tablespoons sunflower seeds
2 plum tomatoes, diced	1 tablespoon extra-virgin olive oil
1 medium cucumber, peeled, seeded, and diced	Salt, to season
½ cup chopped fresh parsley	Freshly ground black pepper, to season
½ cup chopped fresh mint	4 cups baby spinach, divided

1. With a grater or food processor, grate the broccoli into grain-size pieces until it resembles rice. 2. Repeat with the jicama. You should have about 1 cup. 3. To a large bowl, add the grated broccoli, grated jicama, chickpeas, tomatoes, cucumber, parsley, mint, red onion, lemon juice, sunflower seeds, and olive oil. Toss until well mixed. Season with salt and pepper. 4. Arrange 2 cups of spinach on each of 2 plates. 5. Top each with half of the tabouli mixture. 6. Serve immediately.

Per Serving:
calorie: 265 | fat: 8g | protein: 9g | carbs: 44g | sugars: 10g | fiber: 21g | sodium: 138mg

Mediterranean Chicken Salad

Prep time: 5 minutes | Cook time: 0 minutes | Serves 3

8 ounces boneless, skinless, cooked chicken breast	¼ teaspoon freshly ground black pepper
2 tablespoons extra-virgin olive oil	1 cup cooked green beans, cut into 2-inch pieces
2 tablespoons balsamic vinegar	1 cup cooked artichokes
¼ teaspoon dried basil	¼ cup pine nuts, toasted
2 small garlic cloves, minced	¼ cup sliced black olives
3 cherry tomatoes, halved	Tomato wedges (optional)

1. Cut the cooked chicken into bite-sized chunks, and set aside. 2. In a medium bowl, whisk together the oil, vinegar, basil, garlic, and pepper. Add the chicken, and toss with the dressing. 3. Add the green beans, artichokes, pine nuts, olives, and cherry tomatoes; toss well. Chill in the refrigerator for several hours. Garnish the salad with tomato wedges, and serve.

Per Serving:
calorie: 307 | fat: 19g | protein: 21g | carbs: 14g | sugars: 4g | fiber: 7g | sodium: 73mg

Chinese Chicken Salad

Prep time: 10 minutes | Cook time: 0 minutes | Serves 4

2 cups cooked chicken, diced	Two 8-ounce cans water chestnuts, drained and chopped
1 cup finely chopped celery	2 scallions, chopped
1 cup shredded carrots	⅓ cup low-fat mayonnaise
¼ cup crushed unsweetened pineapple, drained	1 tablespoon light soy sauce
2 tablespoons finely diced pimiento	1 teaspoon lemon juice
	8 large tomatoes, hollowed

1. In a large bowl, combine the chicken, celery, carrots, pineapple, pimiento, water chestnuts, and scallions. 2. In a separate bowl, combine the mayonnaise, soy sauce, and lemon juice. Mix well. Add the dressing to the salad, and toss. Cover, and chill in the refrigerator for 2–3 hours. 3. For each serving, place a small scoop of chicken salad into a hollowed-out tomato.

Per Serving:
calorie: 365 | fat: 16g | protein: 27g | carbs: 32g | sugars: 17g | fiber: 9g | sodium: 476mg

Mediterranean Pasta Salad with Goat Cheese

Prep time: 25 minutes | Cook time: 0 minutes | Serves 4

½ cup (75 g) grape tomatoes, sliced in half lengthwise	½ tsp sea salt
1 medium red bell pepper, coarsely chopped	½ tsp black pepper
½ medium red onion, sliced into thin strips	1 tbsp (3 g) dried oregano
1 medium zucchini, coarsely chopped	½ tsp garlic powder
1 cup (175 g) broccoli florets	4 oz (113 g) crumbled goat cheese
½ cup (110 g) oil-packed artichoke hearts, drained	½ cup (50 g) shaved Parmesan cheese
¼ cup (60 ml) olive oil	8 oz (227 g) lentil or chickpea penne pasta, cooked, rinsed, and drained

1. In a large bowl, combine the tomatoes, bell pepper, onion, zucchini, broccoli, artichoke hearts, oil, sea salt, black pepper, oregano, garlic powder, goat cheese, and Parmesan cheese. Gently mix everything together to combine and coat all of the ingredients with the oil. 2. Add the pasta to the bowl and stir to combine. 3. Let the pasta salad rest for 1 to 2 hours in the refrigerator to marinate it, or serve the pasta salad immediately if desired.

Per Serving:
calorie: 477 | fat: 24g | protein: 23g | carbs: 41g | sugars: 6g | fiber: 6g | sodium: 706mg

Blueberry and Chicken Salad on a Bed of Greens

Prep time: 10 minutes | Cook time: 0 minutes | Serves 4

2 cups chopped cooked chicken	1 tablespoon chopped fresh cilantro
1 cup fresh blueberries	½ cup plain, nonfat Greek yogurt or vegan mayonnaise
¼ cup finely chopped almonds	¼ teaspoon salt
1 celery stalk, finely chopped	¼ teaspoon freshly ground black pepper
¼ cup finely chopped red onion	8 cups salad greens (baby spinach, spicy greens, romaine)
1 tablespoon chopped fresh basil	

1. In a large mixing bowl, combine the chicken, blueberries, almonds, celery, onion, basil, and cilantro. Toss gently to mix. 2. In a small bowl, combine the yogurt, salt, and pepper. Add to the chicken salad and stir to combine. 3. Arrange 2 cups of salad greens on each of 4 plates and divide the chicken salad among the plates to serve.

Per Serving:
calories: 207 | fat: 6g | protein: 28g | carbs: 11g | sugars: 6g | fiber: 3g | sodium: 235mg

Salmon Niçoise Salad

Prep time: 10 minutes | Cook time: 30 minutes | Serves 1

salad	potatoes
4 oz (113 g) fresh salmon fillets	2 tsp (2 g) dried rosemary
Cooking oil spray, as needed	2½ oz (71 g) fresh green beans
1 tsp olive oil	dressing
Sea salt, as needed	1 tbsp (15 g) tahini
Black pepper, as needed	½ tbsp (8 g) Dijon mustard
2 cups (60 g) arugula	1 tbsp (15 ml) fresh lemon juice
⅛ cup (17 g) assorted olives	3 tbsp (45 ml) water
½ cup (60 g) coarsely chopped cucumber	½ tsp dried dill
1 large hard-boiled egg	Sea salt, as needed
½ cup (65 g) quartered baby	Black pepper, as needed

1. Preheat the oven to 400°F (204°C). Line a large baking sheet with parchment paper. 2. Bring a large pot of water to a boil over high heat. 3. To make the salad, heat a medium skillet over medium-high heat. Spray the salmon with the cooking oil spray and drizzle the oil on top. Place it in the skillet and cook for 2 to 3 minutes on each side (depending how thick the fillet is), until the outside is an opaque pink color and just barely starts to brown. Season the salmon with the salt and black pepper. 4. On a serving plate, arrange a bed of arugula. On the arugula, arrange the olives, cucumber, egg, and salmon. Set the plate aside. 5. Place the potatoes in a medium bowl. Add the rosemary and toss to coat the potatoes. Transfer them to the prepared baking sheet and bake them for 20 to 25 minutes, or until the potatoes are brown and crispy on the outside. 6. While the potatoes are roasting, prepare a large bowl of ice water. Add the green beans to the boiling water and cook them for 2 minutes. Quickly transfer the green beans to the bowl of ice water. Once they have cooled, add the green beans to the salad. 7. To make the dressing, mix together the tahini, mustard, lemon juice, water, dill, sea salt, and black pepper in a medium jar. 8. Add the potatoes to the salad, toss the salad with the dressing, and serve.

Per Serving:
calorie: 471 | fat: 23g | protein: 37g | carbs: 31g | sugars: 6g | fiber: 7g | sodium: 555mg

Cheeseburger Wedge Salad

Prep time: 15 minutes | Cook time: 10 minutes | Serves 4

salad	chopped (optional)
1 lb (454 g) lean ground beef	dressing
2 medium heads romaine lettuce, rinsed, dried, and sliced in half lengthwise	2 oz (57 g) no-salt-added tomato paste
	2 tbsp (30 ml) apple cider vinegar
½ cup (60 g) shredded Cheddar cheese	2 tbsp (30 ml) water
½ cup (80 g) coarsely chopped tomatoes	1 tbsp (15 ml) honey
	¼ tsp sea salt
⅓ cup (50 g) finely chopped red onion	½ tsp onion powder
	¼ tsp garlic powder
1 small dill pickle, finely	

1. To make the salad, heat a large skillet over medium-high heat. Once the skillet is hot, add the beef and cook it for 9 to 10 minutes, until it is brown and cooked though. 2. Meanwhile, place a ½ head of romaine lettuce on each of four plates. Divide the beef evenly on top of each of the romaine halves. Then top each with the Cheddar cheese, tomatoes, onion, and pickle (if using). 3. To make the dressing, combine the tomato paste, vinegar, water, honey, sea salt, onion powder, and garlic powder in a small mason jar, secure the lid on top, and shake the jar thoroughly until everything is combined. Drizzle the dressing evenly over each salad and serve.

Per Serving:
calorie: 320 | fat: 14g | protein: 32g | carbs: 19g | sugars: 11g | fiber: 8g | sodium: 341mg

Greek Island Potato Salad

Prep time: 5 minutes | Cook time: 35 minutes | Serves 10

⅓ cup extra-virgin olive oil	1 onion, chopped
4 garlic cloves, minced	16 ounces artichoke hearts packed in water, drained and cut in half
2 pounds red potatoes, cut into 1½-inch pieces (leave the skin on if you wish)	
	½ cup Kalamata olives, pitted and halved
6 medium carrots, peeled, halved lengthwise, and cut into 1½-inch pieces	¼ cup lemon juice

1. In a large skillet, heat the olive oil. Add the garlic, and sauté for 30 seconds. Add the potatoes, carrots, and onion; cook over medium heat for 25–30 minutes until vegetables are just tender. 2. Add the artichoke hearts, and cook for 3–5 minutes more. Remove from the heat, and stir in the olives and lemon juice. Season with a dash of salt and pepper. Transfer to a serving bowl, and serve warm.

Per Serving:
calorie: 178 | fat: 8g | protein: 4g | carbs: 25g | sugars: 4g | fiber: 6g | sodium: 134mg

Lentil Salad

Prep time: 10 minutes | Cook time: 45 minutes | Serves 8

- 1 pound dried lentils, washed (rinse with cold water in a colander)
- 3 cups water
- 2 tablespoons extra-virgin olive oil
- 2 teaspoons cumin
- 1 teaspoon minced fresh oregano
- 3 tablespoons fresh lemon juice
- ¼ teaspoon freshly ground black pepper
- 2 large green bell peppers, cored, seeded, and diced
- 2 large red bell peppers, cored, seeded, and diced
- 3 stalks celery, diced
- 1 red onion, minced

1. In a large saucepan over high heat, bring lentils and water to a boil. Reduce the heat to low, cover, and simmer for 35–45 minutes. Drain, and set aside. 2. In a large bowl, mix together the oil, cumin, oregano, lemon juice, and pepper until well blended. Add the lentils and the prepared vegetables. Cover, and chill in the refrigerator before serving.

Per Serving:
calorie: 261 | fat: 4g | protein: 15g | carbs: 43g | sugars: 5g | fiber: 8g | sodium: 15mg

Chickpea Salad

Prep time: 15 minutes | Cook time: 0 minutes | Serves 4

- ½ cup bottled balsamic vinaigrette
- 1 (15-ounce) can chickpeas, rinsed and drained
- 1 cup cherry tomatoes
- 1 small red onion, quartered and sliced
- 2 large cucumbers, peeled and cut into bite-size pieces
- 1 large zucchini, cut into bite-size pieces
- 1 (10-ounce) package frozen shelled edamame, steamed or microwaved
- Chopped fresh parsley, for garnish

1. Pour the vinaigrette into a large bowl. Add the chickpeas, tomatoes, onion, cucumbers, zucchini, and edamame and toss until all the ingredients are coated. 2. Garnish with chopped parsley.

Per Serving:
calorie: 188 | fat: 4g | protein: 10g | carbs: 29g | sugars: 11g | fiber: 8g | sodium: 171mg

Moroccan Carrot Salad

Prep time: 15 minutes | Cook time: 0 minutes | Serves 5

Dressing
- ¼ cup orange juice
- 2 tablespoons olive oil
- 1 teaspoon orange peel
- 1 teaspoon ground cumin
- 1 teaspoon paprika
- ¼ teaspoon salt
- ⅛ to ¼ teaspoon ground red pepper (cayenne)
- ⅛ teaspoon ground cinnamon

Salad
- 1 bag (10 oz) julienne (matchstick-cut) carrots (5 cups)
- 1 can (15 oz) chickpeas (garbanzo beans), drained, rinsed
- ¼ cup golden raisins
- 3 tablespoons salted roasted whole almonds, coarsely chopped
- ¼ cup coarsely chopped fresh cilantro or parsley

1 In small bowl, combine all dressing ingredients with whisk until blended; set aside. 2 In large bowl, combine carrots, chickpeas and raisins; toss to combine. Add dressing; mix thoroughly. Cover and refrigerate at least 2 hours or overnight, stirring occasionally. Just before serving, sprinkle with almonds and cilantro.

Per Serving:
calorie: 310 | fat: 11g | protein: 10g | carbs: 44g | sugars: 12g | fiber: 10g | sodium: 230mg

Greek Rice Salad

Prep time: 10 minutes | Cook time: 0 minutes | Serves 4

- 3 tablespoons fresh lemon juice
- 1½ tablespoons coconut nectar or pure maple syrup
- 1 tablespoon red wine vinegar
- 1 teaspoon sea salt
- 1 teaspoon Dijon mustard
- ¼ teaspoon allspice
- ½–1 teaspoon grated fresh garlic
- Freshly ground black pepper to taste (optional)
- 4 cups cooked brown rice
- 1 cup chopped cucumber (seeds removed, if you prefer)
- 1 cup sliced grape or cherry tomatoes or chopped tomatoes (can substitute chopped red pepper)
- ½ cup sliced kalamata olives
- ½ tablespoon chopped fresh oregano
- 2 tablespoons chopped fresh dill

1. In a large bowl, whisk together the lemon juice, nectar or syrup, vinegar, salt, mustard, allspice, garlic, and pepper (if using). Add the rice, cucumber, tomatoes, olives, oregano, and dill, and stir to combine. Taste, and add extra salt or lemon juice, if desired. Serve as a side or as a hearty lunch over greens.

Per Serving:
calorie: 306 | fat: 4g | protein: 6g | carbs: 62g | sugars: 7g | fiber: 5g | sodium: 751mg

Warm Sweet Potato and Black Bean Salad

Prep time: 5 minutes | Cook time: 35 minutes | Serves 2

- Extra-virgin olive oil cooking spray
- 1 large sweet potato, peeled and cubed
- 1 tablespoon extra-virgin olive oil
- 1 tablespoon balsamic vinegar
- 1 teaspoon dried rosemary
- ¼ teaspoon garlic powder
- ⅛ teaspoon salt
- ⅛ teaspoon freshly ground black pepper
- 1 cup canned black beans, drained and rinsed
- 2 tablespoons chopped chives

1. Preheat the oven to 450°F. 2. In a small baking dish coated with cooking spray, place the sweet potato cubes. Put the dish in the preheated oven. Bake for 20 to 35 minutes, uncovered, or until tender. 3. In a medium serving bowl, whisk together the olive oil, balsamic vinegar, rosemary, garlic powder, salt, and pepper. 4. Add the black beans and cooked sweet potato to the oil and herb mixture. Toss to coat. 5. Sprinkle with the chives. 6. Serve immediately and enjoy!

Per Serving:
calorie: 235 | fat: 7g | protein: 8g | carbs: 35g | sugars: 4g | fiber: 10g | sodium: 359mg

Italian Potato Salad

Prep time: 10 minutes | Cook time: 25 minutes | Serves 8

12 new red potatoes, 3–4 ounces each, washed and skins left on	1 tablespoon balsamic vinegar
3 celery stalks, chopped	½ tablespoon red vinegar
1 red bell pepper, minced	1 teaspoon chopped fresh parsley
¼ cup chopped scallions	⅛ teaspoon freshly ground black pepper
2 tablespoons olive oil	

1. Boil the potatoes for 20 minutes in a large pot of boiling water. Drain, and let cool for 30 minutes. 2. Cut the potatoes into large chunks, and toss the potatoes with the celery, bell pepper, and scallions. 3. In a medium bowl, combine the olive oil, balsamic vinegar, red vinegar, parsley, and pepper; pour the dressing over the potato salad. Serve at room temperature.

Per Serving:
calorie: 128 | fat: 4g | protein: 3g | carbs: 22g | sugars: 3g | fiber: 3g | sodium: 30mg

First-of-the-Season Tomato, Peach, and Strawberry Salad

Prep time: 15 minutes | Cook time: 0 minutes | Serves 6

6 cups mixed spring greens	½ Vidalia onion, thinly sliced
4 large ripe plum tomatoes, thinly sliced	2 tablespoons white balsamic vinegar
4 large ripe peaches, pitted and thinly sliced	2 tablespoons extra-virgin olive oil
12 ripe strawberries, thinly sliced	Freshly ground black pepper

1. Put the greens in a large salad bowl, and layer the tomatoes, peaches, strawberries, and onion on top. 2. Dress with the vinegar and oil, toss together, and season with pepper.

Per Serving:
calorie: 122 | fat: 5g | protein: 3g | carbs: 19g | sugars: 14g | fiber: 4g | sodium: 20mg

Rotisserie Chicken and Avocado Salad

Prep time: 15 minutes | Cook time: 0 minutes | Serves 4

½ cup plain Greek yogurt	1 cup shredded rotisserie chicken meat
1 tablespoon freshly squeezed lime juice	½ medium red onion, chopped
4 teaspoons chopped fresh cilantro	1 large tomato, diced
2 ripe avocados, peeled, pitted, and cubed	4 cups mixed leafy greens, divided

1. In a large bowl, stir together the Greek yogurt, lime juice, and cilantro to make a dressing. 2. Add the avocado, chicken, onion, and tomato and mix gently into the dressing. 3. Divide 1 cup of the greens into 4 bowls and top with the chicken salad.

Per Serving:
calorie: 269 | fat: 18g | protein: 14g | carbs: 16g | sugars: 5g | fiber: 9g | sodium: 93mg

Summer Salad

Prep time: 5 minutes | Cook time: 0 minutes | Serves 4

For The Salad	½ cup chopped walnuts or pecans
8 cups mixed greens or preferred lettuce, loosely packed	½ cup crumbled feta
4 cups arugula, loosely packed	For The Dressing
2 peaches, sliced ½ cup thinly sliced red onion	4 teaspoons extra-virgin olive oil
	4 teaspoons honey

To Make The Salad 1. Combine the mixed greens, arugula, peaches, red onion, walnuts, and feta in a large bowl. Divide the salad into four portions. 2. Drizzle the dressing over each individual serving of salad. To Make The Dressing 3. In a small bowl, whisk together the olive oil and honey.

Per Serving:
calorie: 261 | fat: 19g | protein: 8g | carbs: 20g | sugars: 15g | fiber: 4g | sodium: 184mg

Sunflower-Tuna-Cauliflower Salad

Prep time: 30 minutes | Cook time: 0 minutes | Serves 2

1 (5-ounce) can tuna packed in water, drained	1 scallion, chopped
½ cup plain nonfat Greek yogurt	¼ cup sunflower seeds
1 teaspoon freshly squeezed lemon juice	2 cups fresh chopped cauliflower florets
1 teaspoon dried dill	4 cups mixed salad greens, divided

1. In a medium bowl, mix together the tuna, yogurt, lemon juice, dill, scallion, and sunflower seeds. 2. Add the cauliflower. Toss gently to coat. 3. Cover and refrigerate for at least 2 hours before serving, stirring occasionally. 4. Serve half of the tuna mixture atop 2 cups of salad greens.

Per Serving:
calorie: 251 | fat: 11g | protein: 24g | carbs: 18g | sugars: 8g | fiber: 7g | sodium: 288mg

Make-Ahead Apple, Carrot, and Cabbage Slaw

Prep time: 10 minutes | Cook time: 0 minutes | Serves 6

4 cups shredded cabbage (green or purple, or a mixture)	1 teaspoon mustard seeds
2 cups shredded carrots	½ teaspoon garlic powder
¾ cup sliced scallions	½ teaspoon celery seeds
¾ cup unsweetened apple juice	⅛ teaspoon freshly ground black pepper
⅔ cup cider vinegar	1 tablespoon dry mustard
1½ teaspoons paprika	

1. In a large bowl, combine the cabbage, carrots, and scallions. 2. In a blender, combine the remaining ingredients. Pour over the cabbage mixture, and toss to coat. Refrigerate overnight, and serve chilled.

Per Serving:
calorie: 57 | fat: 1g | protein: 2g | carbs: 12g | sugars: 7g | fiber: 3g | sodium: 68mg

Mozzarella-Tomato Salad

Prep time: 15 minutes | Cook time: 0 minutes | Serves 2

Fresh mozzarella cheese (2 ounces), cut into ¾-inch cubes	¼ cup chopped scallions
½ cup cherry tomatoes, halved	1 tablespoon minced fresh basil
½ cup cannellini beans, drained and rinsed	1 tablespoon extra-virgin olive oil
½ cup artichoke hearts, drained	2 teaspoons balsamic vinegar
¼ cup jarred roasted red peppers	⅛ teaspoon salt
	4 cups baby spinach, divided

1. In a small bowl, stir together the mozzarella cheese, tomatoes, beans, artichoke hearts, red peppers, and scallions. 2. In another small bowl, whisk the basil, olive oil, balsamic vinegar, and salt until combined. 3. Drizzle the dressing over the cheese and vegetables. Toss to coat. Chill for 15 minutes. 4. Using 2 plates, arrange 2 cups of spinach on each. Top with half of the cheese and vegetable mixture. 5. Serve immediately.

Per Serving:
calorie: 199 | fat: 8g | protein: 9g | carbs: 26g | sugars: 6g | fiber: 10g | sodium: 387mg

Garden-Fresh Greek Salad

Prep time: 20 minutes | Cook time: 0 minutes | Serves 6

Dressing	Salad
3 tablespoons fresh lemon juice	1 bag (10 oz) ready-to-eat romaine lettuce
1 tablespoon chopped fresh or 1 teaspoon dried oregano leaves	¾ cup chopped seeded peeled cucumber
½ teaspoon salt	½ cup sliced red onion
½ teaspoon sugar	¼ cup sliced kalamata olives
½ teaspoon Dijon mustard	2 medium tomatoes, seeded, chopped (1½ cups)
¼ teaspoon pepper	¼ cup reduced-fat feta cheese
1 clove garlic, finely chopped	

1 In small bowl, beat all dressing ingredients with whisk. 2 In large bowl, toss all salad ingredients except cheese. Stir in dressing until salad is well coated. Sprinkle with cheese.

Per Serving:
calorie: 45 | fat: 1.5g | protein: 3g | carbs: 6g | sugars: 3g | fiber: 2g | sodium: 340mg

Couscous Salad

Prep time: 10 minutes | Cook time: 6 minutes | Serves ½ cup

1 cup whole-wheat couscous	oil
2 cups boiling water	4 tablespoons rice vinegar
¼ cup finely chopped red or yellow bell pepper	2 garlic cloves, minced
¼ cup chopped carrots	3 tablespoons finely minced scallions
¼ cup finely chopped celery	¼ cup slivered almonds
2 tablespoons minced Italian parsley	¼ teaspoon freshly ground black pepper
1 tablespoon extra-virgin olive	

1. Place dry couscous in a heat-proof bowl. Pour boiling water over it, and let sit for 5–10 minutes until all the water is absorbed. 2. In a large bowl, combine the couscous, bell pepper, carrots, celery, and parsley together. 3. In a blender or food processor, combine the olive oil, vinegar, garlic, and scallions, and process for 1 minute. Pour over the couscous and vegetables, toss well, garnish with almonds, and season with the pepper. Serve.

Per Serving:
calorie: 373 | fat: 15g | protein: 12g | carbs: 51g | sugars: 3g | fiber: 10g | sodium: 34mg

Crab and Rice Salad

Prep time: 10 minutes | Cook time: 50 minutes | Serves 4

1 cup uncooked brown rice	2 tablespoons minced red onion
5 ounces cooked fresh crabmeat, flaked	½ cup plain fat-free yogurt
1 large tomato, diced	1½ tablespoons lemon juice
One 1.8-ounce can sliced water chestnuts, drained	¼ teaspoon freshly ground black pepper
¼ cup chopped green bell pepper	1 head butter lettuce, cored and quartered
3 tablespoons chopped fresh parsley	1 large tomato, cut into wedges

1. In a medium saucepan, boil 2½ cups of water. Slowly add the brown rice. Cover, and reduce the heat to low. Cook the rice for 45–50 minutes until tender. Do not continually stir the rice (this will cause it to become gummy). Just check it occasionally. 2. In a large salad bowl, combine all the ingredients except the lettuce and tomato wedges. Just before serving, line 4 plates with the lettuce, and spoon the salad on top of the lettuce. Garnish with the tomato wedges.

Per Serving:
calorie: 253 | fat: 2g | protein: 15g | carbs: 45g | sugars: 6g | fiber: 4g | sodium: 189mg

Wild Rice Salad

Prep time: 5 minutes | Cook time: 45 minutes | Serves 6

1 cup raw wild rice (rinsed)	¼ cup minced red bell pepper
4 cups cold water	1 shallot, minced
1 cup mandarin oranges, packed in their own juice (drain and reserve 2 tablespoons of liquid)	1 teaspoon minced thyme
	2 tablespoons raspberry vinegar
½ cup chopped celery	1 tablespoon extra-virgin olive oil

1. Place the rinsed, raw rice and the water in a saucepan. Bring to a boil, lower the heat, cover the pan, and cook for 45–50 minutes until the rice has absorbed the water. Set the rice aside to cool. 2. In a large bowl, combine the mandarin oranges, celery, red pepper, and shallot. 3. In a small bowl, combine the reserved juice, thyme, vinegar, and oil. 4. Add the rice to the mandarin oranges and vegetables. Pour the dressing over the salad, toss, and serve.

Per Serving:
calorie: 134 | fat: 3g | protein: 4g | carbs: 24g | sugars: 4g | fiber: 3g | sodium: 12mg

Haricot Verts, Walnut, and Feta Salad

Prep time: 10 minutes | Cook time: 15 minutes | Serves 12

½ cup walnuts, toasted	⅓ cup crumbled fat-free feta cheese
1½ pounds fresh haricot verts, trimmed and halved	¼ cup extra-virgin olive oil
½ cup cooked green lentils	¼ cup white wine vinegar
1 medium red onion, sliced into rings	¼ cup chopped fresh mint leaves
½ cup peeled, seeded, and diced cucumber	1 garlic clove, minced

1. Place the walnuts in a small baking dish in a 350-degree oven for 5–10 minutes until lightly browned. Remove from the oven, and set aside. 2. Steam the haricot verts about 4–5 minutes, or until desired degree of crispness. 3. In a salad bowl, combine the haricot verts with the walnuts, lentils, red onion rings, cucumber, and feta cheese. 4. Combine all the dressing ingredients together, and toss with the vegetables. Chill in the refrigerator for 2–3 hours before serving.

Per Serving:
calorie: 119 | fat: 7g | protein: 5g | carbs: 11g | sugars: 3g | fiber: 4g | sodium: 61mg

Pasta Salad–Stuffed Tomatoes

Prep time: 10 minutes | Cook time: 0 minutes | Serves 4

1 cup uncooked whole-wheat fusilli	parsley
2 small carrots, sliced	¼ cup calorie-free, fat-free Italian salad dressing
2 scallions, chopped	2 tablespoons low-fat mayonnaise
¼ cup chopped pimiento	
1 cup cooked kidney beans	¼ teaspoon dried marjoram
½ cup sliced celery	¼ teaspoon freshly ground black pepper
¼ cup cooked peas	
2 tablespoons chopped fresh	4 medium tomatoes

1. Cook the fusilli in boiling water until cooked, about 7–8 minutes; drain. 2. In a large bowl, combine the macaroni with the remaining salad ingredients (except the tomatoes), and toss well. Cover, and chill in the refrigerator 1 hour or more. 3. With the stem end down, cut each tomato into 6 wedges, cutting to, but not through, the base of the tomato. Spread the wedges slightly apart, and spoon the pasta mixture into the tomatoes. Chill until ready to serve.

Per Serving:
calorie: 214 | fat: 3g | protein: 10g | carbs: 40g | sugars: 6g | fiber: 8g | sodium: 164mg

Herbed Tomato Salad

Prep time: 7 minutes | Cook time: 0 minutes | Serves 2 to 4

1 pint cherry tomatoes, halved	1 teaspoon sumac (optional)
1 bunch fresh parsley, leaves only (stems discarded)	2 tablespoons extra-virgin olive oil
1 cup cilantro, leaves only (stems discarded)	Kosher salt
¼ cup fresh dill	Freshly ground black pepper

1. In a medium bowl, carefully toss together the tomatoes, parsley, cilantro, dill, sumac (if using), extra-virgin olive oil, and salt and pepper to taste. 2. Store any leftovers in an airtight container in the refrigerator for up to 3 days, but the salad is best consumed on the day it is dressed.

Per Serving:
calorie: 113 | fat: 10g | protein: 2g | carbs: 7g | sugars: 3g | fiber: 3g | sodium: 30mg

Thai Broccoli Slaw

Prep time: 20 minutes | Cook time: 0 minutes | Serves 8

Dressing	Slaw
2 tablespoons reduced-fat creamy peanut butter	3 cups broccoli slaw mix (from 10-oz bag)
1 tablespoon grated gingerroot	½ cup bite-size thin strips red bell pepper
1 tablespoon rice vinegar	
1 tablespoon orange marmalade	½ cup julienne (matchstick-cut) carrots
1½ teaspoons reduced-sodium soy sauce	½ cup shredded red cabbage
¼ to ½ teaspoon chili garlic sauce	2 tablespoons chopped fresh cilantro

1 In small bowl, combine all dressing ingredients. Beat with whisk, until blended. 2 In large bowl, toss all slaw ingredients. Pour dressing over slaw mixture; toss until coated. Cover and refrigerate at least 1 hour to blend flavors but no longer than 6 hours, tossing occasionally to blend dressing from bottom of bowl back into slaw mixture.

Per Serving:
calorie: 50 | fat: 1.5g | protein: 2g | carbs: 7g | sugars: 3g | fiber: 1g | sodium: 75mg

Grilled Hearts of Romaine with Buttermilk Dressing

Prep time: 5 minutes | Cook time: 5 minutes | Serves 4

For The Romaine	1 tablespoon extra-virgin olive oil
2 heads romaine lettuce, halved lengthwise	1 garlic clove, pressed
2 tablespoons extra-virgin olive oil	¼ bunch fresh chives, thinly chopped
FOR THE DRESSING	1 pinch red pepper flakes
½ cup low-fat buttermilk	

To Make The Romaine 1. Heat a grill pan over medium heat. 2. Brush each lettuce half with the olive oil, and place flat-side down on the grill. Grill for 3 to 5 minutes, or until the lettuce slightly wilts and develops light grill marks. To Make The Dressing 1. In a small bowl, whisk the buttermilk, olive oil, garlic, chives, and red pepper flakes together. 2. Drizzle 2 tablespoons of dressing over each romaine half, and serve.

Per Serving:
calorie: 157 | fat: 11g | protein: 5g | carbs: 12g | sugars: 5g | fiber: 7g | sodium: 84mg

Chapter 12 Pizzas, Wraps, and Sandwiches

Red Pepper, Goat Cheese, and Arugula Open-Faced Grilled Sandwich

Prep time: 5 minutes | Cook time: 15 minutes | Serves 1

½ red bell pepper, seeded Nonstick cooking spray 1 slice whole-wheat thin-sliced bread (I love Ezekiel sprouted bread and Dave's Killer Bread)	2 tablespoons crumbled goat cheese Pinch dried thyme ½ cup arugula

1. Preheat the broiler to high. Line a baking sheet with parchment paper. 2. Cut the ½ bell pepper lengthwise into two pieces and arrange on the prepared baking sheet with the skin facing up. 3. Broil for 5 to 10 minutes until the skin is blackened. Transfer to a covered container to steam for 5 minutes, then remove the skin from the pepper using your fingers. Cut the pepper into strips. 4. Heat a small skillet over medium-high heat. Spray it with nonstick cooking spray and place the bread in the skillet. Top with the goat cheese and sprinkle with the thyme. Pile the arugula on top, followed by the roasted red pepper strips. Press down with a spatula to hold in place. 5. Cook for 2 to 3 minutes until the bread is crisp and browned and the cheese is warmed through. (If you prefer, you can make a half-closed sandwich instead: Cut the bread in half and place one half in the skillet. Top with the cheese, thyme, arugula, red pepper, and the other half slice of bread. Cook for 4 to 6 minutes, flipping once, until both sides are browned.)

Per Serving:
calories: 109 | fat: 2g | protein: 4g | carbs: 21g | sugars: 5g | fiber: 6g | sodium: 123mg

Grilled Nut Butter Sandwich

Prep time: 5 minutes | Cook time: 8 minutes | Serves 1

2–3 teaspoons almond or other nut butter (can substitute sunflower butter, Wowbutter, or tigernut butter) 2 slices sprouted grain bread	½ cup sliced ripe banana or apple ¼ teaspoon cinnamon ⅓ cup unsweetened applesauce

1. Place a nonstick skillet over medium-high heat. Spread about half of the nut butter on one slice of bread, then top with the banana or apple and cinnamon. Spread the remaining nut butter on the other slice of bread. Close up the sandwich, and place it in the skillet. Cook for 3 to 4 minutes, or until lightly browned. Flip and cook for another 3 to 4 minutes, or until lightly browned. Transfer to a cooling rack (so the underside doesn't soften) to cool slightly, then transfer to a plate and cut in half. Serve with the applesauce for dipping.

Per Serving:
calorie: 332 | fat: 8g | protein: 9g | carbs: 60g | sugars: 20g | fiber: 7g | sodium: 412mg

Thai-Style Chicken Roll-Ups

Prep time: 15 minutes | Cook time: 0 minutes | Serves 4

1½ cups shredded cooked chicken breast 1 cup bean sprouts 1 cup shredded green cabbage ½ cup shredded carrots ¼ cup chopped scallions, both white and green parts ¼ cup chopped fresh cilantro	2 tablespoons natural peanut butter 2 tablespoons water 1 tablespoon rice wine vinegar 1 garlic clove, minced ¼ teaspoon salt 4 (8-inch) low-carb whole-wheat tortillas

1. In a large mixing bowl, toss the chicken breast, bean sprouts, cabbage, carrots, scallions, and cilantro. 2. In a medium bowl, whisk together the peanut butter, water, rice vinegar, garlic, and salt. 3. Fill each tortilla with about 1 cup of the chicken and vegetable mixture, and spoon a tablespoon of sauce over the filling. 4. Fold in two opposite sides of the tortilla and roll up. Serve.

Per Serving:
calories: 210 | fat: 8g | protein: 21g | carbs: 17g | sugars: 3g | fiber: 10g | sodium: 360mg

Tuna, Hummus, and Veggie Wraps

Prep time: 10 minutes | Cook time: 0 minutes | Serves 2

FOR THE HUMMUS 1 cup from 1 (15-ounce) can low-sodium chickpeas, drained and rinsed 2 tablespoons tahini 1 tablespoon extra-virgin olive oil 1 garlic clove Juice of ½ lemon	¼ teaspoon salt 2 tablespoons water FOR THE WRAPS 4 large lettuce leaves 1 (5-ounce) can chunk light tuna packed in water, drained 1 red bell pepper, seeded and cut into strips 1 cucumber, sliced

TO MAKE THE HUMMUS In a blender jar, combine the chickpeas, tahini, olive oil, garlic, lemon juice, salt, and water. Process until smooth. Taste and adjust with additional lemon juice or salt, as needed. TO MAKE THE WRAPS 1. On each lettuce leaf, spread 1 tablespoon of hummus, and divide the tuna among the leaves. Top each with several strips of red pepper and cucumber slices. 2. Roll up the lettuce leaves, folding in the two shorter sides and rolling away from you, like a burrito. Serve.

Per Serving:
calories: 191 | fat: 5g | protein: 26g | carbs: 15g | sugars: 6g | fiber: 4g | sodium: 357mg

Appendix 2: The Dirty Dozen and Clean Fifteen

MEASUREMENT CONVERSION CHART

VOLUME EQUIVALENTS (DRY)

US STANDARD	METRIC (APPROXIMATE)
1/8 teaspoon	0.5 mL
1/4 teaspoon	1 mL
1/2 teaspoon	2 mL
3/4 teaspoon	4 mL
1 teaspoon	5 mL
1 tablespoon	15 mL
1/4 cup	59 mL
1/2 cup	118 mL
3/4 cup	177 mL
1 cup	235 mL
2 cups	475 mL
3 cups	700 mL
4 cups	1 L

VOLUME EQUIVALENTS (LIQUID)

US STANDARD	US STANDARD (OUNCES)	METRIC (APPROXIMATE)
2 tablespoons	1 fl.oz.	30 mL
1/4 cup	2 fl.oz.	60 mL
1/2 cup	4 fl.oz.	120 mL
1 cup	8 fl.oz.	240 mL
1 1/2 cup	12 fl.oz.	355 mL
2 cups or 1 pint	16 fl.oz.	475 mL
4 cups or 1 quart	32 fl.oz.	1 L
1 gallon	128 fl.oz.	4 L

TEMPERATURES EQUIVALENTS

FAHRENHEIT (F)	CELSIUS (C) (APPROXIMATE)
225 °F	107 °C
250 °F	120 °C
275 °F	135 °C
300 °F	150 °C
325 °F	160 °C
350 °F	180 °C
375 °F	190 °C
400 °F	205 °C
425 °F	220 °C
450 °F	235 °C
475 °F	245 °C
500 °F	260 °C

WEIGHT EQUIVALENTS

US STANDARD	METRIC (APPROXIMATE)
1 ounce	28 g
2 ounces	57 g
5 ounces	142 g
10 ounces	284 g
15 ounces	425 g
16 ounces (1 pound)	455 g
1.5 pounds	680 g
2 pounds	907 g

Appendix 2: The Dirty Dozen and Clean Fifteen

The Dirty Dozen and Clean Fifteen

The Environmental Working Group (EWG) is a nonprofit, nonpartisan organization dedicated to protecting human health and the environment Its mission is to empower people to live healthier lives in a healthier environment. This organization publishes an annual list of the twelve kinds of produce, in sequence, that have the highest amount of pesticide residue-the Dirty Dozen-as well as a list of the fifteen kinds of produce that have the least amount of pesticide residue-the Clean Fifteen.

THE DIRTY DOZEN

- The 2016 Dirty Dozen includes the following produce. These are considered among the year's most important produce to buy organic:

Strawberries	Spinach
Apples	Tomatoes
Nectarines	Bell peppers
Peaches	Cherry tomatoes
Celery	Cucumbers
Grapes	Kale/collard greens
Cherries	Hot peppers

- The Dirty Dozen list contains two additional items kale/collard greens and hot peppers-because they tend to contain trace levels of highly hazardous pesticides.

THE CLEAN FIFTEEN

- The least critical to buy organically are the Clean Fifteen list. The following are on the 2016 list:

Avocados	Papayas
Corn	Kiw
Pineapples	Eggplant
Cabbage	Honeydew
Sweet peas	Grapefruit
Onions	Cantaloupe
Asparagus	Cauliflower
Mangos	

- Some of the sweet corn sold in the United States are made from genetically engineered (GE) seedstock. Buy organic varieties of these crops to avoid GE produce.

Appendix 3: Recipe Index

A

Almond Milk Nut Butter Mocha Smoothie /65
Almond Pesto Salmon /50
Ann's Chicken Cacciatore /32
Apple Cinnamon Bread Pudding /94
Apple Crunch /94
Asian Cod with Brown Rice, Asparagus, and Mushrooms /56
Asian Mushroom-Chicken Soup /30
Asian Salmon in a Packet /52
Asparagus and Bell Pepper Strata /15
Asparagus with Vinaigrette /71
Asparagus, Sun-Dried Tomato, and Green Pea Sauté /78
Autumn Pork Chops with Red Cabbage and Apples /47
Avo-Tuna with Croutons /51
Avocado and Goat Cheese Toast /9

B

Bacon and Spinach Egg Muffins /16
Bacon-Wrapped Asparagus /72
Bacon-Wrapped Vegetable Kebabs /40
Baked Berry Cups with Crispy Cinnamon Wedges /92
Baked Chicken Dijon /28
Baked Chicken Stuffed with Collard Greens /32
Baked Oysters /55
Baked Parmesan Crisps /60
Baked Scallops /64
Baked Vegetable Macaroni Pie /23
Balsamic Brussels Sprouts /67
Balsamic Tilapia /51
Banana Bread Nice Cream /97
Banana Pineapple Freeze /92
Bavarian Beef /45
BBQ Bean Burgers /25
BBQ Lentils /26
BBQ Turkey Meat Loaf /34
Beef and Pepper Fajita Bowls /39
Beef Burgundy /40
Beef Roast with Onions and Potatoes /43
Beef Stew /44
Berry Bubble /94
Best Brown Rice /73
Black Bean Soup with Sweet Potatoes /84
Black-Eyed Pea Sauté with Garlic and Olives /75
Blood Sugar–Friendly Nutty Trail Mix /65
BLT Breakfast Wrap /11
BLT Potato Salad /101

Blueberry and Chicken Salad on a Bed of Greens /102
Blueberry Chocolate Clusters /97
Blueberry Oat Mini Muffins /9
Bran Apple Muffins /11
Breakfast Farro with Berries and Walnuts /15
Breakfast Panini /10
Breakfast Tacos /18
Broccoli "Tabouli" /101
Broccoli Cauliflower Bake /72
Broccoli Cheese Breakfast Casserole /18
Broiled Dijon Burgers /41
Brown Rice–Stuffed Butternut Squash /23
Brussels Sprout Hash and Eggs /10
Brussels Sprouts with Pecans and Gorgonzola /70
Bunless Breakfast Turkey Burgers /17

C

Callaloo Redux /73
Calypso Shrimp with Black Bean Salsa /57
Candied Pecans /61
Caprese Eggplant Stacks /76
Caprese Skewers /62
Caramelized Onion–Shrimp Spread /63
Caribbean Haddock in a Packet /58
Carrot Pear Smoothie /13
Carrots Marsala /67
Cashew-Kale and Chickpeas /79
Cauli-Curry Bean Soup /87
Cauliflower Leek Soup /85
Cauliflower with Lime Juice /67
Celery and Apple Salad with Cider Vinaigrette /99
Chai Pear-Fig Compote /96
Charcuterie Dinner For One /52
Cheese Pork Chops /42
Cheeseburger Wedge Salad /102
Cherry Delight /93
Chicken and Vegetables with Quinoa /26
Chicken in Mushroom Gravy /36
Chicken Kabobs /63
Chicken Nuggets /36
Chicken Patties /36
Chicken with Mushroom Cream Sauce /30
Chicken, Cantaloupe, Kale, and Almond Salad /99
Chickpea and Tofu Bolognese /81
Chickpea Salad /103
Chickpea-Spinach Curry /75
Chile Relleno Casserole with Salsa Salad /82

Chili Tilapia /52
Chinese Chicken Salad /101
Chipotle Chili Pork Chops /48
Chocolate Tahini Bombs /93
Chocolate-Zucchini Muffins /19
Cinnamon Wisp Pancakes /12
Cinnamon-Almond Green Smoothie /13
Citrus-Glazed Salmon /51
Cobia with Lemon-Caper Sauce /54
Cocoa Coated Almonds /64
Coconut Chicken Curry /29
Coconut Lime Chicken /30
Coconut-Ginger Rice /22
Coconut, Miso, and Sweet Potato White Bean Chili /84
Coffee-and-Herb-Marinated Steak /45
Colorful Rice Casserole /24
Comforting Chicken and Mushroom Soup /86
Corn, Egg and Potato Bake /10
Couscous Salad /105
Crab and Rice Salad /105
Crab-Filled Mushrooms /62
Crab-Stuffed Avocado Boats /56
Cranberry Almond Grits /16
Cream Cheese Shortbread Cookies /97
Cream Cheese Swirl Brownies /95
Creamy Cheese Dip /61
Creamy Garlic Chicken with Broccoli /35
Creamy Orange Cheesecake /93
Creamy Pineapple-Pecan Dessert Squares /93
Creamy Spinach Dip /64
Creole Braised Sirloin /39
Creole Steak /42
Crispy Fish Sticks /50
Crispy Green Beans /69
Crumb Pie Shell /96
Crustless Peanut Butter Cheesecake /96
Crustless Potato, Spinach, and Mushroom Quiche /13
Cucumber Roll-Ups /60
Curried Rice with Pineapple /22
Dirty Forbidden Rice /26

D

Double-Ginger Cookies /94
Dump Cake /95

E

Easy Cheesy Vegetable Frittata /81
Easy Chicken Cacciatore /32
Easy Lentil Burgers /22
Easy Pot Roast and Vegetables /41
Easy Southern Brunswick Stew /84
Edamame and Walnut Salad /99

Edamame Falafel with Roasted Vegetables /81

F

Farmers' Market Barley Risotto /21
Favorite Chili /88
First-of-the-Season Tomato, Peach, and Strawberry Salad /104
Flank Steak with Smoky Honey Mustard Sauce /44
Four-Bean Field Stew /85
French Market Soup /90
Fresh Blueberry Pancakes /14
Fresh Dill Dip /64
Frozen Mocha Milkshake /96

G

Garden-Fresh Greek Salad /105
Garlic Beef Stroganoff /42
Garlic Galore Rotisserie Chicken /33
Garlic Kale Chips /62
Ginger Blackberry Bliss Smoothie Bowl /12
Ginger Turmeric Chicken Thighs /28
Gingered Red Lentils with Millet /21
Gingered Tofu and Greens /80
Gingered-Pork Stir-Fry /47
Gluten-Free Carrot and Oat Pancakes /17
Goat Cheese–Stuffed Pears /95
Goji Berry Muesli /14
Golden Lentil–Pea Soup /89
Gouda Egg Casserole with Canadian Bacon /18
Greek Chicken /33
Greek Island Potato Salad /102
Greek Rice Salad /103
Greek Scampi /55
Greek Stuffed Eggplant /76
Green Bean and Radish Potato Salad /70
Green Beans with Garlic and Onion /71
Green Chickpea Falafel /25
Green Chile Corn Chowder /88
Green Ginger Soup /89
Green Goddess White Bean Dip /65
Grilled Hearts of Romaine with Buttermilk Dressing /106
Grilled Herb Chicken with Wine and Roasted Garlic /31
Grilled Nut Butter Sandwich /108
Grilled Vegetables on White Bean Mash /79
Grilled Watermelon with Avocado Mousse /95
Ground Turkey Tetrazzini /33
Gruyere Apple Spread /62

H

Haddock with Creamy Cucumber Sauce /52
Ham and Potato Chowder /90
Haricot Verts, Walnut, and Feta Salad /106

Harvest Blackberry Quinoa Bowl   /15
Hearty Beef and Veggie Stew   /90
Hearty Hamburger and Lentil Stew   /87
Herb-Crusted Halibut   /51
Herb-Roasted Turkey and Vegetables   /34
Herbed Spring Peas   /99
Herbed Tomato Salad   /106
Herbed Whole Turkey Breast   /35
Homemade Sun-Dried Tomato Salsa   /65
Homestyle Herb Meatballs   /46
Horseradish Mashed Cauliflower   /73
Hummus   /61
Hummus with Chickpeas and Tahini Sauce   /60

I

5-Ingredient Chunky Cherry and Peanut Butter Cookies   /97
Instant Popcorn   /61
Instant Pot Hoppin' John with Skillet Cauli "Rice"   /79
Instant Pot Tapioca   /96
Italian Bean Burgers   /21
Italian Beef Kebabs   /42
Italian Frittata   /11
Italian Potato Salad   /104
Italian Roasted Vegetables   /68
Italian Tofu with Mushrooms and Peppers   /75
Italian Wild Mushrooms   /67
Italian Zucchini Boats   /75

J

Jerk Chicken Kebabs   /31
Jerk Chicken Thighs   /31

K

Kale Chip Nachos   /64
Kickin' Chili   /88

L

7-Layer Dip   /63
Lemon Chicken   /29
Lemon-Basil Turkey Breasts   /28
Lemon-Garlic Mushrooms   /68
Lentil Bolognese   /23
Lentil Salad   /103
Lentil Soup   /85
Lentil Stew   /89
Lentil, Squash, and Tomato Omelet   /14
Lentil, Squash, and Tomato Omelet   /15
Lime Lobster Tails   /56
Low-Sugar Blueberry Muffins   /61

M

Make-Ahead Apple, Carrot, and Cabbage Slaw   /104
Mandarin Orange Chicken Salad   /100
Mandarin Orange–Millet Breakfast Bowl   /12
Mango Nice Cream   /96
Manhattan Clam Chowder   /86
Meatloaf for Two   /43
Mediterranean Chicken Salad   /101
Mediterranean Pasta Salad with Goat Cheese   /101
Mediterranean Salmon with Whole-Wheat Couscous   /57
Mediterranean-Style Cod   /54
Mexican Tortilla Soup   /86
Mexican Turkey Tenderloin   /32
Mexican-Style Shredded Beef   /41
Mini Breakfast Quiches   /11
Moroccan Carrot Salad   /103
Mozzarella-Tomato Salad   /105
Mushroom Cassoulets   /68
Mushroom-Sage Stuffed Turkey Breast   /35
Mustard Herb Pork Tenderloin   /43

N

Nancy's Vegetable Beef Soup   /87
No-Added-Sugar Berries and Cream Yogurt Bowl   /62
No-Bake Spaghetti Squash Casserole   /76
No-Tuna Lettuce Wraps   /76
North Carolina Fish Stew   /53

O

Oat and Walnut Granola   /14
Oatmeal Chippers   /95
Oatmeal Cookies   /92
One-Pan Chicken Dinner   /31
One-Pot Roast Chicken Dinner   /29
Open-Faced Pulled Pork   /47
Orange Chicken Thighs with Bell Peppers   /36
Orange Muffins   /12
Orange Praline with Yogurt   /92
Orange Tofu   /78
Oregano Tilapia Fingers   /54
Overnight Berry Oats   /10

P

Palak Tofu   /77
Parmesan Artichokes   /77
Parmesan Cauliflower Mash   /72
Parmesan-Crusted Pork Chops   /43
Pasta Salad–Stuffed Tomatoes   /106
Peppered Beef with Greens and Beans   /44
Perfect Sweet Potatoes   /70

Pizza Eggs /13
Pizza in a Pot /31
Poached Red Snapper /51
Pork and Apple Skillet /40
Pork Carnitas /46
Pork Chili /88
Pot Roast with Gravy and Vegetables /40
Potato-Bacon Gratin /13
Potato, Egg and Sausage Frittata /18
Potatoes with Parsley /67
Potlikker Soup /84
Pra Ram Vegetables and Peanut Sauce with Seared Tofu /80
Pulled BBQ Chicken and Texas-Style Cabbage Slaw /34
Pumpkin Soup /88

Q

Quick Moroccan-Inspired Chicken Stew /86
Quick Shrimp Skewers /50
Quinoa Pilaf with Salmon and Asparagus /50

R

Radish Chips /73
Rainbow Quinoa Salad /100
Rainbow Salmon Kebabs /57
Raspberry Nice Cream /92
Red Beans /22
Red Pepper, Goat Cheese, and Arugula Open-Faced Grilled Sandwich /108
Rice Breakfast Bake /16
Roast Chicken with Pine Nuts and Fennel /35
Roasted Delicata Squash /71
Roasted Garlic /69
Roasted Lemon and Garlic Broccoli /71
Roasted Red Snapper and Shrimp in Parchment /54
Roasted Salmon with Honey-Mustard Sauce /55
Roasted Salmon with Salsa Verde /50
Roasted Veggie Bowl /78
Robust Crimson Bean Stew /85
Romaine Lettuce Salad with Cranberry, Feta, and Beans /100
Rotisserie Chicken and Avocado Salad /104

S

Sage and Garlic Vegetable Bake /23
Sage-Parmesan Pork Chops /45
Salmon en Papillote /56
Salmon Niçoise Salad /102
Salmon with Brussels Sprouts /52
Sausage Egg Cup /9
Sausage, Sweet Potato, and Kale Hash /17
Sautéed Garlicky Mushrooms /69
Sautéed Mixed Vegetables /71

Sautéed Spinach and Tomatoes /69
Sautéed Spinach with Parmesan and Almonds /70
Scallops in Lemon-Butter Sauce /53
Sea Bass with Ginger Sauce /55
Seitan Curry /77
Sesame Broccoli /69
Sesame Chicken-Almond Slaw /99
Short Ribs with Chimichurri /45
Simply Terrific Turkey Meatballs /28
Sirloin Steaks with Cilantro Chimichurri /47
Slow Cooker Chicken and Vegetable Soup /85
Smoked Salmon and Asparagus Quiche Cups /12
Smoky Chicken Leg Quarters /29
Smoky Whole Chicken /30
Snapper with Shallot and Tomato /54
Snow Peas with Sesame Seeds /73
Southern Boiled Peanuts /60
Southern-Style Catfish /55
Southwest Tofu /82
Southwestern Egg Casserole /17
Southwestern Quinoa Salad /25
Spaghetti Squash Fritters /9
Spanish Black Bean Soup /86
Spice-Rubbed Pork Loin /41
Spiced Pear Applesauce /97
Spiced Rice Pudding /94
Spicy Beef Stew with Butternut Squash /41
Spicy Cajun Onion Dip /61
Spicy Chicken Drumsticks /29
Spicy Couscous and Chickpea Salad /24
Spicy Mustard Greens /67
Spinach and Mushroom Mini Quiche /16
Spinach and Provolone Steak Rolls /40
Spinach and Sweet Pepper Poppers /71
Steak Fajita Bake /43
Steak Gyro Platter /39
Steak Stroganoff /44
Steak with Bell Pepper /39
Stuffed Peppers /75
Stuffed Portobello Mushrooms /82
Stuffed Portobellos /80
Summer Salad /104
Sun-Dried Tomato Brussels Sprouts /70
Sunflower-Tuna-Cauliflower Salad /104
Sunrise Smoothie Bowl /11
Sunshine Burgers /25
Sweet Beet Grain Bowl /100
Sweet Potato Bisque with White Beans /87
Sweet Potato Crisps /69
Sweet Potato Oven Fries with Spicy Sour Cream /62
Sweet Potato Toasts /14
Sweet-and-Sour Cabbage Slaw /68

T

Tarragon Cod in a Packet /53
Teriyaki Green Beans /68
Teriyaki Rib-Eye Steaks /46
Teriyaki Salmon /57
Teriyaki Turkey Meatballs /36
Tex-Mex Rice 'N' Beans /21
Texas Caviar /24
Thai Broccoli Slaw /106
Thai Corn and Sweet Potato Stew /89
Thai Red Lentils /22
Thai-Style Chicken Roll-Ups /108
Three Bean and Basil Salad /100
Three-Berry Dutch Pancake /17
Tropical Steel Cut Oats /10
Tuna Steak /51
Tuna, Hummus, and Veggie Wraps /108
Turkey Cabbage Soup /33
Turkey Chili /37
Turkey Rollups with Veggie Cream Cheese /63

V

Vegan Dal Makhani /78
Vegetable Burgers /81
Veggie Fajitas /77
Veggie Unfried Rice /24
Veggie-Loaded All-American Breakfast /15
Veggie-Stuffed Omelet /9
Veggies and Kasha with Balsamic Vinaigrette /24
Very Cherry Overnight Oatmeal in a Jar /16

W

Warm Sweet Potato and Black Bean Salad /103
Western Omelet /19
Whole Veggie-Stuffed Trout /53
Wild Rice Salad /105
Wilted Kale and Chard /72
Wine-Poached Chicken with Herbs and Vegetables /28

Z

Zoodles Carbonara /46
Zucchini Hummus Dip with Red Bell Peppers /60
Zucchini on the Half Shell /72

Made in the USA
Monee, IL
20 July 2023

39611587R10066